ALSO BY JOHNNY RICO

Blood Makes the Grass Grow Green

BORDER CROSSER

BORDER CROSSER

One Gringo's Illicit Passage from Mexico into America

JOHNNY RICO

BALLANTINE BOOKS ᴥ NEW YORK

Copyright © 2009 by Johnny Rico

Published in the United States by Ballantine Books, an imprint of The
Random House Publishing Group, a division of Random House, Inc.,
New York.

BALLANTINE and colophon are registered trademarks of Random
House, Inc.

Library of Congress Cataloging-in-Publication Data
Rico, Johnny.
Border crosser : one gringo's illicit passage from Mexico into
America / Johnny Rico.
p.   cm.
ISBN 978-0-345-50383-1
1. United States—Emigration and immigration.   2. Illegal aliens—
United States.   3. Mexican-American Border Region—Description
and travel.   4. Rico, Johnny—Travel—Mexican-American Border
Region.   I. Title.
JV6465.R54   2009
364.1'370973—dc22
2009015488

Printed in the United States of America on acid-free paper

www.ballantinebooks.com

9 8 7 6 5 4 3 2 1

First Edition

Book design by Liz Cosgrove

To Pie—
My beautiful blond volcanic sumptuous
Russian tornado

And once you know the price of the rain in Bolivia, why hell . . .
then you know the answer to everything.

CONTENTS

FOREWORD AND MEA CULPA

In the summer of 2007, I attempted to cross from Mexico into the United States, not through the formal border crossing checkpoints, but instead using the fields, forests, and mountains that connect Mexico to the United States. It was part of my attempt to greater understand and *live* the politics of the border. This book—a curious hybrid of gonzo journalism and storytelling—is a chronicle of my developed understanding and efforts. To this end, I feel compelled to be up-front with my readers regarding some of the more diaphanous literary components necessarily required in the telling of such a tale.

I believe it's a journalist's duty to lay out the facts and details in clear, unambiguous terms, however rote and monotoncus their presentation may be. And it's a storyteller's duty to transform the messy false starts, errant timing, and awkward pauses of real life to something approaching a readable, cohesive, and hopefully entertaining narrative. While I'm sometimes a journalist, as when employed by various magazines, with this work I'm a storyteller. And so here is my mea culpa: this work is nonfiction, but with manipulations to time and sequencing, and an economy for setting and character.

For example, in order to compress two months into three hundred pages, there's a necessary molestation of chronology—there are 1,440 hours in a two-month period and you can't write about each of them verbatim—you have to pick and choose, and in this choice, you inadvertently become an editor, fusing and linking occasionally unrelated moments that are individually important but separated by scenes that aren't. Case in point: in *real* life, I took two trips to the border two months apart. And Patriot Point, as you will later read, was two different visits. But long-winded explanations about sequencing and protracted cutaway scenes to airports don't make for compelling reading, so for the sake of linear storytelling, I've neatly combined them. Which, really, if you think about it, is the beauty of storytelling: we can transform real life into the way it exists within our memories.

Sometimes setting is important, crucial, in fact, to what someone said or did, and in these moments, I've tried to leave it unchanged. But there are other times too, when a particularly important piece of dialogue or action occurs in a moment of contextual indifference, where it doesn't really matter when or where it was said, only that it occurred. These are the moments I've manipulated in my perpetual quest to limit my page count and my subsequent workload.

Additionally, while the words that follow are not fictionalized, they are subject to imperfect memory, conflicting interpretation, and biased perception. I did take notes and have an audio recorder with me, but as is often the case, when the recorder is running, nothing occurs. And then the second the recorder is safely packed away at the bottom of a suitcase, at that unexpected moment when nothing was supposed to happen, that's when everything transpires—thereby forcing the author at his first opportunity, often days later, to attempt to remember the conversational nuances. And sometimes you don't realize something was important until you start typing, and that's the real bitch of it, attempting total recall six months after the fact.

As well, many of the names and identifying characteristics of the people and organizations I've mentioned in the book have been changed. Partly this has been necessitated by those troublesome corporate legal departments that specialize in negating risk regardless of truthfulness, and partly this was done in exchange for information. The individuals and organizations operating on the border have become excessively media-wary and sometimes the only way to access their stories was under a promise of at least an attempted obscurity, however clumsy.

And finally, for the benefit of my reader, dialogue is dutifully restored from real life, where we rely heavily on meaningless statement prefaces (*it's like, you know,* and *I was literally, like, uh, you know, um*), and transformed into something more competent.

Border Crosser!

Enjoy.

Part One

WELCOME TO AMERICA

It was the spring of 2006 when half a million stormed the streets of downtown Los Angeles waving Mexican, Honduran, and Guatemalan flags in protest of a congressional immigration law that would have made being in the United States illegally a felony.

And then, in a complete about-face, there was Title VI of the Senate's Secure Borders, Economic Opportunity and Immigration Reform Act of 2007, a provision that created a class Z exclusively for undocumented workers, granting amnesty to any life-form in the country that met the stringent provision of producing two pieces of identification.

Astute and sensitive observers could feel the Internet vibrate with the faint echo of millions of phantom keystrokes typing as the blogs and message boards on all sides of the issue hummed at a pitched velocity, vitriolic and screaming with anger. Statistics and cobbled evidentiary support were bandied about, flying in every which direction: the undocumented Mexicans were an economic stimulus to the nation—no, the undocumented Mexicans were bankrupting the nation.

On the conservative frequencies of talk radio, which was almost the entire bandwidth, they were hopeful that the tide was turning, that the nation and its government were finally taking a stand against illegal immigration, and did you know that more people died at the hands of undocumented aliens than soldiers died each year in Iraq?

The liberals countered that methods were discriminatory, enforcement of laws racist, and what did this say about us as a people, as a nation?

The issue had become a part of our national pulse—thick, iron-scented, and coagulated in controversy. Along with terrorism and economic crisis, it was one of the new quintessential American questions of the twenty-first century: what was to be done about the Mexicans?

And how one responded exposed the fault lines of a divided nation.

Chapter 1
MIGRANT MOUNTAIN
(MEXICO SECTOR)

In the Big Rock Candy Mountains, there's a land that's fair and bright
Where the handouts grow on bushes and you sleep out every night
Where the boxcars are all empty and the sun shines every day . . .
Oh, I'm bound to go where there ain't no snow
Where the rain don't fall and the wind don't blow
In the Big Rock Candy Mountains.

—"Big Rock Candy Mountains"

I never knew the dark to be filled with so much light.

But as we moved silently and in sequence through the underbrush of the basin, the nighttime sky concealed by the reaching branches that took the form of a camouflaged canopy, the twilight gloom began to percolate and bleed into phantom phosphorescent streaks.

The visibility spectrum was exploding, disassembled into crimson and sapphire shadows that crested across my field of vision, forcing me to stumble.

And as the darkness deconstructed itself, I knew I wasn't going to make it.

I hadn't even crossed the border yet and already I was going crazy, made lame by so small an annoyance as too little light.

I squeezed my eyes shut, hoping for a renewal of vision, and dropped down to the earth—moist and dewy—hydrated by an early predawn mist. I felt confused legs carefully seeking out each step bump into me from behind, followed by distraught falling yells offered in a cascading descending Spanish as the two Mexicans behind me reached out hopefully for branches to keep their footing. Their fall sent the leaves about them flapping in snapping wobbling ricochets. The coyote leading us, disguised under a black ski mask, turned and offered a forced hushed whisper of admonishment.

Shut the fuck up!

But in Spanish.

Which, of course, was a language I didn't speak.

I winced in the darkness; I hated being admonished by human smuggling coyotes.

I moved to the side of the passing line on weary wobbly ankles as I heard the rustling of corduroy pants, soggy sneakers, and the gentle parting of leaves peeling off fabric. I crouched in silence, counting their number as they passed before I moved into the last position.

There were twenty of us in all. Twenty individuals whose names I didn't know. Twenty individuals whom I didn't know anything about except that we were linked by this shared covert journey that made me feel a desperate kinship born out of necessity and circumstance. We were a caravan of migrants, men and women, children and adults, strangers and family, and our temporary cooperation seemed a testament to something profound and invigorating about the potential of civilization. If we could cooperate, entrusting our lives with one other, then it seemed too as if there was potential for the rest of the world to get along, for nation-states and divisive religious sects and warring ethnic enclaves.

The silhouette figure ahead of me suddenly disappeared, merging with the shadows, and I felt the subtle push of panic at my heart, fearing that they had all suddenly disappeared, leaving me alone in the wilderness.

I dropped to my heels on a small vertical muddy incline as I peered into the darkness, my eyeballs hurting as I strained them against their sockets—everyone was still there, just resting quietly, sitting off to the side of the trail, silent save for the panting breaths that came in ragged random bursts. I sighed with relief realizing I wasn't alone and collapsed on my butt, participating in the shared stillness. And it was then, for the first time, that I noticed the cacophony of noise all about us: the screaming crickets, the hum of a light wind rattling the leaves above the basin's rim, and somewhere, the distant sound of water.

It was the sound of the river that made my heart heave heavily in my chest, careening against the side of my rib cage. It was the sound of the river that surged the blood in my circulatory system, forcing it to sprint throughout my body, causing a warm friction of movement within my veins that warded off the stinging chill of the evening. It was the sound of the river that gave rise to the onset of distant panic as my fingers tingled and I flexed them in an attempt to maintain control, taking in low deep methodical breaths.

The river, of course, was the border—our reason for being.

The true test of one's mettle wasn't how you behaved when the panic was a low murmur, but how you behaved when it was a roaring throbbing scream in your temple. How you behaved at that moment was how you defined your character and I was determined to come out glistening and heroic.

I was an American after all.

And I felt I had something to prove to the Mexicans who were wondering why I was here, who stared at me and whispered quietly about me when they believed me to be out of earshot. They were quite sure that no American had ever done this before.

I heard a distant scratch of noise, echoed and repeated, a message being passed down the line, the sound only taking the form of language when it was two people up from my own position. The man in front of me received the message and turned; an imposing shadow within layers of clothed darkness. There was the hot bad-breath blast of chicken and tortillas on my ear and then a precious hastily conveyed whisper of important information.

Spanish, of course.

The man in front of me paused in his backward retreat to his position under a bush to make sure I got it, that I understood. This was important information. We were only crossing the border, for God's sake.

I nodded. I got it.

Except, I didn't get it.

Not at all.

I had no idea what I was supposed to do.

I had no idea what I was supposed to do because I didn't speak Spanish.

And then, one by one, the line in front of me started to rise. I moved to a ready crouch as everyone started to move forward. I followed as we left the impromptu trail, a thin snaking path of broken branches and battered grass created by so many who had come before, and we began moving straight through the brush. The sounds of the river moved closer and I was able to make out the gurgles of the current and volume of the water. My hands were out in front, hanging limply in the darkness to protect my eyes as I pushed through thick foliage. I felt the barbed tears of the bush's thorns rip at my body and clothes. Somewhere down by my hip, I felt the warm flow of fresh blood.

And suddenly—I was falling.

I slid out of the bush and into a pile of Mexicans at the bottom of a five-foot drop, a soggy slope of moss and mud. A boot caught me sideways in the face as its owner started to right himself. There was a break in the overhead branches and a single stream of weak moonlight flashed down onto us where I could see the reflection of racing water just a few meters away.

One by one, we moved across the shallow frigid river, carefully stepping over slippery rocks, our hands balancing on one another's shoulders to weigh against the current. And then, on the other side, we climbed a steep muddy embankment. My heels farted with each step, blasting water as mud shrank and compressed through my toes.

And it was at this moment that I realized my innate and wholesale stupidity: I hadn't brought a clean, dry pair of socks. I should've brought a second pair of socks. It was the sort of thing any semirational thinking person of even marginal intelligence would consider when knowing they were going to be crossing a river.

Who didn't bring a spare pair of socks?

I sighed as we approached the fence, a gnarled threadbare tangle of wire that the coyote held up high as we each crawled under it. Afterward, we congregated at the bottom of a tree, at the lip of the basin's opposite side. A thrash of reeds marked the path of what I assumed would be our imminent ascent.

We were almost done!

And bit by bit, the noise discipline that we had been practicing so effectively was lost. There were hushed whispers and quiet snickers of victory.

Why the hell not? We'd earned it.

In the darkness, I smiled fiercely—a lonely private demonstration witnessed by no one—as I congratulated myself for my success.

And as this comfortable congratulatory platitude settled comfortably within my brain, a screaming siren pierced the night; its volume and careening shrieking pitch such a shift from the subtle soft audible tones of the last four hours that it hit us with the force of an errant surprise overhead thunderclap. Bodies froze with faces made immobile in the middle of grotesque contortions of fear. The siren grew louder until it sounded as if it would split the night itself apart . . .

And suddenly, we were all running—wildly crazily running!

It occurred to me that this too seemed a testament to civilization, how order and discipline could fail in single seconds.

It was every man for himself now!

And because it was every man for himself, I shoved past two young women, knocking them to the ground.

Panic dumped into my body as a toxic poison, released from a flood valve as I raced headlong into the darkness, following shadowy forms, unsure of who I was chasing or where I was going. From my peripheral vision it was blurred hyphenated breaking shadows that coiled and restricted and then advanced, leaping over me. I had the strange feeling that I was in that scene in the science fiction movie where the protagonist had just set the self-destruction sequence on the ship and was racing through claustrophobic metal corridors toward the escape pod while the emergency lights flickered and the ship's overhead intercom counted down the final seconds until total and complete destruction.

I felt my legs trip over rocks and felt a single euphoric second of momentary freefall weightlessness before slamming into the ground, my nails digging into the mud. Just beside me two Mexicans hid under a thick leafy bush. I crawled in on my elbows and squirmed my way beside them as we stared out across the basin, our panting gasps coming in abated halts as we struggled for breath.

The overhead canopy of branches changed color in rapid cyclical flashes of red and blue light that sifted eerily among the leaves, spilling like water down the branches.

"THIS IS THE UNITED STATES BORDER PATROL!"

And then, a coned beam of hot light shimmered heavily from the ridge behind us as it searched the ground, just feet in front of me. I marveled at its cylindrical perfection and watched the luminescent dust kicked up by our rapid escape billow lazily in the light's glare; a silent confession to our sudden and rapid evacuation.

Gunfire.

A girl behind me under the bush giggled.

There was a fierce tug on my arm.

"What the fuck are you doing?" I yelled in a hushed whisper as I was forcefully slid forward through the mud and brought to my feet.

"Take pictures," the coyote responded.

"I don't want to take pictures, I want to hide under the bush," I exclaimed angrily through wheezing breaths.

The coyote only smiled and dropped down to his haunches as he pointed to the top of the hill behind us. I sighed and took up a position next to him as I reached into my bag for my camera. There was more gunfire and then the sound of bulls racing through the reeds toward our position.

The darkness fractured from the flash of my camera as the first Border Patrol agent emerged from the brush and grimaced and shielded his eyes from the explosion of light. The Border Patrol agents, dressed in U.S. Army uniforms and Border Patrol baseball caps, raced past me to a position a few meters beyond the bush I was hiding under and emerged from the reeds on the adjoining side with two young Mexican boys. They laid them on the ground in front of me as they began to search them; the boys giggling throughout.

I moved between them, taking disinterested photos because, in all honesty, I'd rather have been hiding under the bush.

The Border Patrol agents began to beat the boys mercilessly and the boys laughed.

THE PICKUP BOUNCED and jostled over the acne-scarred backcountry road as my fingers itched the edge of the scratchy blindfold.

One gringo, shaken, not stirred. I snickered at the thought.

I felt a hand on mine, a subtle gesture to leave the blindfold on. I sighed and dropped my hand to my crotch where my fingers nervously interfolded themselves among one another.

"Where are we going?" I asked, my voice shy and contrite.

"We are going to a special place," the coyote answered in broken English.

I could feel the weighty stares from the other seven Mexican Border Patrol agents crammed into the back of the pickup truck. These weren't resort city Mexicans from Cancun, or border city Mexicans, or even middle-class urban Mexicans from Mexico City—these were deeply rural Mexicans—poor and agrarian and indigenous. Otomi Indians, mostly. And I, of course, was an American at the government-funded EcoAlberto nature park, at Migrant Mountain, deep inside Mexico's Yucatan peninsula, several miles outside of Ixmilquilpan, a veritable theme park, or border simulation. I didn't really know which it was, as I didn't speak Spanish.

And I was acutely aware that I was one of the few Americans they'd seen in person and in this self-consciousness I wished I was a more imposing specimen, a more succulent sample of my people instead of the lanky uncouth specimen they saw before them.

The pickup truck came to a stop and I felt a network of hands and arms gently lift me up and carry me off the back of the truck. Warm clammy hands took up my own as we moved off the road and I was led down a hill through the brush, all of this realized through smell and sound. And with my mind held hostage alongside my eyes behind the blindfold, I started to feel panicked; no one back in America had the slightest idea of where I was.

I laughed at the memory of a game I once played at a work retreat while a probation officer, the one where you had to "trust" by closing your eyes and fall willingly into the arms of a co-worker. Well, this was that game on a whole new level where you traveled to a Third World country to investigate an illegal alien training camp, which might have only been a theme park, and after arriving at one of the poorest sections of that country, you willingly allowed yourself to be blindfolded and transported in the back of a truck and then marched through the forest to a fate unknown at the hands of a foreign mob.

I felt a firm hand on my belly indicating that I was to stop walking. I squatted down and felt the soil . . . thin velvet blades of manicured grass bent between my fingers. We were in a yard, a cultivated yard, heavily cared for and looked after. Felt like suburbia.

I rose back up as a soothing bad-breath voice spoke into my ear, "Do you feel the light?"

What? Light?

And then a different voice, this time in the other ear, "Do you feel the loss?"

I ripped off my blindfold—if they were going to kill me, I damn well wanted to witness my own death.

I found myself surrounded by a large circle of thirty staring Mexicans, each holding another's hand, myself at the center of their circle. We were in a small valley and there was a soft glow all around us, and as I looked up, I saw the candles—thousands of them—lit upon the encircling mountains. The place had the feel of holiness about it, like that of a sacred shrine or temple.

And suddenly, I understood—I was to be their human sacrifice.

They were direct descendants of the Aztecs, and I'd stumbled upon a secret rural cabal of still-practicing Aztecs who were going to rip out my beating heart as an offering to their Sun God.

The coyote who had been leading us during the border crossing simulation, still wearing his black ski mask, grabbed my arm and moved me to the circle's edge where it broke and rejoined with me as one of its links. I laughed the laugh of exhausted trembling people everywhere who'd just realized they weren't going to die after all.

We were going to sacrifice somebody else.

Which I was mostly fine with.

A second ski-masked coyote, one who had been guiding another team, moved to the circle's center taking two young women with him who held the Mexican flag in place.

And then, everyone dropped hands, hats were removed, and they recited the Mexican Pledge of Allegiance. I took off my own cap and mumbled through it . . .

I pledge allegiance, to the flag, and for the Mexico, for which it stands . . .

The recitation complete, the coyote in the middle began his speech as my own coyote translated for me in a soft purr: "He say, be proud of Mexico. We come from a grand and good people. He say, this is the dream, but you cannot not like the dream or you can like the dream but not be good."

I nodded, pretending that he was doing a good job translating.

And then, the benediction complete, everyone started to clap. I clapped too.

And as the clapping died down, I became increasingly uncomfortable as the eyes of the group started turning to me, expecting a statement.

"Jesus, how about those candles, huh?" I said, hands on my hips, turning in small circles as I looked up at the overhead cliffs. "That's sure something else. Who would've thought it'd be humanly possible to, you know, light so many candles."

"Those candles represent one candle for each person who has died crossing the border," my coyote responded proudly.

"Um, I'm still a bit confused," I replied. "Was this whole thing to deter people from crossing the border or to . . . um . . . train them for crossing the border?"

"It's to make them aware," he responded.

We climbed wooden steps to a small alcove dining area with picnic tables hidden above the yard where Mayan women lay out cookies that had the look of being baked entirely and solely of flour. And these were accompanied by frothy beverages that seemed a combination of curdled milk and yogurt. I was surrounded by a dozen smiling Mexicans who started chatting at me in Spanish, proud of their theme park experience and wanting to know my thoughts as I was handed both a cookie and a mug.

I took a small bite and an even smaller sip; they both tasted awful. I patted my tummy appreciatively and started to put them both down, an action that brought immediate frowns from my hosts. And then, I suddenly remembered a moment in the Army when we had been visiting an Afghanistan tribal elder who had no food for his village yet had managed to provide for us a considerable feast and who had grown greatly upset when we had each taken a simple nimble bite and refused the rest. Our interpreter, a young kid from Kabul in a Raiders starter jacket, had told us that we were acting rudely, that our future relations with the elder and whether he supported the American coalition or the Taliban just quite possibly depended upon our consumption of the food. Even then none of us had decided it was worth the bitter taste of a mouthful of congealed camel's milk, and had, all the same, refused the offer. But I had remembered the disgusted look of both our interpreter and the tribal elder at our bad manners and had promised myself to never again be such a rude little pig.

"No, get that stuff away from me, it's gross," I responded to another attempt to force the cookie and the beverage back into my hands. "No, it's gross, I don't want it!"

The issue of the consumption of the beverage tabled for the moment, I was suddenly barraged with questions in Spanish and broken English by young girls and teenage boys and middle-aged men.

How far had I come to get here?

Did I like Mexico?

What did I think of the border crossing?

And, most importantly, why had I come?

And that was the ten-million-dollar question, why the hell was an American here?

"Tell them, I need to cross the border into America," I said to my coyote.

The coyote parsed my question, "At the point of entry or in the desert?"

"The desert," I responded.

My coyote attempted to dutifully translate. Giggles erupted from the crowd as I smiled, pleased to be the center of attention. It was a funny thing, after all, an American crossing the border like the Mexicans.

THE PICKUP SNAKED slowly down the mountain, the driver using the light of the moon to navigate the hairpin turns and abrupt bends in the rough road. In the rear of the cab, I nodded at each of the Border Patrol agent actors in turn. One with a goatee smiled broadly at me.

It was to him I asked my first question, "So all those candles really represent a death?"

He laughed, and then in the sort of perfect English acquired only from being so frequently in America, responded, "Fuck no, man. That's just some made-up shit. They don't know." He shook his head dismissively at all his country bumpkin fellow Mexicans. He seemed a little embarrassed. "They're all country people, they don't know no better."

"Those coyotes that led us, did they ever cross before?"

"Fucking experts, man. Fucking experts. They cross all the time, back and forth, back and forth. You headed back to the States now?"

"Yeah, starting back first thing tomorrow," I replied. I drifted into silence for a moment before reciprocating, "You? You headed back to the States?" It seemed a strange question in light of our situation, but also curiously appropriate.

"Yeah, I'm leaving ina couple days," he responded casually.

I nodded in recognition of our mutual destination.

I wondered if I should offer him a ride.

MY RUINED SUBARU intercepted a flurried herd of butterflies, pasting them onto the windshield as a deep grin cracked upon my face. There was no time for a requiem. This was a goddamn barrel run. I spilled the speed from this shitty Mexican rental bleeding a building-burning velocity onto the highway behind me while the day retired splashing a sweetly sticky dripping merlot sunset across southern Mexico as I sped north from the belly of the earth and the Yucatan jungle back toward the United States.

This is what life was all about, I thought while I floored the accelerator, ratcheting the engine into a high-pitched scream as I veered erratically into the center of the highway, passing two lethargic slow-moving semis. I swerved back into my own lane just in time to avoid the oncoming traffic that thundered past me with my tires acting as deftly nimble ballerinas, dodging so many dead dog carcasses and the peeling sheaths of rubber that ripped from the inferior tires of the Mexican trucks.

The speed was liberating. And thank the Lord I'd been recklessly careening all day and not a single traffic cop. I was passed by a single vehicle—an unrecognizable SUV with tinted windows—its back adorned with the stenciled image of a haloed crucified Jesus holding twin AK-47s as it headed north up the middle of the highway. I decided to let the vehicle pass me, what with the militant-themed Jesus and all.

This land called Mexico?

It was truly God's country. And I was Iris, the god of rainbows, traveling from one end of the world to the other. I was sunlight, shooting across the galaxy. I was Mad Max, and I would zip across the Apocalypse until the end of time itself.

I would die before I slowed myself down.

And then, a pop from somewhere inside the rental car, just north of the driver's seat and hidden under the hood, as the engine died, my momentum failed, and the speed withered.

I pulled over to the shoulder, my tires rolling to a stop. I got out of the car and looked down the highway in each direction. Steaming mountains in the distance, superimposed by emerald green banana fields and not a car or truck in sight.

"Fuck," I murmured quietly.

THE AMBER GLOW of evening took siege on the small village somewhere in Mexico as I sat beside an outcropping of cat's claw and whitethorn acacia littered with stubbed cigarette butts as the mechanic leaned under the hood of the Subaru, rubbing the battery leads with the rind of a lime. He looked up at me and offered a gap-toothed smile and enthusiastic thumbs-up, which I quickly returned in overexaggerated form as I scanned the village.

A few vaquero Dukes in sharp buckles and wide-brimmed hats sat outside a taco stand in plastic chairs, swatting at encircling flies as cutely tanned children ran about the village among squat stores painted in the fading logos of Pepsi and Orange Crush. A homeless dog with hanging swollen nipples careened recklessly across the road, darting in between speeding semis. Two boys chased each other with machetes, one playfully simulating the decapitation of the other as they both laughed—typical kid stuff.

What was most unsettling, though, was that the village seemed disproportionately quiet, subsisting as an eerily subdued hamlet. It was evening during the week, just after the workday, well before bed, but the village had the character and tempo of a lazily maintained Sunday afternoon where a burning sun might clear the streets until the cooler evening hours.

And then I realized it, the isolated emptied buildings, and the long-ago-abandoned construction projects that years later were still only cinder block skeletons: the village was operating at half its normal capacity. The people had all left. I wondered where they had all gone, but it was a query to which I realized I already knew the answer.

These were the working-poor farmers of the world, industrious and naive. The descendants of the once proud empires of Maya and Aztec who toiled under a sun that seemed a bit hotter each year to produce bare thread crops of coffee and corn and sugarcane, wagering entire seasons' harvests on razor-thin profit margins that barely returned the cost of seed.

And what had changed?

It wasn't the fault of the soil, which had been generous enough for hundreds of years.

No, it was the fault of the seed, the only type available—what they called a "terminating technology"—genetically impotent and from the United States, purposely designed not to reproduce, to force its perpetual purchase year after year. A corporate shill's ingenious and patented idea to wreak devastation on the poor peoples of the world while bumping fiscal year-end profits.

And it was also the fault of that Yankee free trade agreement that imposed tariffs for exported agriculture. Prices and wages used to be set locally, that's how it had worked for hundreds of years and sometimes you did well and sometimes you didn't, but at least you always knew the score. These days the prices were set in faraway countries by men in suits haggling over small percentage points in trade contracts, points that down here on the line where the soles of the feet met soil resulted in real-life worry. And who could compete with American agriculture anyhow? Their farms all tractors and turbines with chemically augmented soil and computer-forecasted crop rotation. Which is how it came to be that food could become a scarce commodity in one of the world's most fertile regions.

And it wasn't just the price of food and seed, it was the price of everything—diapers, clothes, feed for the chickens. The prices keep rising and the wages keep dropping. Same story as everywhere else, but for the time being a wage drop in America was sustainable; south of the border it was absolutely devastating.

Times were tough, no doubt about it.

And I imagined that some of them came back, from El Norte. And when they returned it was in shiny new trucks filled with diapers and toys for the children, and stereos for the boys, dresses for the women. They came with stories of earning hundreds of dollars in a single week!

And I imagined that the minds of the men and the women, descendants of those who had worked and lived off the land for hundreds and sometimes thousands of years, began to wander and peer north as they began to whisper. And as the whisper was regurgitated on anxious tongues eager to spread the message, it built in momentum and strength until it became bright and fierce and loud and something resembling hope as it inspired transformation of the lethargic sufferers into aspiring migrants, delirious with the future.

It was from the north that their people had first migrated, arriving at Lake Texcoco as migrant squatters. And it was to the northern frontier that, throughout their history, folks had returned in times of desperation in search of work or gold. To the north, where so many of the Spanish language already lived and where the land was named in familiar labels like Los Angeles and New Mexico and Las Vegas.

"Dónde está el chicos?" I asked the mechanic, offering one of my few known Spanish phrases as I looked about dubiously and then shrugged my shoulders in an exaggerated display.

Where were the men?

The mechanic stared at me for a moment of contiguous indecipherable judgment before he wiped his hands with an oily black rag and slowly pointed north.

Toward Wisconsin.

Chapter 2

DAY ZERO
(DENVER SECTOR)

The desert of my dreams was flat and vacuous and dark, a shaved geometric plane of dehydrated hardpan turtle-shell mud cakes that stretched into perpetuity. The story of the dream was variable and unimportant and never remembered. The heart of the beast, that which stung and mattered, were the four emotions linked in a burning sequencing transition that stayed with me long after waking.

First, there was pain. The pain of aching throbbing legs, as if running a marathon on a sprained calf, each step across the desert sending crackling bolts of pain up my spine, tingling electricity, jagged and reaching.

Second, there was panic at the searchlights that broke the blackened vacuum from storm clouds in the distant horizon as lighted pinpricks—like God searching, distant and inevitable.

Third was the subtle suggestion of impending panic, teasing and flirtatious.

The panic, though, wasn't about the searchlights; it was regarding an impending moment that had not yet arrived.

It was a moment in anticipation of another moment.

It was the anticipation of . . .

Regret.

Regret for attempting to cross the border illegally.

Regret for what attempting this would do for my life if I ended up arrested, or dead in Mexico.

But the regret never came.

Instead the final emotion was euphoria.

Euphoria as realized in a sunlit forest, or a meadow, maybe. A peaceful meadow—the type with the little daisies pushing petals toward soft sunlight surrounded by svelte blades of grass, pollinating bumblebees gently hovering.

And that was the dream.

And then, I'd wake up.

AND IT WAS back in Denver, curled up on the floor in the dark, wrapped in the sort of scratchy comforter indigenous to thirty-five-dollar-a-night budget motels everywhere, staring at the mottled ceiling, and inhaling deep on ten-cent miniature shampoo, that I thought about my dream and the border. It wasn't hard to realize the dream's underlying Freudian meaning—it was forecasting anxiety over whether I'd succeed or fail in my attempted illegal border entry back into America.

I wanted to know how difficult it actually was to cross as the Mexicans did. I wanted to know what it felt like to forcibly enter a largely hostile foreign country, compelled by dire circumstance, to search for work when there was nothing sustainable at home. I wanted to know for myself if our borders were fiercely patrolled and encircled with strands of barbed wire, or if they were quiet desolate open stretches of desert chirping with lonely crickets. And at the end of all these bemused amused ponderings, there was the question: *Could I do it? Could I, as a soft, white monolingual middle-class American, illegally cross the border?*

It wasn't enough to simply pick an unoccupied point along the long and lanky border and cross over back and forth, a technical demonstration of boundary circumvention. No, the crossing needed to be performed under formal conditions, along an actual migratory route that was used by the Mexicans so that I could feel what they did, so that I could understand their experience.

But more than that, I wanted to intimately understand the border dilemma and the actors engaged in the drama. My plan, such as it existed, was to drive to San Diego, California, and then slowly start making my way east to Texas, and as I went, I'd visit the various players of the border issue. I was going to ride along with the Border Patrol, walk the desert with the open border advocates that published maps for the illegal aliens, visit an underground railroad for Mexican immigrants in El Paso, and hunt for illegal Mexicans with border vigilantes. It was my theory that the only way to truly begin to understand the issue was by full-on immersion—there was drama playing out on the peripheral edge of my nation and I desperately wanted to be involved. And I was also hoping that by visiting these various actors, I'd also be able to gain valuable intelligence about where and how to perform my own border crossing.

I rose from the floor where I was sleeping as part of my last-minute conditioning program and moved to the window where I opened the curtains to streaming sheets of sunlight, another late afternoon in an industrial periphery of Denver, all pluming factories and buzzing Interstate.

"Fuck," I quietly muttered to myself, closing the curtains, collapsing the room once again in darkness as I vaguely remembered the previous night's promises to perform a stage-one life reboot this morning upon waking.

Today, Day Zero of my border investigation and crossing, I was supposed to have gotten up at six A.M. and run three miles as I would do every morning from here until the end of eternity. It was supposed to have been nothing but healthy eating and giving up smoking. All in preparation for the border, of course. I strongly felt that the restructuring of long entrenched habits should coincide with moments of intense change like a border run to Mexico followed by illegal return entry into the United States. The newly desired more healthy habits seemed more likely to stick around if you had a firm memorable date their starting had coincided with.

And today was going to be the tipping point toward the new me.

Except it was already afternoon. I couldn't be expected to run at two P.M.—I had too much to do before I started the drive to California later tonight. I'd have to put it off, not just the jogging, but all of it. Another couple of days, at least. You couldn't start with just half the program, it didn't work that way. It was all or nothing.

Content with my decision to start my life of clean living another day, I shrugged and lit up a cigarette as I climbed from the floor up to the bed and began studying my maps and the known migratory routes used by Mexicans, attempting to cobble together some preliminary plan for my crossing, which, eight hundred miles from the border, was an exercise consisting of equal parts topographical reference and imagination.

Border crossings came in all shapes and sizes. There were river crossers in Texas, fence jumpers in the border towns, short-haul enthusiasts who crossed at points where U.S. roads were only a few miles off, such as along the Tecate Line in southern California, though these points were few and far between. And then there were the long-haul truckers, which seemed to be almost everyone these days, those who crossed in the vacant wide-open desert in Arizona along the Amnesty Trail and the Devil's Highway; no-man's-land, with fifty-mile journeys to the nearest city. And as I sat, reading, thinking, and choosing my border crossing, I was happy because this route selection was a tenderly private moment. What I imagined it would feel like choosing a first wedding dress.

Of course, it was impossible to estimate conditions on the border while in Denver. Like shopping in a catalog for clothes, sometimes you needed to smell the product and try it on, roll it over in your hands before you made a purchase. And consequently, my methodology of the moment was that of best plan evolving—if I saw an opportunity to cross, I'd take it. Otherwise, from San Diego I'd just keep heading east until I ran out of border. My already purchased flight back to Europe, where I lived with my wife as an expatriate, didn't leave from Los Angeles for seven weeks. I had six weeks and six days to work with, an amount of time that seemed more than adequate.

I laughed aloud within my empty motel room at how I had first envisioned my crossing . . .

I would go into Mexico where I would hire a human smuggling coyote who would take me into the United States along with a group of illegal aliens. Sure, it'd be uncomfortable at first since I didn't speak any Spanish and, being a tall skinny gringo, I wouldn't fit in very well, but over time they'd recognize my warm compassionate heart and then, of course, we'd probably end up bonding during the journey into America. We'd probably share our food with one another, giggling as we swapped national cuisine and pantomimed out the meaning of different words in our respective languages. There would be some hard times as we crossed the desert and our legs got tired. We'd snipe at one another, argue a bit as any companions did during long road trips. But by the end of our mutual journey somewhere in the American desert, the women would hug me, and the men would offer me firm handshakes. But then they wouldn't be able to contain their respect and admiration that I, a relatively comfortable American, had taken this journey with them if for no other reason than to experience it, and while still holding my hand, the men would pull me into a tight hug. Of course, I'd be the sober one, laughing amicably at their shows of affection as I patted them on the back to say that it was okay. No, they were right, they probably wouldn't see me again, but they should continue on with their lives anyway. They'd find some good honest work in America making substandard wages, but being Mexican, they wouldn't really know the difference and all would be okay with the world.

It seemed an idea born of brilliance and a tender-loving absurdity, the sort of life-affirming peril that was also a unique empathy-building experience with a people I knew nothing of and had never met. But mostly, it just made for a great bar story. Most likely retold in the same place where the idea had been born, *"Did I ever tell you the story about when I crossed the border illegally with a bunch of Mexicans!"*

And it was funny too because I was white and didn't speak any Spanish.

And, to my surprise, my publisher agreed—it *was* funny!

And unlike the illegals that had to pay to cross, I was being sponsored. And you can't beat sponsorship, you really can't.

And then, like any good writer, after the contract had been submitted and signed off on, I started fully researching my assignment. I reached across the bed and grabbed my manila folder of Internet research as I sorted through and reread the pages for the tenth time:

Nine journalists killed.

Americans vanish in northern Mexico town.

Journalists risk life and limb in northern Mexico.

Gangs force shutdown of newspaper in northern Mexico.

To work and die in Juárez: Scores of young workers murdered.

Human smuggling coyotes kill immigrants in the desert.

Mexico ranked first in the world in manslaughter.

Rampant corruption ties Mexican police to narcotics trade.

Northern Mexico ranked as one of the world's most dangerous hotspots.

Murder on the border as more illegal immigrants turn up dead in the Arizona desert . . .

I considered the details that I had promised myself and my publisher. The details that were necessary for a full feel of the experience; a tourist's sampling just wasn't going to do. Hiring a human smuggling coyote? Oh yes, I had promised I would try that, at least a good-faith effort. Of course, when I had made this promise, I hadn't known that coyotes were typically regarded as drug cartel runners who often abandoned their own clients in the desert to die. Who sometimes raped and murdered them.

Previously, when I thought of Mexico, I had thought of Cancun and Puerto Vallarta—sombreros and sunburns, mariachi bands and tequila. Good times, mostly. But as I had learned, northern Mexico was an entirely different world, one of corrupt police and military, a region ruled by drug cartels that were the de facto law and order. The international nonprofit Reporters Without Borders had recently rated northern Mexico as the second most dangerous place in the world, second only to Iraq. You were fine, of course, when you stayed on the corridors, the motorways, when you stayed within the proper neighborhoods and the tourist shopping districts within the big cities, but it became quite problematic when you started sloughing off into the rural backwoods. That's when, if you weren't lucky, you turned up as a buried news item on page seven of the local paper, another ignored murder or kidnapping statistic. And it was in these areas, unfortunately, that most of the migratory routes started.

And then there was the crossing itself, which, although I hadn't researched it mostly because I didn't want to know, I could only assume was a flagrantly illegal act; probably a felony, which would be an inconsonant decorative award to carry through the rest of my days.

And knowing all this, I smiled leanly in the shadowed motel room as my heart aggressively thumped out the minutes. Ostensibly, I was scared shitless. But underneath the fear, was also a curious and salacious arousal, not unlike the feeling of seeking out pornography—simultaneous shame while being unable to turn away; self-loathing with a hard-on.

I reminded myself there was nothing to worry about. I had overdosed on heroin in Vietnam and survived war in Afghanistan. Going into northern Mexico would be easy . . . it was like going to Ohio. Besides, after my trip to Migrant Mountain in the southern portion of the country, I was formally trained now. All I was missing was my certificate of achievement.

There wasn't anything to worry about.

Not a damn thing.

I reached under the map for my notepad and started writing out a goodbye letter to my wife to be opened after I died as I knew I surely would. It had to be meaningful, important, so that she would read it and cry with joy over the realization of how much I loved her.

I concentrated my thoughts onto her. She was beautiful to look at, definitely: a tiny blonde with a good figure. But certainly there were other things I loved about her? And then it was a cascading torrent of overwhelming emotions, a flood of memories about why, not only was she the love of my life, but why she was also one of the most adorable people I'd ever met . . .

The way she'd be sitting quietly in bed reading, and then suddenly, and without warning, attack me pretending to be a dog or a wild animal, barking in her native Russian. Or the way she'd berate me for forgetting the apple juice outside when we carried in groceries, her angry reproach raising to a hysterical pitch until we were both laughing so hard that our sides ached in pain. The way she never quite heard all the words of her adopted English language, singing, "It's rainy rain, hallelujah!" as she washed dishes, never once realizing she had forgotten to include the word "men." The way she became infuriated with my perpetual yells of

"Time!" Unwilling as I was to wear a watch when my wife was so readily available to be asked.

She didn't just make each day of my life better—she had saved me.

And that is what I needed to express to her, tender loving poetic words that, years later, years after my death in Mexico, she'd read over and over again, remembering her beloved husband as the man who loved her more than anyone else ever had. I needed to express a love so intense that it would stretch from my forthcoming absence to the end of her life, so that at no point during her continued tenure on earth would she ever feel lonely, so that she would be forever enveloped by the love of a single moment.

And so, I wrote:

> *Anna Pie,*
> *You're the best.*
> *If you're reading this, something has happened to me.*
> *Sorry.*
> > *Love,*
> > *Hubby*
> *P.S. Time!*

I wrote an e-mail to an old friend from the Army—to be opened in case of life-altering events. Upon incarceration or serious injury he was to call my wife and calm her. Upon my death, he was to contact my agent and have him try to capitalize on said death with some press release designed to sell a few more copies of my first book: AMERICAN AUTHOR JOHNNY RICO KILLED BY DRUG LORDS IN NORTHERN MEXICO—BOOK AVAILABLE AT AMAZON.COM.

And then, he was to mail my wife her lovely letter.

I didn't care how my things were divided.

I didn't own much anyway.

OUTSIDE THE MOTEL, along the I-70 corridor, where the air reeked slightly of diesel fuel, the semis pummeled the night sending out blasting explosions of air in their passing. To the east was the corn-fed Bible Belt, the Heartland, and the little house on the prairie running all the way to Ohio. To the west were the mountains and, beyond that, the desert with Vegas somewhere deep inside.

I loaded up the back of the pickup truck I had borrowed from my stepfather here in Denver, a rusted orange 1977 GMC half-ton with a bed full of empty soda cans and a bumper advertising the Marine Corps. And despite a failed speedometer and hyperactive needle on the fuel gauge, it was the type of vehicle you wanted when doing reconnaissance on rough border roads and pulling over to talk to Minutemen in the desert.

I reentered the motel room for one last look to make sure I hadn't left anything and grabbed my rucksack. I pulled open its top and grabbed the pistol I had borrowed from a friend of mine who was a district attorney. I studied the pistol for a moment, debating the relative wisdom of its inclusion, before deciding that it was too late to be second-guessing myself and packed it back inside my bag.

I stood to leave and then, quite suddenly, I began to worry about the physical demands of a fifty-mile hike through the desert at the height of the summer burn along places like the Devil's Highway.

Was I truly prepared for this endeavor?

Was this something I could conceivably pull off?

Was I in any physical condition to even attempt such a thing?

I hadn't really exercised much in the last couple of years, but then it had also been just three years ago in the Army where I had excelled at road marches. My long legs had simply endured, pumping out the miles while others had fallen to the wayside. And I was only thirty years old; it wasn't like I was an old man. Surely, I could cross fifty miles of desert.

And as I was about to leave the room, I caught my passing reflection in the bathroom mirror: tall and skinny, forearms spiraling in tattoos, a hinting tease of a beard. I surmised my condition as my angular face frowned and I abruptly dropped to the floor to do some push-ups.

A few push-ups as last-minute conditioning wouldn't hurt. In the Army they had been my favorite exercise during morning training, when I had been able to do eighty at a time.

I burned quickly through the first ten.

I collapsed on number fifteen, winded and out of breath.

Chapter 3
THE GOOD SAMARITAN
(SAN DIEGO SECTOR)

I spent the next morning, afternoon, and early evening moving slowly through the American Southwest, making my way from Denver toward San Diego, avoiding the Interstates and instead exercising a tenuous chain of backcountry roads and highways as I took in the measure of the land, a bronzed tawny landscape between heaven and hell. It was desolate and lonely, intermittent with fierce dull copper mountains, empty coffee-hued dust plains, and ginger craggy hills.

The population density in Massachusetts is 809 people per square mile, in New York it is 401, but out here in the American Southwest, it is 15. A number still skewed radically upward by millions in Phoenix and Tucson and Santa Fe, in its precious few clusters of congregated civilization. In other words: empty and vacuous with lots of places to hide and to get lost and to start over and to find trouble.

And then, outside my speeding truck, the desert began its descent toward another evening.

And then, the darkness fully collapsed, looming, it was just me again, distinct and separate from the land, pummeling hundreds of empty square miles in a rattling coughing pickup truck, my weak headlights dissipating into the oily vacuum of the great nothingness. I smiled warmly at feeling insignificant in the great vacant—swallowed, just a bouncing echo.

I SAW HIM on the side of the road, an hour outside San Diego amid a devastating burnt cocoa landscape of sparse intermittent forest, ripped ravines, and jagged hills. His weathered rusted truck broken down on the shoulder of the Interstate, a tenuous and snaking asphalt artery that cut through the desert. He nervously peered around the hood, attempting a rudimentary mechanical repair while simultaneously surveying the motorway with nervous eyes that stole anxious looks from under the brim of his oversized cowboy hat.

I pulled to a stop.

"Do you need some help?" I asked, overly satisfied with myself at being the type of good person and Samaritan that helped out migrant Mexicans on the side of the freeway.

"Qué?" the old Mexican responded. A frightened gaze overtook his face as he cautiously studied me. He was old, frightened, and frail. His pants were held up by a belt composed of severed rope and I imagined that he was here attempting a late-in-life renewal.

I imagined that he'd come from the Yucatan, just another of the planet's migratory poor—another nobody. I imagined that, back home, he had felt sadness for his wife, who, gracing the cusp of old age, still hadn't yet owned a proper dress, and sadness for his children, who were struggling in adulthood as he had. I imagined that deep down, despite his exterior gentle temperament, burned a fierce and furious anger over the unfairness of it all. That maybe his wife had been suggesting for years that he go to America and he had resisted because it wasn't legal and it wasn't right and it wasn't home, and for this she had quietly hated him—it wasn't a hate born of malice, just one of contempt, the contempt one has for a coward. Because, after all, everyone else had gone and look at the money *those* men were sending home to their families. And, for a long time, he had resisted, but then something had flipped the switch, something had triggered, and this anger had inspired him to risk everything, to beg, borrow, and plead for enough money to pay a smuggler to take him across. He was old and appreciated his mild comforts such as they were, an evening pipe of tobacco, a brief rest at sundown from a long day in the fields, snuggling up to his wife at night, and being here meant none of those, and mild comforts, after all, were important to an old man.

And now in the Estados Unidos, alone and old. This crossing to America was a zero sum game, with nothing less than everything he had and had never earned at stake, and it was being played out in sudden death overtime, in his twilight years. And while Americans his same age were humping their final stretch before retirement, making small adjustments to their 401(k) contributions in order to reach their financial goals, he was starting out as if a young man. Working as a dishwasher, maybe. Or mowing yards despite the painful arthritis and the bad back, whatever it took to be able to send some remittance south to his wife and children, he'd ruin himself in order to help them. He was expendable, and he knew it. But goddamn, if he could just help his family a little.

Yes, I read all that and more in a brief flash in his eyes. I was psychic that way.

I dangled my cell phone out the window, offering it to him, a universal gesture, which he appropriately interpreted before his face revealed a cautious smile and a waving of his hands. No, he'd be fine, it was best if I just went, but thanks anyway.

I nodded, frowning, slightly upset at his refusal of my benevolent offer.

He turned back to the truck's engine, pretending a continued assessment as he waited for me to pull away.

I offered a brief goodbye wave, which he returned as I drove off the shoulder and back onto the Interstate, watching him watch me in my rearview mirror. And as soon as I was out of sight behind a bend in the road, I put on my turn signal and pulled over back to the side of the road, contemplating.

I was thinking about what to do, about exactly how it was I felt about the issue of illegal immigration. It was never an issue I'd been confronted with before, always relegated to the edge of my existence as a problem occurring only on the television. Before I had joined the Army and later moved to Europe after my discharge, I had been a probation officer, someone who never had to worry about my job being taken or my wages being depressed by a Mexican, so it was easy to adopt a knee-jerk liberal impulse. To be humanitarian about it all, assume that they were mostly a good and decent people who were trying to make a better life for themselves, who the rest of us should be helping, not arresting. To appreciate them in the finest of American traditions: the hardworking immigrant searching for a better life, and to hell with it if they had to break a few laws along the point of entry. Everyone broke laws, the corporations, the President. The law was for suckers, the law was just something to keep people in their place while the clever ones ran circles around the system, and it was because most people realized this that there was such widespread sympathy for the plight of the Mexicans here illegally.

I should have just continued on, kept driving, ignored the man and let our two paths diverge. But then I *was* here on the border for a purpose and for a reason. I was here to involve myself in the border controversy. I was here to get dirty. And until I'd tasted both sides of the issue, I wouldn't know how I truly felt about it.

I pulled out my cell phone and dialed the Border Patrol, the number memorized from the frequent billboards that rimmed the Interstate.

"Border Patrol," the dispatcher responded.

"Yeah, I'm on Interstate 8 just west of Pine Valley, and I've got what I think is an illegal alien broken down on the side of the road?"

I offered a brief description of the make and model of the vehicle, the Mexican, and the mileage marker before I ended my call.

I waited quietly on the side of the road, chewing my nails with an agitated disposition until I saw a Border Patrol truck drive past me on the other side of the Interstate, heading around the bend toward my Mexican. I pulled forward to a break in the median rail guard, and did a quick U-turn during a pause in oncoming traffic.

As I drove past, I saw the Border Patrol agent exit his vehicle and approach the Mexican, who had suddenly become desperate, his eyes searching for an escape, nervous as he slowly backed away from the truck. I imagined imminent screaming and bitter fury at so much wasted nonrenewable effort. After all he had risked, after all he had sacrificed, this was his reward and his redemption.

And then, as I'd hoped, a feeling emerged.

My first genuine emotion about the border problem.

I felt bad.

Shit, I thought to myself, suddenly wishing I hadn't called Border Patrol as I saw the trembling Mexican pitch toward tears as he collapsed on his ass into the dirt at the feet of the Border Patrol agent, staring ahead with dull vacant eyes.

Welcome to America, Mexican.

Part Two

THE TECATE LINE

The Tecate Line is a rough and rugged forty-mile stretch of scabrous hills in California's southern fringe, just south of the Campo Indian Reservation and east of San Diego with a reaching breadth that anchors between Jacumba and Tecate.

With Highway 94 less than a mile from the international boundary in parts, it creates a disproportionate funnel effect for incoming illegal aliens and drug smugglers lured by the promise of a short border jump and the chance of a rapid evacuation into the country's interior. Here, entering America is the equivalent of a fifty-meter dash, which makes it one of the nation's premier crossing sites for migratory Mexicans, second in popularity perhaps only to central Arizona.

In the drug enforcement communities they have a title for this directional-specific flow of drugs and money.

They call it a narco corridor.

Chapter 4

NARCO CORRIDOR
(SAN DIEGO SECTOR)

The American government
took away the marijuana.

—"Contraband in the Border," Popular Mexican gangster ballad

I can't even produce a metaphor for the drug world anymore.
I don't even like the phrase the drug world since the phrase implies
that it is a separate world. And drugs are as basic and American as,
say, Citibank.

—Charles Bowden, *Down by the River*

The perceived national threat regarding drugs seems a relic of the past now.

Consigned to the cultural waste bin of the 1980s when Rambo ruled the box office and crack cocaine flooded the inner-city ghettos. Crack, when America still cared. Crack, when America was motivated.

Our perception of the problem, our understanding of the drug epidemic, has become marginalized by complacency and familiarity, replaced on the red carpet as the starlet crisis of the moment by the economy and global warming and terrorism—real problems. Take a survey of public opinion on the most pressing issues facing Americans, and drugs don't even rank anymore. It doesn't rank because we've become acclimated, we've assumed its existence as the cost of doing business in America, as being a thing of inevitability.

The open border doesn't help.

But while the conversation might have dried and died, the drugs never did.

The War on Drugs has been quietly raging for twenty years now—

hundreds of thousands in prison, $75 billion a year in costs, and secret wars with commandos in Colombia—and nothing statistically measurable regarding progress.

Yes, there are year-by-year spikes in the data that are perceived as minor victories; data variance touted as success stories by eager politicians. But in the larger spanning scope and draw of the data as aggregated over two decades, the truth of futility reveals itself: the year is 2009 but it might as well be 1988 all over again.

As William F. Buckley, the father of modern conservatism and the founder of the *National Review,* stated to a panel of lawyers from the New York Bar Association: "We are speaking of a plague that consumes an estimated $75 billion per year of public money, exacts an estimated $70 billion a year from consumers, is responsible for nearly 50 percent of the million Americans who are today in jail, occupies an estimated 50 percent of the trial time of our judiciary, and takes the time of 400,000 policemen—yet a plague for which no cure is at hand, nor in prospect."

It's because of the War on Drugs that, in the 1990s alone, the number of prison inmates grew by an estimated 816,865. A full two million people will be arrested for drug offenses each year and someone will violate a drug law every seventeen seconds.

And if the question is why, the answer is cash.

But researching the profit trails of illegal narcotics raises troubling questions. Questions like why did a Gulfstream jet, known as the "Mayan Express," that crashed in Mexico in 2007 chock-full of cocaine end up being registered to a CIA asset? And why are there modern sparkling shiny happy skyscrapers in Mexico sitting empty with no mortgage owed, sold cheap to U.S. companies by the shell corporations set up by narcotics traffickers?

The further, more complicated answer is that the American economy is as irrevocably linked to the narcotics trade as the Mexican economy. DEA Special Agent Harold D. Wankel explained it once, testifying to the House Banking and Financial Committee about the laundering of drug profits into the U.S. economy: "The use of payable-through-accounts held in U.S. banks by foreign banks makes it difficult for law enforcement to trace the money. These accounts can have hundreds of sub-account holders in foreign countries who have complete access to these accounts but who are unknown to the U.S. bank and maybe even to the foreign bank. The goal of all these schemes is to get the money into the banking system unchallenged."

And once in the banking system, marijuana and methamphetamine dollars become stock in Citibank and Apple. Blood money earned from desperate heroin junkies robbing grandmothers for a fix becomes venture capital for small business, legitimate and sincere. It's not a stretch to suggest that somewhere buried in each 401(k) and pension plan is a bit of cocaine residue.

As Charles Bowden wrote in *Down by the River:* "Centro de Investigación y Seguridad Nacional, the premier internal security apparatus within Mexico, once estimated that if the drug business disappeared overnight, the U.S. economy would shrink by 19 to 22 percent, the Mexican 63 percent. And in 1995, one Mexican drug-trafficking expert guessed that half the motel rooms in Mexico were ghost receipts, counted as sold to launder drug money. I stare at these numbers and I have no idea if they sound accurate or not—no one can really grapple with the numbers because illegal enterprises can be glimpsed but not measured."

The story ends with U.S. drug enforcement as a cottage industry and with millions employed on the back of prohibition and with new prisons going up all the time; hell, you can buy stock in prison construction. Sudden and complete enforcement would mean unemployment for damn near a million people and paralytic economic calamity in the form of instantaneous recession.

In a world of uncertain economic times with fluctuating profits, illegal narcotics are one of the few proven investments, steady and certain. And drug prohibition, like drug trafficking, is industrial and corporate— managed on both sides by MBA graduates attempting to perfect business models as they make rapidly narrowing concentric circles of adjustments, seeking to maximize profits by securing congressional approval for another prison, or breaking in a new drug route across the border. Both sides locked in an incestuous cycle of profiteering, condemning the other while staying mutely quiet about their sick symbiotic fueling of the other. It's the type of problem that no one really wants to go away.

It's what you call a mutually invested interest.

And according to a new 2007 threat assessment from the National Drug Intelligence Center, it was the cartels of northern Mexico that were responsible for almost all of it: the cocaine, the heroin, and most of the meth and marijuana entering the United States these days came from directly south of the border.

I **DROVE THE BACKWOODS** of Jacumba performing some early reconnaissance before my arrival on the border with the vigilantes. I needed to acclimate to the smell of the land. Jacumba, seventy-one miles east of San Diego, is a border town on the fringe of America—a petite mountain village with no center—the sort that came into existence quite by accident when enough people stumbled into living within distant earshot of one another, the sort of place where residents arrived and left drifting like wind-blown shrub brush. Jacumba had been big in the 1930s, an early Hollywood Hot Springs retreat, fanciful and decadent with hotels and spas, but that was before the Interstate passed it by in its routing, relegating the village to a slow entropic death of depleting population and interest.

Now it was dirty with drugs and smugglers and citizens on the take; just another narco corridor. What the *L.A. Times* in a 2006 article said was the number one spot of drug trafficking for southern California. No hotels left, no businesses left and even fewer people, but there were the husks of old cars—shot up and burned out and flipped over, a requiem to long-ago scenes of battle between drug smugglers working the corridor. Jacumba's defenders argue that it wasn't that bad, there had only been a handful of murdered residents in the last ten years. It was a slight defense. There was also only a handful of people who live here.

Like many border communities, the town existed before the border, and there's another Jacumba on the other side in Mexico, created when the border partitioned the village in two; it's a point of some interest that the Mexican police won't visit the Jacumba on their side of the border unless the Mexican Army is with them.

A Border Patrol agent will die here in two weeks.

But this was to be expected.

This was the Tecate Line, after all.

And as I passed the hinterland palaces of the West, isolated ranches, ramshackle trailer parks, and squat homes of peeling paint, the modern inheritors of Western wanderlust, I wondered at the character of those who made the desert their home; they seemed to be purposely hiding out from the rest of us and I was jealous of their anonymity. It also seemed a proper place for conspirators, no one was around to grab on to a careless accidental and dirty thought as they floated through the air.

I admired their necessary self-reliance. Out here, they still knew how to fix a car, hunt their own food, and defend the homestead—primal caveman shit that came in handy when the rest of us were all screaming our dainty little heads off during global economic calamity or nuclear apocalypse—because in the desert you couldn't entrust your protection to the formal institutions of civic society; in the West, folks looked after their own. And although I wasn't quite confident in my ability to look after myself, I certainly appreciated the sentiment.

I haven't lived among the desert people, but I suddenly felt that this was my tribe. I had never felt quite comfortable in the suburban environment I had grown up in. Suburbia had always seemed artificially quiet and serene, a corporate facsimile of small-town America with an unhealthy external fixation on appearance. In the desert, you could keep a goat tied up in your front yard or let a junked-out car slowly rot behind the house. And that was the type of place I suddenly realized I'd wanted to live all my life, where I could finish a beer and drop-kick it into the yard without a care.

I pulled to a stop at a small emaciated rotting trailer home, propped up on cinder blocks and tucked into a grove of trees, encircled by barbed wire and transformed into purposeful and defensible space. A brand-new convertible was parked in the driveway; from my truck I could still catch a whiff of that new car interior. I wondered what type of deranged desert person lived inside. I wondered if I should knock on the front door, ask for an interview. I wanted to ask how the owner felt living smack dab in the middle of a narco corridor. But mostly I wanted to ask why this piece of shit home was being fortressed against invasion by barbed wire and fencing. And then it occurred to me that perhaps that would be the type of inquiry that would catch me a bullet in the gut if said person in residence happened to be employed in the local industry of favor.

And then, as I started my truck back up again and pulled forward, my eye caught the reflection in my rearview mirror: a black SUV with tinted windows further back on the road, crouching to the shoulder, but moving slowly up on me in first gear.

"Shit!" I murmured quietly to myself. I leaned across the truck's cab into the glove box and pulled out my pistol, setting it on the seat next to me—just in case. I built up speed as I drove forward, moving slowly on the road's sudden and abrupt curves. My eyes watched in the rearview mirror as the black SUV copied my movements, keeping pace, disappearing for moments behind clusters of trees and brush before always reappearing again, set back the same distance as before.

I reached a T intersection. I came to a full stop and put on my blinker indicating I was going to turn right, and instead made a left-hand turn!

Goddamn, I was one sneaky son of a bitch!

I immediately floored the pedal, as the engine hummed and rattled, making a desperate dash for the highway.

In my rearview mirror, the SUV was charging, quickly dropping the distance between us.

THE FOLK SONGS, the narcocorridos, the drug ballads, were sung low and heavy like Johnny Cash but with the character and moral conviction of gangster rap. The songs, thousands of them, played across ghettos and bars in places like San Diego and Tijuana, Ciudad Juárez and El Paso.

And somebody was killing their authors, thirteen dead musicians within the last year.

Dissatisfied fans, probably.

Maybe it was Los Zetas. It was a fair enough guess, they were killing everyone: journalists, police, bankers, and anyone dumb foolish enough to think menacing thoughts in their general direction.

You know that old tough-guy euphemism from the movies? *You even dare kill me in a dream, you better wake up and apologize?*

That's Los Zetas.

Yes, they're just another criminal gang, but being an American, you can't quite understand the power they wield and the fear they inspire until you put it into a comparative context. It's not just the Sopranos putting the heavy lean on waste management in New Jersey or the Latin Kings shooting up their own ghettos, affecting the outside world only when a kid from a decent neighborhood occasionally and accidentally takes an errant bullet in the temple.

To really understand it, you have to imagine a U.S. criminal enterprise like the Mafia having enough power to execute the chief of police in San Diego in broad daylight and no one saying a goddamn thing about it. You have to imagine the Mafia physically taking over police stations in mid-sized cities and executing all the officers inside and no one having the power to stop them. You have to imagine the Mafia having more power than the FBI and working in cooperation with the United States Army. And you have to imagine the Mafia inspiring such an environment of fear that *The New York Times*, CNN, and Fox News all remain conspicuously quiet, afraid that their reporters will start ending up as decapitated burnt-out husks.

That's Los Zetas.

And the fear of Los Zetas rivals that of both the devil and Keyser Söze. The mere rumor of Los Zetas being within a several-hundred-mile radius is enough to keep the locals inside their homes and send shop owners scurrying, closing up early, shuttering their stores behind them as they abscond. And when Los Zetas was rumored to be taking up residence within fifty miles of a particular city within northern Mexico, it was said that the economy crashed—no shoppers with courage.

Los Zetas was a small group of deserters from the Special Air Mobile Forces Group, Mexican Special Forces, and they were the strong-arm enforcers for the Gulf Cartel. And they had recently, just within the last few months, decided they were going to be giving the orders, not taking them. And in their corporate split with the Gulf Cartel, there was also a corporate merger, this one with Guatemalan death squads known as Kaibiles, covert military operatives and famous jungle survivalists who were rumored to drink the blood of the animals they killed. And then Los Zetas went on a hiring spree, corrupt cops and crooked commandos, the more vicious the better. And Los Zetas was now a two-thousand-member paramilitary organization.

Their plan was to take over nothing less than all organized crime within Mexico. And to prove it, they were leaving a trail of dismembered limbs and bullet-strewn bodies as they robbed guarded casinos with automatic weapons and took over police stations midday, killing the few cops inside who refused to look the other way, to supply them with uniforms and equipment and weapons.

Not that they needed any more weapons or equipment. Before leaving the military they had ransacked the Mexican Army for all it was worth: grenade launchers, automatic weapons, rocket launchers, antiaircraft embattlements, and, of course, surface-to-air missiles.

Regular business supplies, mostly.

Or, so the story goes.

But the painful part of it all, the real head shaker, was that Los Zetas had been trained by the United States military. Where depends on whom you talked to. Some said at Fort Benning, Georgia, at the School of the Americas. Others said it was the Special Forces center at Fort Bragg. Either way, it seems their syllabus included torture and interrogation techniques, counternarcotics operations, surveillance, close combat training—Los Zetas was supposed to be the cartel cure, you see. They were trained and educated and cut loose into Mexico to hunt down and kill the cartels; tough luck then that they immediately went to work for them. And now, according to a leaked Justice Department memo, Los Zetas, quickly dominating the other Mexican cartels, was rumored to have their sights set on the United States.

Blowback was a bitch.

And already, dead bodies were popping up across Texas, killed utilizing special operations techniques, and there were cokehead Arizona National Guard soldiers letting shipments through. And urban U.S. gang members—the Mexican Mafia, the Texas Syndicate, MS-13, Hermanos Pistoleros—were starting to be discovered with the phone numbers of known Los Zetas contacts on their mobiles during routine arrests. Roughly speaking, plus or minus a few lesser cartels, Los Zetas controlled the eastern part of northern Mexico, Laredo and Juárez, and down south to Veracruz and Acapulco.

Of course, they weren't nearly as bad or as unpleasant as the fellows in the west who controlled Baja California and Tijuana. The Arellano-Félix, or Tijuana, Cartel was a family of brothers whose influence was widely regarded to equal that of the Mexican government. So widely feared were they, it was rumored that when they murdered the Tijuana police chief, they performed the execution in midday on a crowded street without masks or concealment, and not one witness came forward. And their influence didn't stop at the border; within the last two years the Southern District of California of the U.S. Attorney's Office had prosecuted seven American customs and Border Patrol agents on graft and corruption charges.

They specialized in the sort of business arrangements within Mexico that couldn't be refused: accept money or end up dead, but with a family-friendly policy. They didn't kill the potential witness, that person they sometimes left alive, instead they'd kill his mother, his father, his sister, his brother, his wife, his son, his daughter, his cousin—and on it goes. They killed a family of eighteen once. Eighteen family members in a single day. One wonders what that guy did to piss them off.

And these Arellano brothers, they were slicers and dicers, they liked the knives, the sharp objects. Ripping and tearing flesh could bring about the most amazing epiphanies from previously information-constipated individuals.

The thing about arresting them—everyone knew where they were—it's just that it couldn't be done. The brothers traveled with a small army. It wouldn't be so much an arrest as an attempted seizure of bin Laden at Bora Bora.

THE HEADLIGHTS OF the SUV lit up in a rotating revolving strobe of red and blue as I pulled over to the side of the road and I quickly covered the pistol with my jacket. I sat nervously, quiet, trying to calm myself so that I would pass the brief investigatory interview that was about to occur.

From my driver's side mirror, I saw a plainclothes officer get out of the SUV in body armor, his hand on his sidearm as he approached my window, hanging back at the rear of the truck.

I rolled down the window and peered out, temporarily blinded by the afternoon sun.

"Can I help you, Officer?"

"Just was wondering what you were doing around here?" the thickly mustachioed officer replied as he peered into the interior of my truck's cab and looked into the pickup bed.

"Did I not use a turn signal or something?" I asked, wondering how I had attracted this attention onto myself.

"Nope."

"I didn't break any laws?"

"Nope."

"Just wondering what I was doing out here?"

"Yep."

I wrinkled my face as I moved my head back inside the truck's interior.

This was different.

Normatively within the United States police officers had to have a reason to pull you over, witness a law or traffic violation or have reasonable suspicion that the vehicle stopped had been involved in the commission of a crime.

"So?" the officer asked.

"Yeah, so?"

"So what were you doing out here?"

I laughed, suddenly getting it—I was on the Tecate Line and that was reasonable suspicion enough.

"I'm not cartel if that's what you're thinking," I replied, suppressing a laugh, which I assumed to be of the infectious variety, the sort that would make the officer laugh too so that we could both have a good chuckle over this incident before he let me go. "Actually, I thought you were cartel."

The officer didn't smile. "Well, you say you're not cartel."

I felt a twisted tinge of pride that I could be mistaken for cartel.

"I'm not, honest to God."

And then the smile I was seeking, hesitant and subdued, emerged on the officer's face. "Why? You'd tell me if you were cartel?"

"I think so," I replied, unsure if I would.

I **SPENT THE NIGHT** at a sodden and filthy motel on the side of the Interstate where the "o" was hanging haphazardly from its parking lot sign and because there were no other guests and because it was only thirty-five dollars a night. The woman who checked me in was dressed only in a nightshirt as she scratched and sniffed her red nose, her pupils dilated as she bounced around the office high on something illegal and fresh from the border, while attempting to find a registration form.

Afterward, I moved to my room, which was decorated in a stained shag carpet with chipped artificial wood paneling and sheets that I knew, even without the benefit of a ultraviolet light, to be dribbled with creamy cum stains. I slid back the curtains and stared into the darkened distance where the border lay lurking—where Los Zetas was now battling it out with the Arellano-Félix Cartel of Tijuana. A giant pissing contest to see who could pump the most product into the ol' Estados Unidos and between them six hundred deaths just within the first six months of this year, seventy of them police officers and journalists. This mattered, because the territory that ran right up to the fence, out in the desert, away from the U.S. customs ports, is where they were waging war, and that was where I needed to go if I wanted to cross the border here in southern California.

I pressed RECORD on my audio recorder and spoke: "Day one of the border, day one of my investigation into southern California as a possible crossing site. Spending the night almost on the border, and tomorrow I go looking for border vigilantes. I'm hoping both to get their story so that I can understand border security from the micro perspective, and also that they'll be able to provide me with some valuable advice and intelligence on the probability of a successful crossing here at the Tecate Line." And then as an afterthought I added, "I do hope though to not run into Los Zetas or Arellano-Félix."

I slept on the floor in my sleeping bag while I watched reruns of *Matlock* through the static-infused television with the bent rabbit ear antennae, my neck cocked at an awkward and uncomfortable angle as I ate a gas station Subway sandwich.

And at the curb, just outside my motel, just below my window, is where they recently found another dead body, an encobijado, victim of the nearby border war, this one a Mexican and wrapped neatly in a blanket like a tortilla.

Chapter 5

THE PRISONER OF PATRIOT POINT

(SAN DIEGO SECTOR)

Old men and old coyote dogs
boil their dreams in the sun
—"Coyote Morning," author unknown

To what better purpose?
To what better end?
In Little Dog we trusted . . .

The sun was timid and hesitant, hanging on the horizon, still deciding which way to go in this early morning hour: mild balm or furious furnace. But moment by moment, she was looking ever brighter and it was my guess she was going to go with the later choice what with this being the desert and the height of summer and all.

There wasn't much time left so as I drove the dirt roads leading to the border, I rehearsed the scene of my introduction to the Minutemen, the border vigilantes. I pretended an impenetrable self-confidence and practiced saying my name, simple things that to others with normal social skills come easily. I reminded myself of my talking points: NASCAR and my military service. Like any good actor, I needed to be able to sell myself convincingly.

The Minuteman Project had started in April of 2005 under the tutelage of Jim Gilchrist, a retired Marine and certified public accountant from San Diego. The organization was self-billed as a group of patriotic citizens concerned about the federal government's failure to secure the border against an unending tide of illegal immigrants from Mexico. Often carrying weapons, purportedly for their own protection, they patrolled the border in support of the Border Patrol, their own role limited to simply observing and reporting the movement of illegal aliens across the border and occasionally providing first aid or water to the illegals when needed. They took their name from the everyman citizen militias of the Revolutionary War— also known as Minutemen—who were ready on a minute's notice to defend against the invading British. During the first border surveillance operation of the Minutemen outside Naco, Arizona, a onetime event mostly designed to draw media attention and raise awareness of the illegal immigration problem, the planners had stated they were careful in vetting volunteers to filter out racists and those with a criminal record, filling their ranks mostly with law enforcement and former military personnel, people who had training with firearms and discipline.

But then the original Minuteman Project became fractured in its top leadership as one of the project's co-founders, Chris Simcox, formed his own rival organization called the Minuteman Civil Defense Corps. And the organization, and the idea, kept splintering, like a spreading crack in a pane of glass broken beyond the point of containment. It had become an honest-to-God social movement, enlisting thousands of volunteers across the nation. Soon there were state chapters and breakaway groups all across the country, each borrowing on a variation of the Minuteman label, some allied together in a loose confederation, others in direct rivalry with one another.

And just recently, the Southern Poverty Law Center had designated the Minutemen as a hate group. My own research had turned up a trove of criticism leveled against various splinter groups for supposed acts of violence and intimidation toward illegal immigrants. Nowadays, if you believed what the Internet said, some of the groups were being heavily infiltrated by the Aryan Nation and the type of vehemently anti-government militias made famous by Timothy McVeigh.

The Minutemen I was visiting weren't the police officers that had joined Gilchrist's original movement. The Minutemen on the Tecate Line were a splinter group. And from everything I had read, they were a group far down along the fractured fault of Minutemen organizations; the sort that didn't adhere to policies vetting against undesirables.

I had interviewed Jim Gilchrist the previous day in San Diego so that I could arrive unannounced at the doorstep of the Minutemen hoping to be able to bandy his name about in a bid for some unearned trust. And Gilchrist had spent most of the morning informing me of a litany of horrors that were being inflicted upon our nation by our Mexican neighbors to the south . . .

Fifty years ago, immigration policy drove numbers, Gilchrist had informed me, but today the numbers drove policy. The increase of immigration was reshaping the language and the law to dissolve any distinction between legal and illegal aliens and, ultimately, the very idea of national borders. There were whole armies of illegal foreign-born criminal gangs in Los Angeles from places like El Salvador and Guatemala and Honduras. Yet should a cop arrest an illegal gang-banger for felonious reentry, it was the cop who would be treated as a criminal, for violating the LAPD's rule against enforcing immigration law. And the LAPD ban on immigration enforcement only mirrored bans in immigrant-saturated cities around the country, from New York and Chicago to San Diego, Austin, and Houston—"sanctuary policies" that prohibited city employees, including the cops, from reporting immigration violations to federal authorities. These laws testified to the sheer political power of immigrant lobbies, a power so irresistible that police officials shrank from even mentioning the illegal alien crime wave.

This here illegal immigration problem, it cut as many ways as you could think. It was a security issue, an economic issue, a cultural issue, a political issue. Hell, it was even a health and education issue; damn hospitals and schools were going broke all over the state.

In short, the country was fucked up.

"John, as the number of illegal aliens increases, at the current rate of invasion of at least five million per year, by the year 2025, there will be more illegal aliens occupying U.S. territory then there will be citizen voters," Gilchrist had explained. "The consequences will be staggering. Right now there are roughly 33 million aliens occupying U.S. territory, that's one in ten, when you have 40 percent of your population that's illegal, it will be impossible without an incredibly horrific civil war to dislodge them and make them return to their homeland . . . and they will do what the KKK did back in the Deep South in the 1920s. They'll get control of the system. The KKK became your mayors, they were in your city councils, they were your police chiefs and sheriffs. They were your business owners and academicians. The sole goal was to engage in racial supremacy. The same thing will happen here, when you have 70 to 80, maybe 120 million people from Mexico and Central America with the common bond of language and culture, they will literally be changing our culture and our economic system to fit their model for their country, for their homeland, and a weak cowardly Congress and a weak President with the wave of a magic wand will grant them all amnesty and immediate citizenship because it'll be out of fear of sheer numbers of 100 million people rising in the streets. That citizenship will entitle them to voting rights where they will support candidates that support Latin America agendas. And that is how they will conquer the United States without firing a shot and they will use our own Constitution and our own lax enforcement of the rule of law against us and the United States will be history. About 5 million get in per year undetected, 75,000 a week, that's close to four reinforced Army brigades entering illegally each week. And that number's going up."

It was like preparing for the Apocalypse. Every family needed to have a basement full of bottled water and a well-stocked larder of food, the Mexicans were invading!

I brought my truck to an abrupt halt. I was at the border. Before me stood an eight-foot brown metal fence, cutting a ragged boulevard through the desert. It was an odd demarcation, one that looked out of place as it divided a land against itself. It seemed an arbitrary division, it was the same desert on both sides of the fence, the same plant life, the same animals, the same geography, but the fence, that was the line in the sand that was not to be crossed; an artificial man-made construct on which so much perceived importance was structured.

A little further down to my right, I saw a couple of men next to pickup trucks unloading dirt bikes in a flat pasture. Minutemen, I figured. I was appropriately nervous. I felt as if the Minutemen would instantly recognize my subdued liberal impulses—my disinterested patriotism, my advocacy for gay rights, my ambivalent religious faith. They'd probably act friendly to my face while they secretly conspired behind my back to have me killed. And then a few days from now, I'd end up dead in the desert. And that'd be just fucking great. I drove over to their position and rolled down my window. Two men with Confederate flag hats holding beers looked at me strangely. The Confederate flag and beer . . . that was pretty much what I had been expecting to find.

"You two Minutemen?" I asked, my voice trying hard to sound casual and confident as they appraised me suspiciously.

The first one laughed. "No. You're looking for Minutemen?"

"Yeah," I replied. "Do you know where I can find some?"

"What sort you looking for?"

His question took me by surprise.

I hadn't known they came in different flavors.

The answer to his question, of course, was that I was looking for the reasonable type, the sort that adhered strongly to the original concept of the Minutemen who would welcome a man or woman of any political ideology, faith, or sexual orientation. The type that would care nothing about befriending a reasonable person such as myself who was somewhat socially liberal.

"I'm looking for the craziest sort there is," I replied.

They both laughed.

"Head up to the top of that mountain," the second one responded. "That's Patriot Point. He's the craziest of all of them. Last man standing, I reckon. He's crazy even by Minuteman standards."

I followed the angle of his finger to a distant peak where I could just make out the top of a U.S. flag flapping atop a towering pole.

Crazy sounded like exactly what I needed.

MY TRUCK STRUGGLED FORWARD, its ancient engine straining against the steep pitted incline of rocks, gravel spitting out the rear tires as I eyed the precarious draw of the mountain that loomed ahead of me. I offered a silent prayer and let off the gas as the truck started to roll backward. I felt for a spot of even traction and applied the full force of one flip-flopped foot to the accelerator. The truck lurched forward, the wheels gripping, and I slowly started to climb the last fifty meters.

And then, breaking like a shy dawn peering over and around the rocks—I came to know Patriot Point, looming like a wrecked garage sale.

Patriot Point seemed cobbled together by piecemeal appropriation: there was the 1960s-era Winnebago, its orange paneling muted to a pale yellow under years of bleaching sunlight, and the massive green Vietnam-era Army transport truck conjoined into a larger structure, the space between them acting as an impecunious patio. There was also the horse trailer that had been converted into a walk-in pantry, and the porta-potty, and the barbecue, and everywhere patio folding chairs and pock-marked Formica tables, and all of it covered by the sort of military camouflage netting meant to conceal positions from aerial photography. And just beyond, adding a garnish of respectability, a towering metal pole where an American flag curled and lapped listlessly, buoyed on weak winds.

I applied the brakes, got out of the truck, and immediately felt weak under the penetrating glare of the desert sun as beads of perspiration slid across my forehead. The sun played fiercely in the desert and didn't seem shy in sharing.

Just thirty meters further, off the tip of the peak, was the rusted metal border fence, Mexico rolling out on its downward slope. From up here, it seemed as if you could see to Chihuahua.

And in front of it all, at the precipice of the point, in a comfortable and colorful lawn chair, slouched an immobile shirtless wrinkled old man with a shock of wild white hair and a bushy mustache, his leathery skin beet red from the sun.

Is he dead? I thought to myself.

He's dead, I was sure of it.

I'd arrived to find a dead man.

I sighed as I looked back down the slope, appraising the route back off the mountain. Maybe if I got back down quick enough I could pretend I hadn't found him.

The door to the Winnebago slammed open and a barking angry dog raced toward me, kicking up a cloud of dust as it crossed to my position before suddenly transforming into happy-smiling panting enthusiasm upon making contact.

At the sound of the barking, the man stumbled awake with a fit, his face betraying surprise as he struggled to compose himself, sitting up astutely and peering out the scope that sat on a tripod in front of him as if he had been doing this the entire time.

He looked over at me cautiously as I offered a tenuous wave and let the dog sniff my hand.

"Hi," I said. "My name's John Rico, I'm a writer covering the illegal immigration issue. Was wondering if I could speak with you for a moment?"

The man was silent as he appraised me, shaking off the final residue of sleep before a scratchy hoarse voice grated by a lifetime of cigarettes asked, "You a reporter?"

"Something like that," I replied nervously. And then, as an afterthought, "I just got done meeting with Jim Gilchrist."

The old man spit in the dirt, "Jim Gilchrist is a low-down dirty dog."

"Yeah, that's what I thought," I replied agreeably. "He was a jerk." I spit in the dirt too.

He wore a suspicious scowl on his face and I suddenly had the strong feeling that he was going to duck behind the cover of the Army truck and emerge with a rifle and start shooting at me. I rapidly started to develop various contingency plans that involved leaping off the side of the mountain and doing a combat roll toward the border fence where I'd hide under the rock outcroppings.

"What's with the T-shirt?" he asked suspiciously.

I looked down at my own chest, suddenly realizing that my Minuteman Civil Defense Corps T-shirt, which I'd worn to inspire yet another level of unearned trust, might be having the opposite effect of being a divisive instrument due to incestuous political infighting that I knew nothing of.

"It's just a T-shirt," I replied smiling meekly. "I don't know no better."

There was a long pause as he studied me. Deciding my fate, perhaps. I swallowed hard as I was observed, waiting for judgment.

"We don't recognize the Minuteman Civil Defense Corps around these parts," he explained.

"Oh, I don't either, not at all. They're full of shit, everyone knows that," I explained.

And then, his entire demeanor suddenly shifted and he exclaimed, "Hell, come on over, amigo! Have a seat. Welcome! Welcome to Patriot Point!"

He led me between the truck and the Winnebago where the canopy provided shade and pulled out two lawn chairs as he lit a Camel and dug into a cooler of lukewarm water for two Pepsis, handing me one. I sat down as I eyed his interior courtyard, a motley mess of military and camping gear, trash, empty soda cans, and cigarette butts littering the ground. A long table was filled with opened boxes of food and spilled coffee cans that ran the width of the Winnebago. Overflowing trash bags were tied off to the edge of the truck.

I knew about this type of living—the sort that happened quite by accident when one started living alone for too long without human contact. My apartment had turned out the same way during several experimental episodes of self-imposed isolation.

"I think you caught me in the middle of my midday siesta," the man laughed, throwing on a stained shirt and a Vietnam-era Army jacket with captain's insignia as he tied off a few garbage bags in a feeble effort to make the place look more presentable. "We power nap up here, amigo! It's twenty-four/seven at Patriot Point, amigo! Twenty-four/seven, yes, sir," he said as he tossed me a Mountain Minutemen T-shirt. "Here put that on, make yourself more respectable."

"Why don't you like the other Minutemen?" I asked as I changed shirts.

"They all let the cartels scare them off, for one. For another, they're not committed to the cause," he explained. "They're just in it for the fame and the glory."

I laughed a little too early and he shot me a look.

It wasn't a joke.

"Is that just a jacket or is that your rank?" I asked, clearing my throat, eager to change the subject.

"Yes, it's my rank. You're speaking to a captain of the Mountain Minutemen of Jacumba, Tecate, and the Mountain Empire."

"How many Mountain Minutemen are there?"

He was quiet for a moment before the embarrassed reply as he took a seat, lighting up another cigarette, "Just myself."

His dog started to sniff me and he offered a firm kick to the dog's ass. "That's Freckles, don't mind her." Freckles moved to her master and he affectionately took her face to his own and offered her a kiss. "Yes, you is one *ugly* dog, aren't you! You one goddamn *ugly* dog!" And then, forgetting his manners, he suddenly extended a hand and said, "The name's Robert Crooks, but everyone around here calls me Little Dog. Little Dog of the Mountain Minutemen. I'm a captain without men."

"John Rico," I replied, returning the handshake.

"What do you want to know, John Rico? Anything you want to know, I'll tell you. I'm an open book, John. I don't have anything to hide."

"Why don't you start by telling me about your operation here and how you got started?" I asked, crossing my legs and readying the pen in my hand.

"What we have here . . . is . . . a sophisticated . . . neighborhood watch," Little Dog replied, his words expelling in a slow, deliberate, methodical reply as if he has been waiting his whole life for this moment and practicing for years at appearing thoughtful. "I used to be out in Arizona with. the very first Minuteman Project but Jim Gilchrist fired me. How you can fire a volunteer I don't know, but I wasn't content to sit on a tailgate banging my drum. I was a little too aggressive for their standards, so they fired me and I asked myself, and prayed on the matter, where can I make a difference? And that's when I set up shop here on Patriot Point. Had this Army truck here donated by Border Patrol and was living under that for a couple of months until the Indians donated the RV." Little Dog looked around his encampment, realizing all that he'd managed. "Guess she's coming together quite nicely now. You see, John, what I'm trying to do here is make the vigilante pill more polished for mainstream America—"

And then the radio in his seat's cup holder came alive: "We got four inbound committed, about four hundred meters off the 240 marker, over."

A sly smile crept over Little Dog's face as he winked at me, his bushy white eyebrows folding like wings into a steep downward almost vertical position, which give his smile the tone of terrible gleeful and exuberant menace.

Little Dog and I moved to the front of the encampment, dragging our lawn chairs behind us as he leaned in to the scope and sought out his prey. He sat back and motioned me over to look as he responded into the radio, "Yep, I see them. You want to hit the button?"

I squinted into the eyepiece to see four Mexicans running past some boulders they had been using as cover.

"Well, I'll be damned," I said leaning back up. "That's pretty neat."

"Yeah, they're about ready to jump the fence," the other voice on the radio said. "Let's pop her."

"I'll call Border Patrol," Little Dog replied. He switched out the radio for a cell phone he kept tied around his neck with Army 550 cord and dialed. "Hello," he said with an informality born out of frequency. "Yep, it's Little Dog. We got four out by the 240 marker, about two minutes inbound. Okay, you too. Later."

"How often do you see them like this? Daily?" I asked.

Little Dog let loose a loud bellowing chest-rattling laugh. "Daily? Amigo! This is every other minute, amigo! This is nonstop! They come through here by the thousands each day, day after day. It's a damn war, amigo! This is the flood, and I am the rock upon which the flood crashes!"

I must've looked surprised because he readjusted the scope to a new position. I looked through to see a well-manicured expansive ranch house in Mexico, isolated and alone in the desert, two flashy new black Mustangs in the driveway, the house surrounded by barbed-wire fencing.

"You see that? That's the cartel," Little Dog explained.

"Someone's looking back at me," I replied, noticing a Mexican man in Duke hat and boots standing in the long twisting gravel driveway with binoculars staring back at me.

"Yeah, of course, they watch us, we watch them, they watch us watch them, we watch them watch us watching them!"

Little Dog adjusted the scope a bit to focus on a white truck driving on rural dirt roads within Mexico.

"What's that?" I asked.

"That's tonight's shipment."

"Shipment of what?"

Little Dog roared with laughter. I *was* wet behind the ears!

"That's the dope, amigo! That's the dope! All day long, all night long, all of it across the border. Open twenty-four hours a day, seven days a week, three hundred and sixty-five days a year! They don't sleep and neither do I! This is the funnel point for all of southern California, amigo! To the west you've got suburbanization and flat desert where you're visible, to the east you've got the Saharan Empire and the Yuma Flats, you'll bake in those goddamn sand dunes. No, right fucking here! This is the Mountain Empire, amigo! You've got Tecate to the west, Campo right below us, and Jacumba to the east! This is it! This is where *everyone* enters into California! Goddamn you've got the fucking goddamn Highway 94 less than half a mile from the border here! That's nothing but a hop, skip, and a jump for little Julio! This is where they want to cross!"

And looking out upon Mexico, I could immediately see that he was right. Being from Colorado, I didn't know if the slight rotund rocky hills and ravines I was looking at deserved to be called mountains, but they did offer a lot of places to hide. It was where I'd want to cross if I was an illegal. It was also, I decided, where I wanted to cross as an American— the quarter-mile sprint to the highway and back to my truck was a luring and enticing offer. I was riveted by the idea of a fifty-mile movement through the desert at the Devil's Highway, but I was also pragmatic. The Tecate Line seemed an offer too good to pass up.

"This daytime traffic is the nonbusiness hours. You want to see rush hour traffic, you stay awake at night."

I leaned back from the scope. I was a bit shocked. If what he was telling me was true, well, it all seemed a bit . . . brazen.

"I knew there was drugs on the border, but I thought it was . . . I don't know, pushed back a few miles," I offered.

"I don't give a good goddamn about little Julio coming over to work the lettuce fields, amigo! That's not the problem! It's the damn cartels, my friend! This all here, this country of southern California and northern Mexico, it's not run by the U.S. and Mexican governments, it's run by the Arellano-Félix cartel! They're running so much meth, heroin, cocaine, marijuana through this fucking border it's enough to fill up the whole goddamn country. We got AK-47s coming through, bodies, human smugglers, fucking everything, my friend! It's a wide-open border, amigo! Shit, just last week they caught a 180-pound dope shipment just a half-mile away in a big truck being driven right over the fence off a ramp. Shit, there was a big gun battle between the cartels not a hundred meters from the point just down that hill there not a month ago. We got Mexican military making incursions into the U.S. down by Jacumba, and Leland and I . . . that's Leland on the radio, next mountain over . . . just a few months back we alerted Border Patrol to a bunch of dope peddlers crossing, they intercepted them, got them to name names, got to the captains of the Félix Cartel, three months later Coast Guard pulls one of the Félix brothers off a fishing boat in the Sea of Cortez. That's how it works, my friend."

Little Dog collapsed into his lawn chair at the front of the encampment, looking out into Mexico as he lit another Camel. "The prisons are going crazy right now, San Quentin and Chino, they're all on lockdown because they're not getting their supply, because we're stopping it right here on the Tecate Line!"

"That's pretty impressive," I responded.

"The Jacumba Indian nation, the tribe that owns the casino up the road? They're all a bunch of meth dealers and car thieves, but the old ones, you know, the wise ones? They had this history, this story mythologized into legend back from the olden frontier days that someday a group of men would come to the mountain and free the evil within it . . ." Little Dog paused quietly as he waited for me to make the connection.

I didn't.

"The Mountain Minutemen!" he roared, laughing, connecting the dots for me.

"Oh right, you're driving off the evil . . . okay, yeah, sure, I get it," I responded, shaking my head at my own stupidity as Little Dog laughed at my incredulousness.

"Wow," I replied, my fingers writing furiously. "Evil and mountain, got it." I winked at him as I dotted the final "i."

"Listen to this," Little Dog said. He turned the dial of the radio and I could hear rapid-fire Spanish being spoken. "That's the cartels, amigo! They're talking about you!" Little Dog roared with laughter as he saw my face grow slack and pale. "Shit, them damn coyotes get on the radio all the time, keep me up half the night, '*Hey Grandpa! You blinked, punto! I come kill you, punto!*'"

Little Dog stood abruptly, faced Mexico, grabbed his balls and screamed, "COME GET YOUR FUCKING CHICKEN BURRITO, MOTHERFUCKERS!"

He turned back around smiling as he retook his seat, arching his eyebrows as if to suggest that we sure showed them, and seeing only confusion on my face explained, "They get a chicken burrito once they're caught by Border Patrol before they're transported back to Mexico."

"What the hell are they talking about me for? I just got here! I'm not involved in all this!" I shrieked, only slightly aware that I needed to modulate the tone and pitch of my voice as I was starting to sound like a little girl. "I don't want cartels talking about me!"

I was very disturbed that the cartels were talking about me.

"That's why they're talking about you, amigo! They're noticing a new car on Patriot Point, they're looking you over, checking you out!" Little Dog stood and did a little bouncy hip-gyrating dance as he laughed hysterically, shaking flip-flopped feet back and forth in an impromptu cha-cha-cha.

Little Dog walked to the edge of the plateau and waved his arms in the air and yelled, "Welcome to the nightmare! Listen up, amigo. You take this story and you tell it to all the people in the rest of America, tell them they need to clean out their ears! Abre los ojos, mi amigo! Open your eyes! This is the Tecate Line from Tecate to Jacumba!"

I smiled. He was a funny guy.

"Yeah, um, about the cartels talking about me . . . that doesn't mean anything does it?" I asked nervously as I craned my neck and tried to peer into Mexico hoping to be able to see them. "I mean, they'll stop after a few minutes, won't they?"

I was giving the cartels two minutes to talk about me and get it out of their system. Two minutes, no more.

"Amigo, if you don't want dangerous, you've come to the wrong fucking place! See this?" Little Dog moved to his truck where he pointed to a rumpled swath of metal across its hood. "Sniper's bullet, was trying to take off my fucking head." He disappeared into the Winnebago and returned a moment later with a smaller scope, its tripod destroyed by another bullet. "See this? Shots have been fired, my friend. When I was in the Army we called that an act of war. We've got half a million people in Los Angeles waving foreign flags on U.S. soil, if that's not an invasion, I don't know what is."

"What do you do when they shoot at you?"

"Fire back, goddammit!" Little Dog barked, before he retrospectively considered his comment and added, "Not that we do any of that around here. God forbid someone should die. But this is a war and the cartels took the first shot, I'm not going to say we use weapons, but let's just say

we have a liberal rattlesnake abatement program around these parts!"
Little Dog erupted into raucous laughter, his face collapsing into nothing
but bushy eyebrows and mustache, brought together by a pinched face.
"It's better to be judged by twelve than carried by six, amigo. We only got
two rules out here, first rule is stay alive, second rule is don't shoot anyone you don't have to."

It seemed a sane and reasonable response.

"Shit, they've already come over the fence and poisoned two of my
dogs." He eyed Freckles, who cocked her own head curiously, returning
his gaze. "Suppose they'll be coming for her soon enough."

And then Leland's voice from the radio: "We got fifteen moving due
northeast, just south of Machete Mountain."

Little Dog took up his position behind the scope as he responded,
"You want to dot the 'i'?"

"I'll place the call," Leland said through a blast of static.

Suddenly, I heard the whirl of an incoming swooping helicopter. Little Dog stood erect at the military position of attention, offering a firm
salute as the helicopter skirted the edge of Patriot Point, pulling a hard
U-turn to avoid flying into Mexico. The helicopter's co-pilot returned the
salute and over the radio was the co-pilot's voice, "Little Dog, you get
more ass than a Sunset Boulevard hooker!"

As the helicopter traveled the length of the border fence, Little Dog
cocked one thumb backward after them, "That's the Border Patrol. Everyone up here knows me, hell I got the captain of the Border Patrol bringing me newspapers every morning." He was quiet for a moment of
consideration as he stood, hands on hips, staring into Mexico. "This here
should be a goddamn national monument, because it's at Patriot Point
where the resistance started, this is the line of no retreat, the demarcation between the kill zone and civilization, the point where the movement to take back our country began! That's what the Border Patrol calls
me, the Prisoner of Patriot Point, because I've been up here perpetually
for a year and a half. First time I left the point was just a few months ago,
had a heart attack so I went to go stay with my dad until Leland started
getting shot at, so I raced back."

"How long you going to stay up here?" I asked.

"Until the border is secure," he replied gruffly. "Or until I die,
whichever comes first. For a penny or a pound, you heard that before?
For a penny or a pound? It comes from the old privateer days when they
went out on the old naval vessels, pirates and such, to rape and plunder.
When they signed on, it was for a penny or a pound, they were in for the

duration and that's what I'm doing, I'm here for the duration. I got my Social Security check, I got my recliner and my television up here and my air-conditioning. I can either sit on my ass back in Santa Barbara and slowly die or I can sit on my ass here and do something about it. Shit, I'm fifty-seven years old, my biggest trick is waking up each morning and there ain't no U-Hauls in heaven, you know what I'm saying, you can't take it with you, so what's the point? Why the fuck not, amigo?"

Why the fuck not, indeed!

I studied him intently as he sucked on a Camel cigarette as he surveyed Mexico with intermittent glances between the scope and a pair of binoculars, looking all stoic in the wind shear, as he let the first silent moment since we met fall between us.

He was absolutely insane.

Made delusional by too much isolation as he wallowed in his sun-baked delusions of grandeur.

I loved him.

Leland's voice on the radio: "Twelve more crossing the border, inbound and committed."

"The end's almost upon us, amigo," Little Dog said. "Pretty soon it's going to all be over. Us, them, everyone, everything. We're on borrowed time. The world's getting tired at the edges and she's about ready to collapse in on herself."

It certainly seemed that way.

A concussive clap of gunfire echoed throughout the valley below us. I arched my eyebrows asking if we should be alarmed.

Little Dog waved away my concern with one limp-wristed wave. "That's just Leland killing rattlesnakes." He winked at me. "Rattlesnake abatement."

THE SUN CRESTED the sky, broiling the desert beneath its glare, as the illegals continually crossed into America. Little Dog had been right, it wasn't an hourly event, it was an every other minute event. And already, just six hours in, I could feel the icy touch of distant insanity. I imagined being at Patriot Point day after day, week after week, month after month, an unending shift without sleep or shower performed mostly in isolation save for sporadic radio contract with Leland, and all of it under the gaze of a burning sun god. I understood his condition and in this understanding I began to forgive him for his eccentric madness.

And already my casual indifference to the illegal immigration problem was radically skewing to recognition that perhaps the open border wasn't just an issue that needed attention, but a crisis on the verge of catastrophe. It wasn't a feeling or opinion based on rational facts or hard data, rather it was formed by the visceral punch in the gut that came from seeing firsthand the perpetual onslaught of so many foreign nationals moving into our country. Whether they were here to abide by the law and only quietly work, as proponents argued, or whether they were a criminal force depleting our resources, as opponents argued, was immaterial. The point was that as a nation, right or wrong, we *did* have laws governing who we would allow into our country, and to see such flagrant violation of the laws and nobody doing anything about it was unsettling. Already I had lost track of the numbers who had crossed, most of whom had *not* been apprehended by Border Patrol . . .

NUA . . . No unit available . . .

. . . and my mind reeled when I considered the collective effect of this assault on the border as realized over months and years.

And *this* was only a small portion of the border, one fixed point upon a 1,950-mile stretch that covered four states. Understanding that the Mountain Empire and the Tecate Line received disproportionate traffic as a funnel point for illegal immigration because of the possibility of a rapid dispersement due to Highway 94 being less than a mile from the border did little to compensate against the intense feeling of anger at seeing my nation so easily infiltrated by foreign citizens. Illegal immigration suddenly seemed like an issue that each and every American should be concerned with.

And here on the Tecate Line, illegal immigration was intimately tied to drug smuggling. Carrying a bundle of dope to the other side was the necessary price of admission for many illegals too poor to afford alternate payment, and too powerless to refuse the offer.

And on the U.S. side, save for the occasional Border Patrol truck, it was undefended, guarded only by one old man and his dog who survived only on a Social Security check and donated groceries; fueled by equal parts nicotine and righteousness.

Little Dog spent the afternoon showing me his operation. A smaller plateau just below Patriot Point operated as a makeshift landing zone for helicopters. A satellite dish routed cable television into his Winnebago. He illustrated his plans to make an outdoor projection theater when football season started.

And slowly, I started to envision myself living on the line, here at Patriot Point. I imagined calling home to my wife and trying to break the news that I had decided to stay a year in Campo, California. When she inevitably got upset and asked why, I'd tell her about the allure of Patriot Point, how somewhere within the heat and the sweat of the day, it held a certain unidentifiable attraction—a purpose and reason for being.

I felt as if I had arrived.

I was home.

I WAS ON the phone with Agent Lloyd Easterling of the California Border Patrol Public Affairs Office. I was looking for some official judgment. "You know you've got Minutemen getting shot at down here?" I asked.

There was a slight pause on the other end of the phone and then, "We got Border Patrol agents getting shot at too."

And then another long pause.

"Yeah, okay," I responded before I hung up.

I rubbed my temple where the headache started to build as I felt my brain baking in my skull from the unrelenting heat. I had asked Little Dog to talk and talk he did. What I hadn't counted on was how lonely he had been up here at Patriot Point, how much he needed someone just like me to ask him what he thought; they were burning opinions he had wanted desperately to share for years.

For hours now he had gone into excruciating detail about the linkage of every criminal element and enemy that America had and how they were all interconnected and how border security was the single solution to all that ailed our country. Cuba, the Islamo-fascists, the communists, it was all related to the lack of a fence. He offered me rambling artificial statistics that he made up on the spot and excitedly recalled stories about Jacumba, where the shit had been serious, and this here at Patriot Point this was fucking retirement compared with Jacumba and if it hadn't been for the damn Border Patrol kicking them past the 220 marker and out of Jacumba, he'd be making a real difference. Everyone knew that it was that side of the Tecate Line where the shit was heavy.

"John, the thing of it is this," Little Dog said as I nodded reflexively, my head perpetually bobbing up and down to convey understanding as I tried not to listen. "We've got thirty million illegal foreign nationals in our country who don't speak the damn language, who don't have allegiance to this country, who don't have real skills—you think we're getting their doctors and lawyers? Hell no! We're getting their criminals, their unskilled migrant farmworkers! And the thing of it is, I ain't a racist, I got no problem with immigrants or Mexicans, but if you're going to enter my country, then by God do it at the port of entry and announce your intentions!" Little Dog collapsed into his seat as he lit up another Camel. "America's losing her way, John. She's slowly dying and no one cares, that's what's so bad about it. No one cares. You got me, a dog, Leland, and some worthless Campo Minutemen down the other way, and that's it! Why is it *our* responsibility to defend our country's borders from invasion? Why aren't others out here helping? Why isn't the government doing something about this? Why have the damn laws in the first place if you're not going to enforce them? You think I want to be out here? I've got better things I could be doing . . . I don't want to be here, but I swore an oath to protect this country, and a good soldier never forgets an oath."

"Uh-huh," I replied wearily, not even bothering to take notes anymore.

"And did you know they have training camps in Mexico for illegal aliens?"

"Sure they do," I replied.

"Sure as fuck they do. Place down in the Yucatan, read about it."

I sighed.

Little Dog put out a cigarette on the ground and lit up another and replied, "Let me tell you how I got started in all of this . . . I was out in Santa Barbara talking to my VFW post commander, I asked him, 'Hey, Bob, you hear about this Minuteman thing that's starting in Arizona?' And Bob says to me, 'Yeah, it's a long-distance beer run!'" Little Dog bellowed with laughter, his frosty mustache twirling and twitching, his voice booming two decibels too loud for his body. "So I get on my CB radio and I call out, 'Hey, can anyone give a patriot a ride?' A feller gets on there and says, 'Where ya going?' I tells him, 'I'm on my fishing boat, heading out to Tombstone, Arizona, to join up with the Minutemen.' He tells me he's going to pull over off the side of the Interstate to take a nap and if I can get there by the time he wakes up, he'll give me a ride. And he does, all the way down to a TA truck stop in Ontario where I caught a ride to Tucson and then another straight into Tombstone . . . John, it was a beautiful thing, my feet never even touched the ground. And it was then that I realized that my being here was divinely inspired by God. That I was the rusty wrench in God's toolbox sent to plug the leaks on the border. This here is a spiritual thing. We have to stop the evil that prevails on the other side of the border. The illegals, they know about me. These other so-called Minutemen down east of us, they're the weekend warriors. They're not committed, not like me. I'm what you call proactive. I don't just sit up here, I . . . engage . . . the . . . enemy. I . . . want . . . them . . . to . . . fuck . . . with . . . me! This is my country, bring it on motherfuckers. You want an asshole contest? Start here! I'm fifty-seven years old. I got a few years left! The illegals call me Commander Chico of the Yanquis, the el vigilante de las fronteras!"

"Yep," I replied, nodding my head in agreement.

Little Dog was quiet as he studied me, observing my indifferent reception to his boasts.

Little Dog pinched his unfinished cigarette between two fingers and flicked it behind me to the dirt, his face curling into a menacing smile: "You want to take a ride?"

WE TRAVELED THE border road in his old rusted Ford pickup as it twisted and turned and Little Dog talked about how you couldn't trust your neighbor or your fellow man, not in America, not anymore. They'd just as soon shoot you in traffic than hold a reasonable conversation. And in New York, they had whole generations of African American communities ruined on the poison that was entering the country right here at the Tecate Line and wasn't it a real tragedy? And in San Francisco the fags were parading in the street, proud of their own sin, reveling in their debauchery. And on television they are marrying people they'd just met five episodes earlier. And the atheists wanted us all to turn away from God—it never used to be like this. And had I ever read the Bible?

America was dying, you see.

America was losing her way.

And he wasn't going to be a part of it. He couldn't stand idly by while his country slowly devoured itself from within. Sooner or later, everyone had to make a stand, draw a line in the sand and say they would no longer accept it.

He was making his stand at Patriot Point.

I started to see him as a prophet—a mad messiah of the desert. He reminded me of the Japanese soldiers found in the jungle years after the war had ended, still serving the Empire.

He told me of his life before Patriot Point with the purposeful vagueness of one hoping to conceal a great many facts. After the Army, he had returned to Santa Barbara and become a fisherman before he was slowly forced into an early retirement by the corporate fisheries with their nesting cages and cheating technologies. And there were allusions to former wives and hard drinking and children that he no longer knew. It was the life of a perpetual hell-raiser and one seemingly filled with much regret—regret that was being atoned for through this late-in-life service to his country, a service that provided him with his reason for being.

On my right-hand side we passed another encampment composed of a crumpled RV and a pickup. A grizzled unshaven large man wearing stained sweatpants and a John Deere cap waved with one hand as he chambered a rifle with the other.

"That's Leland," Little Dog explained, returning the wave as we passed.

We drove for another minute and then suddenly Little Dog slammed on the brakes of the truck as he pointed them out to me—a group of six or seven Mexicans hiding just fifty meters away in the rocky outcropping of boulders above us on the Mexican side of the border—waiting for us to pass before they made the one-mile dash to the highway.

"FUCK YOU, MOTHERFUCKERS! FUCK YOU!" Little Dog screamed out his driver's side window.

"Look, there's a second group," I said, my eyes suddenly focusing and realizing that another group of at least ten were hiding just beyond the first group.

Little Dog gave them the finger and screamed, "GO BACK TO FUCKING MEXICO YOU FUCKING MOTHERFUCKERS!" His reddened face trembled with apocalyptic rage as his body shook. The truck lurched forward and I looked over to realize that his feet were trembling, slipping off the brake. Little Dog's breathing came in hyperventilated gasps as he turned his attention back to the road and inched the truck slowly forward.

For Little Dog, the border issue couldn't become any more personal. It was an issue he had devoted his every waking moment to until it had twisted into an obsession. And every time a non-U.S. national passed illegally into America, it became not only a violation against his country, but a violation against his purpose and reason for being. It was also cyclical and self-serving: the more they crossed, the more intense the necessity of his being on the border.

Ahead of us, a Border Patrol truck drove toward us, riding the same border road that paralleled the fence. Little Dog pushed off to the shoulder of the road as the Border Patrol vehicle came to a stop next to us.

"What's going on, Jeff?" Little Dog asked. "You got two groups right behind us up in the rocks."

Jeff looked uninterested. "Yeah. Another twenty or so back there," he said, motioning ahead of us. "I'll just drive back and forth, we'll let 'em bake out here in the sun for a while, what do you think?" He smiled as he looked up and wearily evaluated the sun.

"How's business?" Little Dog asked.

Jeff laughed, shrugging indifferently. "Usual, you know. How's business at Patriot Point?"

"Same," Little Dog replied. "Nonstop, all day."

"Yep," Jeff said casually, anxious to break from Little Dog and drive aimlessly.

"Well, take care," Little Dog said, putting the truck in gear, slowly sliding forward.

"Yep," Jeff responded.

"Jeff's a good guy. Methodist, I think." Little Dog drove forward along the road. "Take a look up here to your right."

On my right, down a long sloping valley was a large empty ranch house.

"That used to belong to a lady who asked for our protection. Her family had called Border Patrol on the coyotes a few times so they started poisoning all her horses and her dogs, trying to break into the house each night. I assigned it to some guys in the Campo Minutemen when I was a captain over with them but the guys who were supposed to guard it got scared when they heard the coyotes were going to kill them. The coyotes killed all her horses and the lady left the place unsold and moved to Montana or somewhere. Take a look here on your left."

On our left was Machete Mountain, a barren hill of gravel and sagebrush that had the distinction of existing in between Mexico and the United States. The border cut perfectly across its summit, cleaving the mountain in half and forcing it into dual citizenship. At the pinnacle of the mountain's peak was a U.S. flag, fixed onto a granite marker and laying claim to the land.

"The cartels take the flag down, I put it back up," Little Dog said. "It's like contested territory in trench warfare, like in the First World War . . . but without the trenches."

Machete Mountain had gotten its name after Little Dog had been attacked there by a drug runner with a machete.

I grimaced. A machete attack sounded bad. "How'd that end?" I asked.

Little Dog smirked. "Never bring a knife to a gunfight."

I nodded, not really wanting to know more.

"Take a look up here," Little Dog said.

"What happened to the fence?" I asked as we drove to the west side of Machete Mountain's downward slope and there was only empty desert.

"That's the end of it. Ain't no fence from here to Tecate."

My mind reeled, not quite understanding that there *was* no border fence.

"Now you tell me why after fifty years of illegal immigration they ain't got a goddamn border fence over but a tenth of the goddamn border?"

"Well," I said slowly as I examined the terrain, "it's a rough environment. It'd be difficult to build. Then I'm sure you got all types of ranches, and state parks, and different states, lots of jurisdictional difficulty. Plus, it'd be expensive, that's almost two thousand miles to build a fence through all types of different—"

"Bullshit," Little Dog interrupted me.

I was quiet. It *was* bullshit.

This was the United States, we had put a man on the moon, we had military bases in almost a hundred countries around the world, and we had built the Interstate Highway System, 47,000 miles, and had completed most of it ten years.

The only conceivable reason that a border fence didn't exist was because it wasn't a priority.

"NAFTA," Little Dog replied solemnly. "They want to make North America one big free-trade zone without borders, they're planning a superhighway from Guatemala into Canada so the corporations can get rich while they let the nation bleed. You heard about the amero, yet? New currency. Going to combine the peso and the dollar."

I didn't know about his North American free trade conspiracy theory, but it certainly seemed that some ulterior motive had to be in operation that would allow a rich First World country to have such open borders with a poor Third World country.

Or, maybe it was just that the actual border fence as it currently existed was ineffective so why build more of it? After all, it wasn't as if the Mexicans couldn't simply climb. I didn't know the answer to these questions, only that it was unsettling to look out the windshield of the truck into the desert and not know where America ended and Mexico began.

On the mountain above us, the Mexicans waited quietly for the fury to pass as they broiled in the desert sun.

LITTLE DOG BROUGHT the truck to a stop and the wicked smile came over his face again. We were at the entrance to a train tunnel that was buried deep into a mountain, linking the two countries.

"You ready for a little reconnaissance?" he asked as he reached over my lap into the glove box and pulled out a .45 pistol. "You're about ready to see the true meaning of the word 'proactive.'"

"What?" I replied nervously as we got out of the truck. "Reconnaissance . . . in Mexico, you mean?"

Little Dog roared with laughter.

And as we approached the tunnel's entrance, Little Dog mumbled about the interconnectedness of the problems of civilization and original sin and how the prices at the supermarket were all linked together in one large incestuous mess with illegal immigration.

I found that he was starting to make sense in a twisted sort of way.

"Who owns this country, John? Do the Mexicans own it?"

"No, Little Dog," I replied.

"Do the Islamo-fascist Muslims own it?"

"No, Little Dog," I replied.

"Who owns it then?"

"We do, Little Dog," I replied.

"Goddamn right."

Little Dog entered the train tunnel and I followed into Mexico.

Chapter 6

HOLLER, IF THERE'S HELL
(SAN DIEGO SECTOR)

We sprinted along the darkened train tunnel as I kept close to the curvature of the walls behind Little Dog, who kept both hands gripped on his pistol, maintained at the low-ready in front of him like a well-trained soldier, the barrel pointed toward the dirt. I followed with the fingers of my left hand pointed like an imaginary gun, my own pistol being left back in my truck at Patriot Point.

The light diminished, leaving us in an escalating darkness that stank of feces and urine.

"Mexican bathroom," Little Dog replied to a question unasked, chuckling to himself.

Little Dog was quiet amid the silence. The only sound that of the repetitive slap of the back of my flip-flops hitting my heel with each step.

Fuck, I'm in flip-flops, I thought to myself as my feet stumbled into a pool of what I hoped was water. I made a mental note that the next time I went on a covert surveillance operation in Mexico I should at least wear some tennis shoes.

At the tunnel's midpoint, somewhere deep under the mountain, a chalk line on the wall designated the border between the U.S. and Mexico.

Little Dog knelt down behind a small outcropping in the tunnel wall and pulled out a knife from his belt. He held up a plastic jug of water, which he cut down the center before tossing it casually behind him where the water gurgled into the clay. He picked up several bags of food—bread and tortillas—and scattered them around the tunnel floor before he started moving toward the tunnel's end.

I kicked a lone piece of bread as I passed; a feeble token gesture of agreement.

Take that, Mexicans!

Soon we were at the mouth of the tunnel, inside Mexico. Little Dog immediately moved the pistol to his overhead twelve o'clock as he scanned the area in front of us before he moved forward.

And suddenly, I was rippling with fear, my heart colliding with my rib cage as it beat wildly. The thing of it is, we *weren't* alone. Just moments earlier while on the border road we had passed at least forty Mexicans. In fact, the very mountain we were climbing out from the bottom of was covered with Mexicans.

Of course, despite Little Dog's horror stories of the coyote guides he had described as psychopathic killers, I still assumed that most of the Mexicans on this mountain were only poor migrants, so desperate for a chance at a better life that they were willing to endure the heat and Little Dog, the Minutemen, and the Border Patrol. If anything, we didn't have anything to fear from them, it was they who should fear us.

We, after all, were the ones now in *their* country waving around a pistol.

It felt rude being in Mexico uninvited. I wondered if the Mexicans felt rude when they crossed into America.

"You smell that?" Little Dog asked as he moved off the train tracks and into the brush.

I did smell it. And I instantly knew what Little Dog was talking about as I eyed the buzzards overhead rotating in concentric circles above our position.

"It's a dead body," Little Dog said. "You want to go find it?" he asked as he stomped through the underbrush, his head peering back and forth hoping to find the dead body.

"That's okay," I replied, putting my hands in my pockets nervously as I rocked back and forth on my toes. I sniffed the Mexican air and decided I didn't like Mexico, what with my crazy chaperone and the stink of dead bodies everywhere.

Little Dog crouched down behind a boulder and motioned me to his position where I squatted down as he pointed to a valley with a small ranch, a half-dozen cattle along its perimeter edge.

"You see that building? That's cartel."

"How do you know?" I whispered, mostly because the moment seemed to warrant a whisper.

"I went into Mexico and investigated their business license. They're listed as a dairy. But how many damn cows you count out front?"

Six. I only counted six damn cows out front.

We watched the cows eat and the building silently sit as I grew increasingly anxious. Little Dog snarled and spit as he cursed under his breath about Mexicans and the state of America.

"Maybe we could head back?" I asked. "I'd stay longer but I didn't know we were coming out here and I'm only in flip-flops."

Little Dog looked down at my feet and nodded.

Flip-flops were no good in Mexico. That was for damn sure.

"Yeah, all right," he responded.

And as we crossed back into the United States undetected, I looked for the Border Patrol. I waited for us to be apprehended for entering our own country illegally. I *wanted* us to be apprehended for entering our own country illegally.

But the valley, and the desert, were barren and quiet.

And just like that, I had inadvertently performed my first border crossing.

I decided that the first one didn't count.

THE COOL OF the night overtook us as the last tendrils of the sun disappeared under the horizon and the shaded charcoal clouds on the horizon loomed ominously as if to suggest the portent of bad news moving on down the line.

"You're about ready to see the gates of hell open wide, it's a flood at night, amigo," Little Dog said. "No use even trying at night. Leland and I try to switch out staying up at night. The coyotes got a ten-thousand-dollar bounty on both our heads."

"Think we need the lights tonight?" Leland asked, an edge of concern in his voice as the wind whipped up the dirt at his feet. Leland looked like an oversized child who needed a bath, pudgy in stained elastic-band sweats, red-hued bristled gristle for a beard.

Little Dog curled his lip as he considered the matter, tasting the air to see which way fate was blowing. "Don't know that we have enough gasoline left in the generator. We gotta be conservative with the juice we have left until Mark can get back up here to fill us up."

Leland nodded his head in agreement. "Still, wouldn't hurt to light them up for a few minutes, let 'em know we're here."

"Yeah, all right," Little Dog replied as he started to move back behind the Winnebago to the generator.

Behind me the generator coughed to life and a moment later floodlights emanated out from the base of Patriot Point in all directions, burning brilliantly in the early night before Little Dog killed the generator and the lights quickly dimmed like a fast-falling star.

"Well, amigos, I'm turning in for the night," Little Dog said, slapping his hands on his knees as he rounded the corner. "Holler if there's hell," he said before entering his Winnebago and closing the door behind him.

Leland sighed as he stared out at Mexico, hands in his pocket, reveling in the cold dressed only in his T-shirt.

"You think there's any real danger tonight? I mean, they're not going to come over tonight are they? Into camp?"

Leland was quiet for a long time as he considered my question before he finally said, "No . . . I think you'll be all right." He started to say something, to contradict himself, but seemed to think better of it and added, "Nah, you'll be all right, I guess."

I wasn't reassured.

He again was quiet for a long while and then said, "You want to see something horrible?"

"Always," I replied. I wasn't lying either, I loved horrible stuff.

He entered his truck, retrieved his laptop, and set it on the cot next to me. After the laptop cycled through its start-up, he turned the screen so that I could see it, a gesture I correctly interpreted as one of careful intimacy.

He played an audio file of a speech he said was made by the Hispanic advocacy group Nation of Aztlán during the half-million-strong march that had occurred in Los Angeles earlier in the year:

> We remain a hunted people. We have a destiny in this land that has been ours for forty thousand years! We're a new Mestizo nation! This is our homeland! We cannot, we will not, and we must not be made illegal in our homeland! We are not immigrants who came from another country! We are migrants free to travel the breadth of the Americas because we belong here! We are millions! We just have to survive! We have an aging white America! They are not making babies, they are dying! It's a matter of time! The explosion is in our population!

He moved through digital photo collections of illegal immigrants captured in obscene poses, grabbing their crotches and spitting at passing traffic. He showed me video clips of children at a school in Texas pledging their allegiance to the Mexican flag. Images of the U.S. flag being paraded upside down beneath the Mexican flag at public rallies by immigration advocates. He cycled through endless articles about illegal aliens murdering U.S. citizens, molesting small children, getting drunk and killing good decent American people. People on their way home from church, maybe.

It was immigration porn, and he was a pervert.

We spent the next hour browsing his collection as Leland moved closer to tears. When he was finished, Leland snorted derisively and said, "Our country's being invaded by a foreign nation and nobody even cares. Think of it, already Los Angeles, Chicago, Washington, D.C., San Diego . . . cities all across the country are becoming sanctuary cities where you can't ask about immigration status. Isn't that insane? It's against the law to enter the United States illegally, but the police are *not* allowed to investigate the commission of a crime? Why are there sanctuary cities for foreign nationals inside the United States? Why the hell do they think America is their Aztlán?"

His reference was to a popularized ideology of reconquista within certain radicalized leftist segments of Latino politicking. It was the idea that their heritage extended beyond that of Mexicans, to a larger genus of Mesoamerican peoples that, like the indigenous Native Americans, had belonged to this land for epochs before the arrival of the white man. In other variations, it was the north that played the role of ancestral home to the Mexica people before they first migrated south. In either case, the rearass of America belonged to them. It was also an idea of increasing popular acclaim with Mexican nationals. A 2002 Zogby poll reported that 58 percent of Mexicans within Mexico proper believed that the American Southwest should be returned to them. And it was an idea promoted and fielded by the intelligentsia of the Chicano nation in El Norte, and self-proclaimed Chicano-Marxist terrorists. And now, the idea of Aztlán was taking on momentum, and gravity, gaining in political solidarity, becoming serious, a real honest-to-God thing that more people believed all the time.

And why wouldn't the Mexicans believe such a thing? It hurt them nothing to think this way and it felt good to be owed the land of the superpower neighbor to the north. It also offered one more justification for crossing, and humans are always searching for justification.

I thought about how nicely convenient it would be to be able to join up with the long-ago ancestral bloodlines of whoever was owed something. I made a mental note to myself to offer up some blood in the future, to get a genetic ancestry mapped out—surely I belonged to some group that had an accruing benefit I could jump in on. Even if a little long division was necessary to realize my relation.

I decided not to remind Leland that the annexation of Texas occurred, more or less, by President James Polk ordering the U.S. Army to march to the Rio Grande to pick a fight. It seemed slightly treasonous to suggest historical impropriety. Regardless, it all seemed silly since the Mexican War had been like a billion zillion years ago.

"Why are there sanctuary cities for foreign nationals inside the United States?" he asked again, offended by my silence.

I didn't know the answer to his question but responded anyway. "I guess it's because those cities have big Hispanic populations. It's become politically untenable."

Leland snorted angrily. "Goddamn right it's politically untenable. This whole country's politically untenable . . . My father worked construction his whole life, and we weren't rich, but he was able to support a family. It was enough that my mom could stay home and look after us kids. Now, with the wages being as they are . . . Shit, when I first got to Vegas I was making ten, fifteen bucks an hour roofing, and that was back in the early 1990s. Now you'll be lucky if you can make seven bucks because of the illegals. What happened to the working man?"

I didn't know how to answer.

I didn't know what had happened to the working man.

He took his computer, got into his truck, and drove off down the length of the border road toward his camp and I was alone.

I climbed into the back of the green Army truck, which was filled with dirty clothes, sweet with the stink of sweat and body odor. I pawed at the pile of clothes like a cat, making a nest of sorts before I lay down, propping up a pair of jeans under my head as a pillow.

As I stared up at the stars, always more prurient and virile within the desert away from the dilution of city lights, crackling with subtle menace, I thought back about all those throughout the long arc of history who had looked out upon these same stars: the original Mesoamerican migrants who had wandered south from the Alaskan land bridge, the hundreds of indigenous Native American tribes who had called California home, the Spanish, the Mexicans. The gift of the stars was that all one needed to gain some proper perspective on their place within the world was peer upward. It made the very idea of land ownership seem ridiculous and trivial; like two fleas with a half-day lifespan arguing over possession of a dog.

No, the only true test of ownership that mattered was the one I had learned in the Army. In war, you didn't get to claim land as being under your control until you sent in the infantry, until you had boots on the ground. And as cosmically unfair as it might have been for the Native

Americans, who ostensibly were more civilized, once the Europeans had boots on the ground in equal numbers plus one to that of the indigenous populations, the land had been lost.

The Native Americans lost it.

The Mexicans lost it.

And now *we* were losing it back—which, if I was being perfectly honest, almost seemed fair.

And then, I heard the metal border fence flex and bang. I sat up in my bed of dirty clothes, my ears listening to the scratch of the wind against the surface of the night as I heard the furious scurrying of footsteps moving toward my position.

They were entering the camp!

The cartel had been talking about me and they hadn't liked the way I looked and now they were coming for me!

I was seized with a sudden and severe paralysis, unable to move and unable to breathe or exhale, rigid and immobile. I recognized the precise second the adrenaline dumped into my bloodstream. It felt toxic and ungainly, inebriating.

I heard a scuffed movement against the outside of the truck . . . they were right next to where I was sleeping!

And then came the voices in hushed whispered Spanish, just below the bed liner of the truck's raised cargo hold—fiercely muttered murmurs, a conversation deciding something in a heated angry debate, probably whether or not to kill me.

My mind reeled as I thought through my options. I wanted to scream, to wake up Little Dog so that he could come charging out of the Winnebago with a blazing rifle in each hand, but my voice was trapped and choked. I was silently suffocating in my paralytic fear—my limbs not responding to my body's commands for sudden and swift violent motion.

I breathed in deeply as I decided to implement the same plan I held on reserve in case I ever ended up seeing a poltergeist or an alien—I would charge them! The theory went that both ghosts and aliens were so used to inspiring fear in humans that they would be taken off guard by a crazed charging human running toward them in a flying tackle.

I listened intently, feeling each silent breath I took course throughout my body in a quiet shudder. And then I heard a coffee can rattle and fall to the ground—one of them had clumsily knocked into the table . . .

And then I was a fury of clothes as I ripped up my bed and jumped over the side of the truck!

My face locked into an angry growl—my best war face—my hands extended like claws as I charged them!

"AHHHHHH!!!!" I screamed.

But no one was there.

At my feet, the coffee can rolled buoyed by the wafting breath of the dark. A few paper cups were knocked off the table by the wind, falling to the ground where they joined the Folgers can rolling underneath the Army truck.

And then there were the voices again. This time from the handheld radio tied off on Army cord and hanging from the bed of the truck; voices that belonged to Mexicans maneuvering out in the darkened desert. The fence flexed again, releasing a loud wobbling ricochet, but it was only the fence cooling and contracting after a day of exposure to intense heat.

I sighed as I climbed back into my dirty clothes hamper that doubled as my bed.

Yes, I felt silly, but I also felt prepared—if the Mexicans *did* try to cross, well, my war face would be waiting for them.

I SLEPT UNEASILY, waking hour by hour throughout the night, seized with the irrational fear that I'd been abandoned. That at some point during my sleep, Little Dog had quietly snuck away, stifling laughter as he went, leaving me alone, unprotected and unguarded.

It was my dream of crossing the border—of distant insanity, pain, panic, and awaiting euphoria. But the euphoria didn't arrive. Instead it was the feeling of being pushed out of comfortable space. Of Spanish laughing. It was the feeling of being overrun.

I awoke at the sound of the gunshot.

And it was at this moment that I decided I wasn't crossing in southern California. There was just too much going on.

I sat up, my blood pressure dropping, careening. It came from somewhere close by. While I'd had only a brief passing familiarity with the smell of corpses, I could recognize a gunshot instantaneously. In the infantry, all we did was shoot weapons.

I peered over the top edge of the truck as I stared out into Mexico into the darkness. Mexico stared back, a fierce inky vacuous void—a black hole that was going to suck me over the side of the truck and swallow me.

Was I the one being fired at?

I heard the soft trembling hum of an engine and a moment later a Border Patrol truck raced by Patriot Point along the border road, its headlights off. Another one followed a moment later.

Another gunshot.

I threw myself over the side of the truck to the space between the truck and the Winnebago and lay on the ground in the dirt, peering out from behind the tires. I waited for a moment before I stood up and raced into the Winnebago, stubbing my foot on the entry step as I yelled, "Little Dog! We've got shots fired! We've got shots fired!"

"Lemme alone," Little Dog replied, rolling over and going back to sleep in his cot above the driver's seat.

I frowned as I stumbled back out of the Winnebago, picking up his gun as I went. In Afghanistan when someone yelled that shots were fired, people responded. I sat in one of the plastic lawn chairs and tried inserting each of my toes in sequence into the gun's barrel as I stared at the truck tires waiting for another shot.

The truck had really big tires and I wondered what size they were.

They looked like a real bitch to change.

Chapter 7

THE KINGFISH AND OTHER NEFARIOUS CHARACTERS
(SAN DIEGO SECTOR)

I woke slowly to blue sky overhead as I sat up, my eyes wincing and my joints stiff. The temperature was already one hundred degrees and I was covered in sweat, baking all morning in my dirty clothes hamper. With some accuracy I could guess the time of day to the hour simply by feeling the glow of the sunlight on my arm. It felt like ten in the morning.

"Good morning, sunshine," Little Dog said below me from his lawn chair as he watched the border and sorted through his mail. "There's an open can of ravioli for breakfast if you want it. It's been a busy morning—we already had two try to hop over at the electric tower down on Leland's end and we got a group of five or six out there circling, chatting on the radios, trying to decide when they're going to hop." He sighed. "It's like farting into a hurricane, John."

I climbed down from the truck stifling a yawn as I moved across the graveled peak on bare feet to Little Dog's side.

"Aligainy from the Campo Minutemen's on his way over, going to show you around today. You just stay clear of the rest of those Campo fucks, they ain't proper Minutemen."

"Okay," I responded groggily, wiping the sleep from my eyes. "What are you doing?"

"Just going through my fan mail," he replied. "This is a fairly typical morning, I'll get up at four or five, check the generator, have my coffee, and read my fan mail. Did I tell you about my program I started up in Santa Barbara? One of the achievements I'm most proud of is a program I call 'Minuteman Minors'—it's where we take inner-city kids at risk for drugs and try and get them interested in illegal immigration and the border . . ."

I laughed crazily at the idea of Minuteman Minors before Little Dog shot me a look to shut the hell up.

"**WHAT'D THAT LITTLE** Julio tell you?" asked the first Campo Minuteman, comfortably slouched in a lawn chair with his leg over the side as he swatted at mosquitoes, his U.S. Army hat crooked on his head.

"He told me to fuck off!" another replied, this one with a parrot on his shoulder.

A third one, a fat man in military fatigues said, "Goddamn Julio."

Everyone laughed.

We were in a small culvert shaded by a grove of trees where the Campo Minutemen, each wearing a holstered firearm, had made base camp, a motley collection of campers, RVs, and pup tents that more resembled a Gypsy camp than some base of military operations.

Aligainy exited a small, disheveled pup tent, waving in the air his Motorola radio, which he had been searching for since we reentered his aging rusted Ford Taurus with its filthy interior of fast-food wrappers and dirty clothes. He pulled out of the campsite and gunned the gas, and we swung over a rise in the border road, bouncing along the rocks as we went.

Aligainy was in his early twenties, his wild long hair sticking straight up into the air, held in place not by styling gel, but only by the desert dust that caked his cargo pants and Minuteman T-shirt. He offered nothing but congenial shy smiles that he wore awkwardly under his circular John Lennon eyeglasses, his hands always in motion, animated and explaining unspoken addendums to his statements as if a sign language interpreter.

"You living in here?" I asked, pulling a flattened paper Burger King cup out from under my ass.

"Well . . . here and that little pup tent down in the gulch with the Campo Minutemen . . . Little Dog doesn't consider them real Minutemen, but I think they're all right guys. Been here about two months, yeah? It's all right, I got Internet access at the library and there's a state park about eight miles away we can take showers at. I got a case of Chef Boyardee ravioli in the trunk . . . that's all you really need up here. We used to take showers up at the Indian casino. They let us take showers for two dollars, yeah? Stancheck, he's this retired electrician, some naturalized Yugoslavian immigrant with a .45 strapped to his chest, he complained to the Indians that we were defending the nation's borders so we should be able to get showers for free and they cut all our shower privileges after that—that was the first big rift between the Mountain Minutemen and the Campo Minutemen, I guess."

"So what brought you out to the border?"

Aligainy gripped the steering wheel tight as if to accentuate his emotion about this whole border debacle and he struggled to deliver a meaningful yet angry diatribe on the subject. "Well, I'm just really angry, you know, really furious, at the whole illegal alien thing. It's just awful. Awful, I tell you. I guess I'm about the angriest Minuteman you'll find out here."

I nodded, staring at him curiously from the passenger seat.

"Really? You don't seem that angry."

"No, I'm angry. Shit. You know those terrorists that wanted to bomb Fort Dix? They came across the border. I'm concerned about the terrorist connection," he continued.

"The terrorist connection?" I asked dubiously.

"Sure, the terrorists are coming through here all the time."

"Is that a fact?" I chuckled sarcastically.

"Sure is," Aligainy replied. "In 2005, Border Patrol apprehended 165,000 people from countries other than Mexico. Of those, 650 were from special interest countries . . ." He was quiet and then leaned across to my seat and explained, ". . . that's the Middle East, yeah? They just caught an Egyptian crossing in New Mexico, some Syrians here in California."

I responded to his claims with a doubtful gaze.

"What, you don't believe me?"

"I don't not believe you, I'm just a little cynical to believe everything they say about terrorists and the War on Terror," I explained.

"The information's all out there. You just gotta know where to look."

"That's convenient," I responded, not yet knowing that in just a few months, *The Washington Post* would publish a series of articles explaining that, indeed, the cartels had agreed to take terrorists across the border and that terrorist types had also planned to blow up Fort Huachuca, an Army base in southern Arizona, and all while sightseeing.

"You don't have to be a genius to connect the dots, yeah? Al Qaeda's protected by the Taliban in Afghanistan, Afghanistan is the number one poppy cultivator in the world. Taliban sells that to fund their operations. Cut away to Mexico where the biggest source of heroin in the United States is coming over that fence."

"Yeah, so what?" I argued, not seeing the connection.

"How'd the dope get from Afghanistan to Mexico if they ain't connected, yeah?"

I was quiet as I considered his argument and realized I had no rebuttal.

It made sense. The Taliban had the heroin, but the Mexicans distributed it. They had to know each other, at least tangentially. Maybe they were MySpace friends. And if terrorists weren't crossing the border yet, it wasn't a stretch to believe that it was quite possible considering the already existing business connections.

"Well, I'll be damned," I said, shaking my head, suddenly convinced.

"The illegal aliens are ruining this country," Aligainy explained again in his artificial anger. "Nobody can make a living anymore because of the artificial wage deflation. People back where I'm from in Pennsylvania, they think the illegal immigration problem is five guys hanging outside a Home Depot in Tucson, Arizona. They don't realize it's the drugs, it's the terrorists, and they don't realize how many are coming over. It's been a real eye-opener being down here, I'll tell you that."

Aligainy brought the vehicle to a stop in a forested ravine as he pointed into the woods. "They travel these trails down here a lot at night. I usually come over here at night and talk to the coyotes on the other side of the fence. They're some pretty smart guys."

"You talk to the coyotes?"

"Sure, all the time. They'll ask me if there's any Border Patrol around, I'll ask them how many people they've got with them. We'll talk about the weather or whatever while they wait for a good moment to cross." He paused for a moment before adding, "I better give Kingfish a heads-up that we're coming up, I don't want to get shot."

I concurred. "That sounds reasonable."

Aligainy drove forward out of the ravine around a bend so that we were on another point of high ground. Aligainy stopped the car as he pointed to a blue delivery van atop the ridge opposite us.

He grabbed the radio and said, "Kingfish, this is Aligainy. We're headed over to your area of operations, over. Don't shoot."

KINGFISH CUT A striking figure with his crackling smile peering out under the fedora, one eye sheathed under a black pirate's patch, a pistol tucked loosely into the waistband of his cargo pants. Kingfish stood on the edge of the cliff looking out over his kingdom, his arms folded as he cackled, explaining his operation in scientific terms. Whereas Little Dog had been emotionally constipated fury, Kingfish was precision methodology.

He pointed out the topography laid out below, the high points of elevation and the ravines, how when conjoined with the displacement of shadow and sun, and the natural geography of the land, natural paths of migration emerged.

He explained the migratory patterns of the Mexicans as if he were a zoologist offering an explanation on the Discovery Channel—how they shifted with the seasons in recurring cyclical patterns and sometimes during the time of day. He explained the typology of the different species, how migratory behavior was affected by group size and whether they were carrying narcotics or not. The larger groups of migrant workers played it more conservative, you see—they moved incrementally like inchworms, hiding as they went, and they did this because they had women and children with them. The smaller groups of drug runners tended to be young men—they were sprinters and kept to the early morning and nighttime.

Kingfish explained how his specific placement at geographic overwatch positions could deter traffic, reroute smugglers into areas heavily patrolled by Border Patrol. Police and urban planners did the same thing, mapping crime statistics onto overlays of city maps, watching how increased police presence in some neighborhoods only diverted illegal activity to other areas. Crime, like illegal immigration, had volume and substance; it was like water that could be rerouted but had to flow somewhere.

He explained how the job of a Minuteman was like that of illumination in a darkened parking lot; it was a posture of deterrence. Sure, he had been shot at a few times, who hadn't? The point was if you utilized proper technique, one could pretty much force the Mexicans to a prechosen path where they would eventually be apprehended by Border Patrol, further in-country—and all without rising from the patio chair.

It was just one big chess game.

With pieces that spoke Spanish.

"Yes, sir, the Mexicans are like electricity." He turned back around to smile at me. "They both take the path of least resistance."

I turned from Kingfish to Aligainy and we shared a moment of incredulity at the statement we had just heard, but then Aligainy, realizing this shared expression might betray his early political statements, quickly erased his facial posture of agreement and transformed it into an ugly grimace as he spit in the dirt and growled, "Damn Mexicans."

A LIGAINY AND I sat in Campo's single diner, a small mom-and-pop operation, the sort you found in old movies and small-town America with the soda fountains and red-checked tablecloths. We sat at the counter, straws in our mouths as we sucked on root beer floats. Aligainy pointed out the drug runner in the adjacent booth having chicken fried steak and suggested in a hushed whisper that we should follow him if I was up for it.

I looked at my watch and replied, also in a hushed whisper, "I want to but I have to meet up with Leland in a half-hour."

Aligainy bristled. "What's Leland doing that can't wait? I can tell you exactly where he'll be four hours, six hours, or ten hours from now, which is sitting at his camp or hanging out with Little Dog."

"I know, but I'll feel bad if I don't show when I said I would," I whined. And then, noticing my defense hadn't been effective in convincing him, I added, "I want to follow the drug runner, I really do, but my afternoon is already full."

Aligainy shrugged. We'd have to follow the drug runner another day.

I sighed. That seemed to be the case.

"How long you going to stay out here?" I asked.

"About another month or so, yeah? I don't know, really I just . . ." Aligainy paused and also sighed, his hand moving abruptly to his forehead as if pained.

"I know, brain freeze, right?" I laughed as I took another bite of ice cream.

"No, not brain freeze," Aligainy said, sighing again, looking down at the countertop in frustration before leaning across to me and saying, "Okay, half the stuff I've told you about me has all been lies, but it wasn't personal, not in an intent to deceive or anything, it's just that I was in character, and you forget yourself sometimes, you know?"

"Um, sure," I replied, not understanding at all what he was talking about.

"I'm not really a Minuteman, brother." He paused for appropriate dramatic effect. "I'm undercover."

"Undercover?"

"I'm an undercover liberal," he replied, the pressures of his hidden ideology weighing heavy upon him.

"No shit?" I excitedly replied. "I'm undercover as one of them too!" I shook my head at the crazy way of the world.

"I'm also an undercover journalist," Aligainy said firmly, awaiting my reaction.

"Get the fuck out of here!" I yelled a bit too loudly, causing the drug runner to glance over at us.

"Well, how about that. Two undercover liberal journalists. I suppose you should start calling me Andre. Aligainy is just my code name," he said, tipping his root beer float.

"Nice to meet you, Andre," I replied, clinking his glass in a toast.

And then, he told me his story . . .

On a whim, Andre had decided to drive across the country to spend the summer on the border with the Minutemen. They were the sort of group that would provide for good pictures, and he was a photojournalist. And Andre had done this with almost no money in the bank for the return trip to Philly and no exit strategy.

These sorts of confessions amaze me.

Who did this? Who embarked upon a journey they had no way of returning from?

He shrugged his shoulders as he chugged his root beer. These were unimportant details.

He would fund his way back to Philly over time. Maybe by selling some photos to the Associated Press. Maybe by selling his Ford, worn and well trodden though she was.

This is what he does, he informed me.

He told me of a promising career in Philly. Some award-winning photographs that had been syndicated across papers nationwide. The Amish school shootings? The photo of the mother with all the microphones in her face with her hands spread out? That was his. And perhaps you remember some frequent and popular shots from the Sago Mine disaster? Those were his too.

That was how he made his living. Sucking off the misery of others. I laughed when he said this, because I *too* liked being within the vicinity of the suffering of others. It was vicarious drama, you got a contact high without having to participate yourself.

"You have to take me with you when you leave," Andre announced firmly.

"Come again?"

"You have to take me with you. I could take pictures for your book.

I have my own car, we could just form a little convoy across the desert, split the cost of motel rooms. You're what . . . you're just driving around the border region talking to people, right? You've done the Minutemen, now it's on to other groups, right? And your overall purpose is what?"

I shrugged. "You know, to understand the border."

Andre snickered and leaned in close as he marveled at our similarity. "That's great! I want to understand the border too, so that works, you know, that's like perfect with me. I'm all about trying to understand the border." He peered slowly around the interior of the diner, as if to make sure there were no Minuteman spies, and then added in a hushed whisper, "I have to get out of here! They're driving me crazy!"

I made rapid calculations in my head regarding the probable consequences of accepting the company of a liberal undercover photojournalist that I didn't know. I started to speak when the drug runner got up to leave. Andre and I abruptly quieted and turned away from one another, staring forward across the counter as we pretended an inordinate and focused interest in our root beer floats, waiting until the drug runner left before we turned back toward each other.

"Yeah, they're driving me a bit crazy, too," I concurred as we both stared sullenly outside the diner, both of us sighing at those crazy border vigilantes we had become entangled with. I mulled for a moment longer and said, "Agreed. I can't tell you when, might be in the middle of the night. Just . . . well, just be ready."

Andre assured me that he would be.

"WELL, IT AIN'T MUCH, but it's home," Leland said laughing, holding an SKS assault rifle as he lit up a cigarette and took a seat on a folding chair next to a table that looked out over the border. *Home*, as he called it, consisted of yet another broken-down RV, and a car of an indiscernible make or model that had been completely disassembled, its parts lying around in the dirt. Leland's brother, a pimply teenager in a long faded black Metallica T-shirt, watched us talk from the steps of the camper, not participating, just staring.

"Been down here about six months. Was in Vegas when I had a little sticker on my truck that said *Speak English* and a bunch of Mexicans pulled up behind me at six-thirty in the morning on my way to work, and five of them jumped out and threw a tape measure right through my window," he said, motioning to his truck with the still broken window. "They didn't like my bumper sticker, I guess. Got on the Internet and saw a crazy old man playing king of the mountain and decided to come down and join him."

Leland smiled as he saw my eyes drawn to the weapon. "I've been shot at, I get my life threatened every day, they come on the radio saying they're going to kill me every night. *Vato—you're dead! You're dead!* So I don't get very far away from my firearms. After they shot at me from three hundred yards, I figured I'd better get something that could reach out and touch a little further. It's not that I want to kill anybody, but I'm making a statement and I'm not going to get killed doing it."

"How do you sleep?" I asked.

"I don't," he replied. "I can't leave, take a shower, they'll cut my cords, take down my lights. I don't think I've gotten more than four hours of consecutive sleep since I got here six months ago. If I catch 'em in the camp, I'm going to kill 'em. I don't want to kill nobody, but I've got squatter's rights. I've been threatened so many times, on the radio all night, *I'm gonna kill you! I'm gonna kill you!* Fuck that, I'm going to kill them."

"Leland, listen, I have a question for you, and it's going to appear to be a bit strange. But just out of curiosity's sake, if an American, a white American, like you or myself, decided to go into Mexico at one of the ports of entry, and then hop the fence back into America like the Mexicans do it, what do you think their chances of success would be?"

Leland laughed before blurting out his response: "None! Hopping the fence is easy, not sure what Border Patrol would do catching an American hopping the fence, but I doubt they'd just toss you back like they do with the illegals. But you wouldn't survive over there, that's all fucking cartel territory, man. It's all divided up by coyotes that would just as soon slit your throat and rob you as look at you. If you stayed in a car I suppose you could drive the back Mexican roads and maybe be okay, but once they caught you traipsing around out there . . . it'd be fucking over."

I nodded and sighed. "That's what I thought. You ever hear of the Devil's Highway? Say you had to cross either there or here, into the United States, where would you want to cross?"

Leland laughed. "I'm an American citizen though."

"Yeah, but say you had to, like your life depended on it sort of deal."

Leland considered my question and then responded. "Here. Highway's close, no desert to kill you. Why do you ask?"

I avoided the question by asking another. "What's up with the scope? Mexico's that-a-way, right?" I asked, nodding my head at his scope, which was pointed to the west, parallel to the nonexistent fence.

Leland took a drag from his cigarette and smirked. "We gotta crazy fucker down there. Some old guy pretending to be a Minuteman, but Little Dog and I think he's working for the cartels."

"No shit?" I replied as I peered down into the valley to see a pickup truck and a small camper that seemed devoid of life.

"Yeah, no shit. He doesn't work with us, for one. I mean, Little Dog's got his beef with some of the other Minuteman groups up here, that's fine, but in the end, we're all in it together, and we all need to work together, but this guy won't even talk to us. He doesn't ever call Border Patrol, and he spends most of his time watching us or the road behind him while talking on his cell phone."

I sighed. I'd have to go and make contact, of course.

"Well, you want me to go talk to him?" I asked.

A big grin came to Leland's face. "Fuck, yeah! Find out what's up! I'll cover you from up here with my rifle."

THERE WERE FIVE of us surrounding the heater: Little Dog, Leland, Andre, myself, and a local rancher named Dick Buck. The residual glow from the heater's orange grille reflected eerily in the enclosure between the truck and the Winnebago under the camouflage netting, offering just enough light to illuminate hovering faces that belonged to bodies concealed by the encroaching darkness. There was the sound of Bic lighters flicking and lighting, and cigarettes being sucked, and the popping fizz of soda cans being opened in repeated succession.

And this is what was called a positive feedback loop.

The Minutemen complained about the state of the world, and without the presence of dissenting opinion, everyone fervently agreed, and because the proffered viewpoints had found positive agreement, they were reaffirmed, this time with a bit more intensity—it was one big incestuous ideological closed-circuit loop.

Myself? I was just racking my brain trying to figure out how to escape this crazy place.

"It's a goddamn crisis down here and ain't nobody in America who cares about it," Dick Buck said angrily. "I'm a rancher. I've got to check my fence every other day because those goddamn Julios tear it down. Ranchers in Kansas have to check their fence once a month . . . maybe. My own wife can't even check the mail past five o'clock in the evening. I can barely afford to stay in business because of where I'm located, but this is my land that I own, and I'm supposed to move because of foreign nationals illegally in my own country?" Dick was reed-thin and looked fiercely indestructible as if poured from hardened concrete. "Shit, just the other day saw three little Julios just the other side of the goddamn fence, got themselves a little goddamn campfire going. And this was right after Little Dog here had found those goddamn smugglers coming out of the bush out by Dawson's place, so I fucking put the truck in park, hiked through the goddamn desert, jumped that motherfucking fence, and walked straight into their goddamn camp, holy Jesus you never seen such a commotion! Why I starts screaming at 'em, 'Hey, goddamit! Let's talk about this! Come on back and let's talk about all this, motherfuckers! Well, ol' Julio was running back to town to suck on ol' María's titty, so I put out the fire and walked back to my truck!"

Little Dog and Dick Buck laughed while Andre and I pretended to.

"Campo guys saw four cross into camp the other night," Andre added, clearing his throat and presenting himself in character.

"Those Campo fucks ain't proper Minutemen," Little Dog angrily replied. "Present company excluded." Little Dog turned to me. "And John, I want you to stay clear of them. You got no business associating with them Campo fucks."

"Yes, Little Dog," I said, eyeballing the distance to my truck, which was parked only a few feet away, and estimating the time it would take me to race to it, start the engine, and start off down the mountain.

"You should've seen Little Dog when he was out in Jacumba. He was out there crawling around in the bush for months, tracking narco-traffickers, setting out filament wire, slicing tires, rattling the goddamn leaves doing the Little Dog Two-Step!" Dick Buck said laughing.

"What's the Little Dog Two-Step?" I asked.

Little Dog snickered proudly. "You got these drug couriers come in on horses, cartels toss the drugs over the fence, they come in on the horse, race and pick it up, drop it in a Dumpster somewhere in Jacumba. Well, I'd be waiting behind a large boulder, and when that horse races by . . ." Little Dog stood to pantomime the cocking of a shotgun. "Twice into the air. You see what I'm saying? Little Dog Two-Step. That horse . . ." Little Dog rolled with laughter at the memory, barely able to finish his sentence. "That horse bucked that ride and took off across the desert with him hanging from the stirrup!"

"Sounds like Jacumba's pretty crazy, why aren't you guys over there?" I asked.

"Border Patrol kicked us out," Little Dog replied. "Too dangerous."

"You can't even go there as a U.S. citizen," Dick Buck added angrily. "I was driving my pickup truck toward Jacumba, ain't nothing but flophouses and narco-traffickers, anyway. Goddamn Border Patrol stops me, asks me what's my business, says I can't go in. I'm like are you fucking for real? I'm inside the United States of America and you're telling me there's places I can't go inside my own fucking country?"

"Little Dog ever show you the YouTube video he made?" Leland asked. "Little Dog made this video, it's all fake, but he made this video of a Minuteman killing a drug dealer and burying him out in the desert." Leland laughed, collapsing into his chair. "Shit, that kicked up a fire-storm!"

"I had CNN calling me wanting to know if I was killing people!" Little Dog exclaimed excitedly. "As soon as I told him it was a fake, a way to draw attention to the border . . . click, they hung up. But I'll tell you what, John, it worked. They had that fucking thing playing nonstop on Telemundo all down through Mexico and Latin America. This is psy-ops, amigo."

I laughed at their comments, feeling guilty as I did. It wasn't that I thought they were racists so much as simply misguided. Yes, I decided— they were simply well meaning but misguided, but not necessarily racist.

"Want to show you something." Little Dog went into his Winnebago and came back out a moment later with a small noose. "Speaking of psy-ops. I like to hang these along the border fence . . ."

Well, maybe they were racist.

Just a little bit.

I T WAS TWO in the morning when I snuck into the bivouac site of the Campo Minutemen, slowly creeping my way across the rocks and gravel. The Minutemen were all asleep, locked inside pickup trucks and campers where the shades were pulled tight. I quietly admonished them for their lack of discipline while on guard duty; there was a group of seven about ready to cross not fifty meters from here.

I knocked gently on the passenger-side window of Andre's car as I looked rapidly around to make sure I hadn't woken anyone, the last thing I needed was to be mistaken for an illegal alien breaking into camp. Andre woke slowly, his eyes squinting as he shook off the sleep and rolled down his window.

"It's time!" I yelled in a hushed whisper.

Andre's eyes lit up, his body suddenly charged with energy as he began rapidly putting on his shoes. Neither of us was being held as cap-tives, yet we both shared in the unspoken feeling that it was better to qui-etly abscond than to announce our intentions.

Andre packed his tent and belongings quickly into his car, his hands working in a furious rapid tempo as he disassembled poles and packed clothes while I stood guard against Minutemen and Mexicans.

And then, we were gone, swallowed into the desert night where the coyotes chattered on the radio frequency, taunting the Minutemen who slept soundly in their beds.

Chapter 8

THE MINUTEMAN T-SHIRT EXPERIMENT
(TUCSON SECTOR)

An hour later and we were in the Indian casino just up the road along-side the Interstate. Fat suburbanites from Tampa paced industrial-strength carpet with Aztec illustrations as they worked the swing shift, plugging quarters into slots, blindfolded and dumb in their furtive quest for a mid-night awakening of the American dream.

At the bar, Andre listened carefully as I spoke.

I had decided that if we were working together, he needed to under-stand my entire purpose for being on the border.

"Well, I'm writing a story about illegal immigration and its players, but . . ." I paused, attempting to think of the best way to frame what I was about to say. "That's not the whole reason I'm out here."

"You don't want to understand the border issue?" Andre asked dubiously.

"Oh, no! I do! Don't get me wrong, but that's just part of it." I was silent for a moment and then, I offered my confession: "I need to cross the border."

"Like the Mexicans do it?" he asked smiling sweetly, breaking into his giggles.

"Like the Mexicans do it," I concurred shyly. "It's not so much a bor-der investigation, as a border investigation mixed with also attempting to illegally circumvent our nation's border security apparatus. I even took a class in Mexico and everything."

"Shit, you're all trained up!"

"I guess so," I replied, shrugging my shoulders.

"I like it!" Andre exclaimed. "All right, lay it on me, where we going next, yeah?"

"Western Arizona. Little place called the Devil's Highway," I said as I smiled, happy I had some companionship as I pulled out my road atlas and spread Arizona out over the bar, pointing to a tenderly small swath of land between the Barry Goldwater Air Force bombing range and the Tohono O'odham Reservation.

"Ohhh! Sounds ominous," he replied, laughing.

"It is, actually."

And then I told him. I told him about the fifty-mile movements through the desert. I told him about the frequent and routine deaths due to dehydration. I told him about the drug smugglers who controlled the corridor.

My recitation complete, I smiled smugly in anticipation of imminent praise over my reckless abandon.

"You're a fucking idiot," Andre snapped angrily, all his humor depleted.

"What?" I replied, confused, a stupid smile still lingering on my face.

"You're going to get yourself fucking killed. You want to do fifty miles in 120-degree heat in the middle of the desert in July, yeah?" Andre erupted in dismissive laughter at my silly plan.

"Well, I did it in Afghanistan, I suppose I can do it here," I replied tersely, more than a bit offended as I packed away Arizona, no longer interested in sharing my vision.

"Illegal aliens *die* in the desert doing that route, my friend! Burning, exhausting, heat of the day, cold of the night!"

"Yeah, but they're not trained!" I whined. "They're pregnant women and old men, right?"

"And you're trained?" Andre asked, eyeing my slender frame with suspicion.

"Yes! What the hell, you think I'd try something like this if I wasn't?" I replied defensively, wondering again if I was indeed trained.

"You sure that's only fifty miles?" Andre asked suspiciously.

And suddenly, I was worried. Maybe it wasn't fifty miles?

I pulled the map back out and studied it for a single confused moment before grabbing my beer mug, holding it up to the map's mileage marker where I placed my finger at the ten-mile mark, and then placed my beer mug along the Mexican border.

"Yeah," I nodded to myself, somewhat confident in my estimation. "Fifty miles give or take fifteen."

"You're a fool," Andre replied evenly. "What's the hurry, anyway? We can always come back and you can kill yourself then, but I want to get something in before you die."

I nodded.

It did make sense to complete more of the investigation before I died.

And besides, the Devil's Highway was about the toughest border route there was. Ignoring the thrill inspired by the risk it posed, it seemed better to attempt the first crossing in Arizona where all the other migrants crossed. If most of the Mexicans were crossing in central Arizona, south of Tucson, then it suggested that they knew something I didn't.

I decided to follow the Mexicans.

"Forget the Devil's Highway," I said to Andre as I shoved away the map, somewhat embarrassed I had brought up the idea in the first place. "Let's keep going to Tucson."

I DESCENDED ALONE into the desert proper, intending to meet up with Andre the day after tomorrow. I was in Arizona now, where the cacti patrolled the desert, which was now colored in an amber orange tint, ragged cliffs breaking like skyscrapers from the earth, distant and magnificent and looming. I listened to Fox News and National Public Radio podcasts on my iPod. I stopped to take pictures at the abandoned remnants of civilization—broken and boarded diners from a bygone era, trailer parks along the outer rim of civilization, and a drive-in movie theater with a ripped screen that had been left behind when a local community had long ago suddenly absconded like the ancient Anasazi of Mesa Verde.

I pulled out my audio recorder and offered myself a future memo of explanation. "I've entirely ruled out making any manner of border crossing attempt in California. There were simply too many players on too narrow a border—cartels, Border Patrol, Minutemen—having some privacy is important. Like taking a bowel movement or something, crossing the border is an embarrassing thing and a trouble-causing thing and it just needs to be done alone." I clicked the recorder off, thought of a final addendum, and quickly flipped it back on. "I've met a guy named Andre. He's somewhere in the desert."

Directly south of me, covering a full quarter of Arizona's southern border, was the Barry M. Goldwater Air Force Range where A-10s, F-16s, and Marine Corps Harrier jets practiced air-to-surface weapons deployment, bombing, and strafing. The Mexicans still crossed. I winced at the idea of running through the desert while F-16s dropped Daisy Cutters behind me.

I looked out my passenger-side window as I sped the Interstate, contemplating the desert, and the border, wondering how many illegal aliens were in the distant mountains and hills, attempting to cross at any given imaginary parallel intersection.

The Mexicans and I shared the same goal: crossing the U.S. border. But as I drove, I wondered if the experience was a feasible thing to even attempt to replicate. After all, there were qualitative differences of condition that differentiated our shared task. I was a U.S. citizen, for one. A U.S. citizen with free movement on both sides of the border, able to perform reconnaissance prior to my crossing so that I'd know in advance the territory I was moving into. I had GPS and maps, for another. Advantages not shared by my Spanish-speaking brothers.

But then the Mexicans also had the benefit of being led by the human smugglers who knew the territory better than any park ranger or Border Patrol agent—smugglers who had made the same trip dozens of times, which was better than any map or GPS. And while they could disappear quite easily into the United States, I would stick out in woeful contrast back behind the enemy lines of Mexico. Whereas their biggest threat was getting picked up and taken back over the border, my biggest threat was being killed in Mexico.

I decided that it was actually the Mexicans who owned the home field advantage.

I**T WAS DURING** the drive from California to central Arizona that I developed the Minuteman T-shirt experiment. And the Minuteman T-shirt experiment was simply this: for the next few days, I would wear a Minuteman T-shirt and baseball cap. That and my truck was newly adorned in Minuteman bumper stickers I had acquired online before my trip for the purpose of being able to blend in with border vigilantes.

And that was it.

It was a very simple experiment.

I considered it an educational experiment in my attempt to understand the border; playing with Minutemen was one thing, but pretending to be one of them was entirely something else. Many Minutemen went about day-to-day life wearing their various paraphernalia, often adorning their trucks with bumper stickers, advertising their political position wherever they went. But the difference between them and myself was that I was an excessively sensitive soul. I assumed I would feel more trepidation and uneasiness about wearing these items because of the likely offense it would cause the people I would meet whom I would reflexively empathize with.

Or, at least, that's how the experiment worked, in theory.

I **QUICKLY ADDED** up the mileage and the money I had spent on gas so far. I carried the four, subtracted the current mileage from the mileage at the last gas station I had visited, and sat quietly stunned as I realized I was getting only fourteen miles to the gallon.

I sighed as I pulled into the gas station. Borrowing the truck was supposed to have been saving me money, not costing me more than it would have to rent a car.

Inside the gas station, I smiled at the fat Hispanic lady who worked behind the counter. She smiled reflexively in response before her eyes moved up to my Minuteman cap and my T-shirt and her smile faltered and became forced, angry.

I winced. The Minuteman T-shirt experiment was working and I was feeling awkward.

A pleased smile emerged on my face, not because I was offending the woman, but because I was feeling ashamed, which, after all, was the whole point.

"Thirty-seven, sixty-eight," the fat Hispanic clerk sternly told me.

I glared at her, pretending to be a racist bastard, and handed her the pretty credit card with the mountains.

I went back outside to the truck and turned the ignition.

Nothing.

Not even a grunting grind showing an effort on the truck's part.

I tried it again, hoping for a different result.

Nothing.

I sighed and climbed out of the truck and popped the hood and peered inside, pretending that I knew what I was looking for. Maybe there would be a wire loose that obviously fit into a circuit it had popped out of. Or, maybe, as I hoped, there would be a big flashing red "reset" button centered evenly and prominently over the engine itself and I'd simply have to press it.

No such luck.

On the pump opposite me, a large burly man of considerable girth in the form of many plied alcoholic beverages during the evening hours was driving a new Ford F-250 and wearing a U.S. Marine Corps T-shirt as he appraised my situation. His eyes moved over the Marine Corp paraphernalia on the truck and then to my Minuteman T-shirt.

He smiled. He walked around the pump and extended his hand. I had gained points without even talking to him.

"How you doing?" he said. "Looks like you're having some problems here."

"Yeah, she won't start," I replied.

"What do you think is wrong with her?" he asked.

"I think her doohickey is shot," I replied, smirking.

He frowned and I could tell I was starting to lose the points I had just accumulated.

"Might be your starter, on old trucks like this you just have to kick 'em sometimes. Try kicking yer starter and see what that does for ya."

"Right," I replied evenly, wondering where my starter was.

The man paused as he waited for me to kick my starter.

I started banging on various engine parts with my fist.

He slowly nodded his head no.

I smirked uncomfortably as he pointed underneath the truck.

I climbed on the ground and slid myself under the truck where I started kicking randomly.

"It's over here, on your right side," he offered with a scowl.

I moved to the right side and started blindly kicking.

"That should do it," he said.

I climbed out, got inside, and turned the ignition—the truck started right up. I leaned out the open doorway and waved. "Thanks! I really appreciate it!"

He frowned and waved dismissively, yeah, whatever—all my points of unearned Minuteman goodwill had been squandered by lack of comprehension about basic mechanics, but I didn't care, the truck was running.

I WAS HEADED toward Tucson and at eighty miles an hour, the truck shaking and rattling in its settings, the hitchhiker on the side of the road was visible because of the curve in the road for only a few seconds before I blew past him. He was Hispanic and looked like trouble—not because he was Hispanic, but because he was out here in the desert in the middle of nowhere, a hundred miles from civilization without a backpack. That and he was covered in tattoos. He looked like the sort of person you'd expect to find just recently released from prison. But I was also covered in tattoos. It was prejudiced to reject someone for their tattoos.

I pulled over to the side of the road. Picking up hitchhikers was stupid. Anyone could tell you that, especially in this day and age of instant murder and unprovoked assault. I'd have to take my chances. It was an excellent opportunity to test out the Minuteman T-shirt experiment in close quarters. It was more scientific that way, if you tested a theory in various environments.

I watched him in the rearview mirror as he broke into a sprint toward my truck as I made some room in the passenger seat, packing up my things into my rucksack and sliding it to the middle of the cab floor.

I thought for a moment about the gun and then reached into the glove box and pulled it out. It just wouldn't do to have a hitchhiker in the passenger seat with a loaded gun accessible right in front of him. I looked around myself, searching for a place to put it.

The waistband? I thought to myself.

No, I couldn't bring myself to mimic that gun-toting caricature.

I decided to slide it under my seat.

The Hispanic man arrived at my passenger-side door as I reached over and unlocked it. He had a shaved head and was big and brawny and dressed in a torn button-up dress shirt that covered a faded T-shirt advertising some long-ago rock concert. He stank slightly. Tattoos encircled his fingers and wrists and peeked out onto his neck from under his collar.

He didn't smile but instead only muttered thanks as he settled.

I pulled forward onto the Interstate as I watched him study the interior of the truck from my peripheral vision. Seeing what was available to steal, maybe.

"Where you going to?" I asked.

"Tucson," he replied. "*Is that okay?*" he added a little defensively, making me almost afraid to say no.

"That's fine," I replied, swallowing hard as he turned to me and appraised me for physical fitness. "I'm heading to Tucson, myself." The judgment in his eyes told me I came up lacking, that he had decided he could take me if he needed to. I mostly agreed with his assessment.

And then, I noticed him leaning forward and reading my T-shirt and cap.

He collapsed into his seat frowning.

He didn't follow the ideological creeds of the Minutemen.

An uneasy silence hung between us as I drove and he stared out the front windshield.

"Don't you have a radio?" he asked.

"AM frequencies only. Old truck," I muttered.

"Oh," came his reply.

From my passenger seat, he twitched and fidgeted. As if resisting an urge or coming down off of some drug, or struggling internally.

I shook my head and damned myself for picking up a hitchhiker.

This was going to end badly. Real badly, I could feel it. At some point, before the end of the ride, he was going to attack me. I was sure of it. And then, I'd have to defend myself.

Which would mean shooting him.

In the face.

And then I'd have to explain that to the authorities and tell my district attorney friend that his gun, the one he kept tightly locked in his home for personal protection, had been used to kill someone. And that would surely mean the end of my Vicodin access.

I didn't think I'd have much trouble with the authorities after I shot my new friend. Arizona was liberal with the gun laws. Open carry in most of the state. You could shoot to kill around these parts if you were defending yourself or your home.

But then, of course, there was the slight complication that I was wearing a Minuteman T-shirt and he was Hispanic, which would make the police think the murder had been racially motivated. I imagined trying to explain the purpose of the Minuteman T-shirt experiment—that it had no racial overtones, but that it was a part of my desire to understand the border. It wasn't an explanation that would go over well.

I assumed that after he attacked me, as he surely would, and after I killed him, as I surely would, it might almost be irresponsible to myself and my wife and my family to call the police. That was the type of incident you wanted to dump on the side of the road and leave in your rearview mirror.

Except for the blood splatters in the car, the broken window, the tire tracks in the dirt speeding away. The application of forensic science to reveal evidence I knew nothing about.

I sighed. This was getting very complicated.

I reached under the seat with one free hand and flipped the safety from on to off.

"THANKS, MAN, I really appreciate you giving me a ride," he said standing by the passenger-side door in a parking lot on the far outskirts of Tucson.

"Are you sure?" I replied. "I can give you a ride the rest of the way across town, I guess after all . . . maybe."

"No, it's cool, you're not going to that side of town and I don't want to put you out, you took me this far and saved me a lot of walking. A bus will come in a few hours and I can just take that. Again, thanks."

And with that, he shut the door and waved, walking across the parking lot toward a bus stop.

I frowned, angry that he hadn't tried to attack me.

AT AN ARBY'S in Tucson, I offended three Hispanics on staff, two of them young men who looked as if they wanted to kick my ass. At the gas station, where I was already forced to fill up again, I offended another clerk and a family of four getting out of their minivan. And at each offense, I struggled mightily to constrain undulating smiles and frowns—trapped as I was between laughter and sadness.

And all of it, every angry stare, every quiet mutter, it all fed me.

And I greedily consumed it.

I ENTERED THE LOBBY of a clean but cheap motel in Tucson on the right side of the Interstate on the wrong side of town. Rooms were only forty dollars a night. I was in line behind an Amish couple, the man dressed with the suspenders, the woman with the requisite bonnet. They were asking to borrow an ironing board. The young studious bright-smiled Hispanic man behind the desk helped them to the door, carrying the iron before handing it off, and he turned to me, noticing the Minuteman T-shirt and cap. His smile briefly faltered before quickly returning as an artificial model of the previous.

My experiment was working. I was feeling a sickly tension. I wasn't relaxed. I felt both embarrassed for him and ashamed at myself. And because I felt bad, I decided to compensate by being overly nice. I responded to everything he said with an ingratiating sincere thank-you and deep yearning smile.

"And you'll be in room number seven, that's just behind this office," he said, sliding the key across to me, his eyes quietly judging my assumed ideological positions.

"Thank you *so* much!"

I took the key and walked through a neatly trimmed courtyard behind the office to a series of rooms, with a bright freshly painted white exterior. I inserted the key into the door and then heard a rustle of noise inside and felt the presence of someone rushing to the door. The door was flung open to reveal another Hispanic man, this one shirtless with long stringy hair and covered in tattoos, reeking of cigarettes. Behind him in the disheveled room there was a stoned naked woman lying in a mess of covers, watching television.

We stared at each other uncomfortably as I backed up a few feet to check the room numbers on the adjoining rooms.

"Uh, this is my room?" I said.

"Fuck!" the man yelled before slamming the door in my face.

I walked back around to the lobby where a bell rung as I entered.

The Hispanic clerk entered from a back room, still eyeing my T-shirt, still forcing the uncomfortable smile.

"There's someone in my room," I said.

He sighed and shook his head, immediately knowing the problem. He looked flustered and scared at imminent confrontations I knew nothing about. He reentered the back room and exited back into the lobby, this time accompanied by a wide-hipped flustered Native American woman.

"Should I call the police?" the woman asked. "I told them not to come back. I told them!"

"I'm very sorry," the clerk said, his eyes still on my T-shirt. He was genuinely upset. In part, I imagined, because I was white and this was a predominantly Hispanic part of town and these were Hispanic customers and I, being someone who was obviously racist, was only having all of my errant and erroneous predispositions reinforced by the vagrants in my room.

"No, it's no big deal. Truly!" I replied happily, trying desperately to show him that it didn't bother me and that I didn't interpret this one experience as a negative blemish on his people.

I was given a room adjacent to the one I had previously been assigned and as I moved my stuff into the room, I heard yelling from next door between the clerk and the occupants. I grabbed the pistol and moved to the door where I peeked outside to see the clerk backing away from the man, who had opened the door and was now on the sidewalk.

"Don't touch me!" the clerk screamed, backing away more as the shirtless man with the tattoos charged a few feet toward him like a lumbering ape before stopping short. "We're calling the police!"

The shirtless man considered this and appraised his distance from the clerk, making fateful decisions with long-reaching consequences.

I switched the selector level on the pistol off of safe. I was a helluva shot to tell the truth. A sharpshooter qualified by the Army. I prayed silently that the shirtless man would charge the clerk, that he would tackle him, pull a knife maybe, and that I would be able to show the clerk how exactly not racist I was, by charging to his rescue.

I wanted to save him.

I needed to save him.

To show him that I wasn't racist, you understand.

The Minuteman T-shirt thing was just an experiment, and didn't he know that?

The shirtless man relented and went back into the room, slamming the door. From the other side of the wall I could hear him and his female companion start to move about the room, packing, getting ready to vacate the premises. They screamed at each other, yelling obscenities.

A few thumps hit the wall, domestic ricochets in the form of flying debris.

I frowned as I attempted to block out the noises emanating from the other side of the wall and get down to business as I pulled out my laptop and notes. I turned on my audio recorder and made another note: "After dismissing California, I've decided to go with the money shot, where everyone crosses, south-central Arizona on the Amnesty Trail. Tomorrow I'm meeting back up with Andre and . . ."

From the other side of the wall, more shouting.

I sighed and stood up and banged on the wall. "Hey do you mind?"

I sat back down on the bed and realized I couldn't plan my next move with the hotel manager still thinking I was a racist. I went into the bathroom to take a piss and while standing over the toilet, caught my Minuteman reflection in the mirror.

And then suddenly, completely to my own surprise, I ripped off the Minuteman T-shirt and threw it in the trash. I moved out of the bathroom and scoured in my duffel bag for my Mexican T-shirt. It read: "I love Mexicans"—but with a heart instead of the word "love."

I paced the room trying to think of a reason to go back to the lobby. And then, not being able to come up with anything better, I grabbed my map of the state of Arizona. I entered the motel lobby as the bell rang above the door. The clerk was getting off the phone with the police.

"Can I help you?" he asked, eyeing me suspiciously.

"Yeah, how do I get to . . . um . . ." I stammered, having no idea where it was I wanted to get to as I tried to think of the name of a city in Arizona. "How do I get to Phoenix?" I asked, looking inquisitively at the map.

The clerk pointed to the Interstate just outside the motel that I had entered from.

"Just take the Interstate."

"Hmm . . . yes, I see," I replied, nodding at my map as if it all made sense suddenly. "Well, thank you again for all your help! I *really* appreciate it."

As I left, I caught him eyeing my new T-shirt.

He smiled and so did I.

Part Three

THE AMNESTY TRAIL

The Amnesty Trail, which encompasses both the Buenos Aires National Wildlife Refuge and the Coronado National Forest, is an oblique rectangle formed by Sasabe and Nogales in the south and Three Points and Tucson in the north, framed on the sides by Interstate 19 and Highway 286, which both run north to south.

The Amnesty Trail, along with the eastern half of the Coronado National Forest on the other side of Interstate 19, which runs to Sierra Vista, is the single busiest portion of the United States border. It disproportionately counts for almost half of all apprehensions of illegal aliens.

The allure is that in the first thirty miles closer to the border, the geography is mountainous with thick forests; lots of places to hide and disappear. And the allure is also Phoenix and Tucson, the primary difference in attraction from San Diego and Los Angeles being that the southern California border was narrow and more easily defended through choke points like Tijuana and the Tecate Line.

The Amnesty Trail is also a corridor fully filled with the remnants of civilization and suburban subdivisions that grow like moss on the edge of I-19, which stretches from Tucson all the way down to the border. And then there is Arivaca, a small ranching community set in the middle of the national parks. And there are service roads and highways, more chances to surrender if you encounter trouble.

It is almost what you'd call a sweet deal.

Except that unlike in California where a border run means a simple nimble sprint to the finish line and the nearby highway, here a border run means Tucson, Eloy, or Phoenix—somewhere the migrants can dissipate, disappear in the wretched masses and get lost in the shuffle. A point past the numerous choke holds and checkpoints set up to the south. Here a border run means an endurance haul of sixty miles through the country's most severe temperatures.

And as if to prove the difficulty and sour the milk, God keeps sending the Mexicans home to heaven, leaving their dead bodies behind, which lie like dust-covered scarecrows in the desert . . .

Chapter 9

A BODY A DAY . . .
(TUCSON SECTOR)

They went through a lot of water, Chrissy explained. A lot of Mexicans equaled a lot of water. Your average person was supposed to drink eight servings of eight ounces a day. In the desert in July, you were supposed to drink one hundred ounces every four hours, and on regular rotation.

"Most immigrants only cross with a single jug of water," Chrissy explained. "It's all they can carry, and they're out here, three, four, five days sometimes. If we didn't have these water points out here, we'd see more dying every day." She paused for a moment allowing Andre to take a picture and then added, "We're finding a body a day, as it is."

Chrissy opened the spigot of the blue industrial plastic water tank that was hidden from the road by a small slope and outgrowth of wild brush, and the water gurgled to the floor of the desert in frothy chugs, quickly transforming the dirt into mud.

We had to empty the tanks before we could refill them, Chrissy explained. And it was necessary to empty and refill the tanks every few days. If you didn't, the sunlight started to ferment coliformic bacteria—*Escherichia, Citrobacter, Klebsiella, Enterobacter*—nasty bugs that'd play hell on the intestinal tract of a crossing Mexican.

Chrissy, heavily tattooed on neck and arms from her more indiscriminate youth, was now involved in the Latino community as a rehabilitated rebel. She was an organizer. She was a voice, fierce and proud. She even worked with at-risk youth and was majoring in college in African American studies. Just another typical Republican.

Next to her, prepping the larger water tank used for refilling on the back of the pickup truck, were Jasmine and Debra. Debra was a political science college professor who had an academic textbook coming out on the Minuteman movement, an organization that she explained was inherently racist. She had even gone so far as to attend a public rally once where some of them had shown up.

Jasmine was one of her graduate students, finishing up her dissertation on some complex topic that I couldn't quite wrap my head around, but it had something to do with advancing an argument to adopt natural systems of law as opposed to codified systems of law that were biased toward existing power structures. Whatever the idea was, it showed real promise and feasible application to the real world.

And the three of them together were volunteers for Humane Borders, one of many nonprofits within the region that had developed to aid and assist illegal aliens from Mexico, most of which were linked to one another through cooperative national and interstate partnerships. Aiding Mexicans was the new civil rights movement—God's work, important. Some organizations filed lawsuits in an attempt to stop legislation or enforcement of the immigration laws, other organizations ran camps in Mexico offering first aid and border training. Humane Borders put out water in the desert. They were also the same organization that had famously published maps guiding the migrant Mexicans through the desert toward safety and water.

"How do the illegal aliens know where to find the water?" Andre asked, winking at me, knowing it was the most important question on my mind.

Debra turned sharply from her untangling of the hose and said, "I'd advise you not to call them illegals. You may use the term 'migrant,' or 'Mexican,' if you prefer, but not 'illegal.' No human being is illegal."

I snickered, thinking she was joking. Right, of course, no human being was illegal in that abstract way that rock stars intended when they sang to raise money for famine relief in Africa, but in the real world there were laws and lawbreakers, right?

Debra didn't return the snicker.

"Uh, sorry," I replied. "Um, the migrants. How do the migrants know where to find the water?"

"We're a border ministry. We publish maps. They're disseminated by churches in Mexico, nonprofit organizations. The information gets out," Debra explained.

"And how would one get a copy of these maps?" I asked politely, trying not to appear too interested in figuring out how I could obtain one of these said maps.

"If you need one, you'll know where to find it," Chrissy said.

I frowned. I did need one, as a matter of fact, but I still didn't know where to get one.

"A mile from here is where they found a seventeen-year-old Guatemalan girl just last week," Chrissy explained sadly, peering off into the desert forlornly as she inserted the hose into the tank and opened up the spigot on the back of the truck. "She was pregnant, trying to come into the country to meet her husband and child, who were already here." Chrissy pointed in a new direction. "Over there, we had a whole family: mom, dad, kids. They all just ended up lying down together in the desert and dying." She whirled and pointed again. "Down south, another body, no one could identify or make out the gender of that one."

I cringed at the mention of the family. I imagined them back in Guatemala or Mexico, making eight dollars a day and food not much cheaper than here in the United States. I imagined the husband and wife talking quietly at night in their bed, some tin shack at the peripheral edge of a shantytown, speaking in low-hushed murmurs after the children were asleep, wondering about the United States as they held each other in bed, wondering if they should try or if they should stay. They were young and new to the world and, at this point, their love for each other and their still-young children was a thing of terrible beauty and indestructible.

And when the family started off in Mexico, I imagined them excited and beaming, elated at the prospect of realizing the potential for their children, who were laughing. And mom and dad were getting along. They weren't fighting, but smiling as they bribed the children to behave with promises of future gifts earned with American dollars. They were even holding hands again after that nervous dustup right before leaving home. And everyone was happy because this was a grand adventure and they were doing it together, as a family.

In America now and the husband is nervous, frightened in his role as provider as they crossed through the desert, afraid for his children and his wife and himself, afraid for the future. But the fear is still tinged with an ever diminishing hope. But for the moment, it's enough to sustain.

Thirst comes first.

The children whine about it, but then they whine about everything. His wife was silent, although she too was licking her lips. But the thirst wasn't yet a real problem, just enough to be a distant anxiety. But it gets lost in prioritization because there are thousands of distant anxieties and, in any case, there isn't much that can be done about it.

And they keep going, because that's the dream and because the family was and had been subsisting on dreams for a long time now. The mother, with each step, she's dreaming of the school her children are going to attend, and someday, maybe, college. The children, they're dreaming of the toys they've been promised. Father, he's just dreaming of his kids eating well. And maybe of a new stereo, or a car.

Then the migraines and the dizziness—the migraine is because your brain is carpet-burning against the top of your skull. Millions of irreplaceable brain cells blinking out every minute while your eyes dry up, threatening possible and permanent blindness.

And then the children, getting increasingly tired with each step, begin to cry. They're crying because they're tired and thirsty and hungry, but most of all, they're crying because they can see that daddy is scared, guessing at which direction to go. And with each desert precipice they crest, there's another promise broken as he attempts further encouragement, his confidence manufactured and artificial; his words lies. Children know when a smile is working.

It's just over the next hill. I promise.

Then the back pain and joint stiffness starts. This is caused by a water shortage in the spinal column as the discs that cushion the vertebrae rub without lubrication. And that developing sharp pain in the abdomen? That's what is known as fecal impacting, your shit solidifying into a rock and hanging heavy in the gut. Hallucination, lack of coordination, and kidney failure still to come.

And as they keep going, the screaming starts. The parents start screaming at their children, hating them for the forced responsibility. The children hate their parents for making them suffer. And the parents hate one another, each accusing the other for each wrong decision.

And in that way, the desert evaporated their love.

They died hating. I was sure of it.

Their demise was one of lingering procrastination, slow and steady as blood cells exploded and evaporated, losing viscosity and speed while each system of the body started to click offline, one after the other toward death. And when they left, they went out the same way they entered the world, curled into the fetal position, clutching their stomachs.

These people I was with putting water out in the desert? They were doing good work.

Regardless of what one thought of the illegal immigration (migrant) problem, at least stopping the deaths in the desert seemed to be a no-brainer.

"Oh yeah, we have all types of problems," Chrissy explained, breaking me from my morbid vision and bringing me back to the moment. "We have militant groups come out and put bullet holes in our water tanks, they just shoot 'em up . . . with bullets. We have another guy that comes out here putting a Spanish sticker on them that reads poisonous so the migrants won't drink it."

Debra shook her head angrily. "They should be brought up on murder charges as far as I'm concerned."

"And what's really awful is that the Border Patrol sometimes sit out and stake out these water points to catch them when they go to drink," Chrissy angrily added.

"Well," I replied thoughtfully. "Maybe, that's for the best. If Border Patrol can find them, then at least that gets them out of the desert and somewhere safe, right?" I felt happy, participating in a conversation of peers, of people who cared. In the debate over illegal immigration, the ideological lines had been drawn, and the teams had been picked, and I smiled because I had finally found my team, the side on which I belonged.

"What do you mean by that?" Chrissy asked, her face pinched in a crumpled folded cheerful smile.

"Well, if Border Patrol apprehends them, then at least they'll live, right?" I replied, looking around me for some shared agreement.

"But . . ." Chrissy started, her voice wavering in pitch and velocity, tipping toward aggression. "But then the migrants won't come to get our water . . ."

She capped her statement with a sincere smile to let me know that she wasn't angry. Not yet.

I eyed Chrissy nervously as I carefully offered my response: "They can still come, they'll just have to get a ride back to the border. But I mean, that's the point, to live, right? That's why you're doing this?"

"Oh, how traumatizing," Debra said, shaking her head as she contemplated a ride back to the border.

Chrissy was quiet with a frozen prolonged look of incredulousness. "I don't think you get it." She turned her attention back to the water buffalo, snaking in the hose as she quietly shook her head over all that I did not understand.

Debra smiled politely and then said, "The reason they are dying is *because* of Border Patrol. It's because of our border policies that are forcing them to cross in the desert and are directly responsible for these deaths. We receive numerous reports of abuse by the migrants regarding Border Patrol. They're not given medical treatment, they're not fed."

"No, they're fed," Andre explained, matter-of-factly.

Chrissy and Debra shared a look of contemptuous contention before Chrissy sarcastically sneered, "No, I don't think that's right."

"No, they are. I was in Campo and the Border Patrol there had water and crackers in their truck. I saw the crackers with my own eyes," Andre insisted eagerly.

"No, that can't be," Debra said politely, pursing her lips as Jasmine laughed.

Chrissy shook her head, the same way you might if dealing with a slow child, or a retard, maybe. "No, that's not right. They're not fed."

"No, they are . . ." Andre started to say when he noticed my wincing face—we didn't know where their water points were yet, we still needed them! He quickly repealed his argument, "Um, maybe you're right."

An uncomfortable silence overtook us as I moved behind a cactus to take a GPS reading of our current location as Andre struggled with the silence, wanting to speak. When I reemerged a moment later, sliding the GPS in my cargo pants pocket, he asked, "Um, do you not believe in border security? I mean, we do have a right to guard our borders, yeah?"

Jasmine sighed. "It's such a complex issue, you can't reduce it to being for or against the border, and most people, unfortunately, are very ignorant of the actual issues." She shook her head in dismay at our ignorance, unable to continue as she moved to help Chrissy shut off the spigot on the back of the truck as Chrissy started to pull the hose out of the tank.

Debra patted Jasmine on the shoulder and stepped forward, as if a baton had just been passed, and continued: "We're not against border security. We're just against bad border policy. We can have border security without terrorizing the local populace, without harming and terrorizing the migrants. We're for a more compassionate border security."

I nodded.

It certainly sounded good.

But I wasn't quite sure what compassionate border security looked like.

What with the cartels and the organized crime syndicates.

"IT'S AN ISSUE where we need to put people first," Debra said as we drove on a back dirt road toward the location of the second water point. Debra was up front with Chrissy, who was driving, while I was in the rear of the extended cab with Jasmine and Andre. "These are human beings, not commodities, not dollars, not pesos. I mean, what is a border, anyway? Borders are being redefined all the time. Wildlife doesn't adhere to borders, pollution doesn't adhere to borders, technology, communication, and transportation doesn't adhere to borders. Nothing does, the economy doesn't, but yet we still want to have human beings adhere to borders."

I must confess: I was confused.

"The border's in place to make some people a lot of money and to marginalize another group of people," Debra explained. "It's about how the borders are connected that's problematic. They're connected in ways that benefit some to the detriment of others."

"So you don't want any borders at all?" Andre asked, just as confounded as I was.

"Why not?" Chrissy asked.

"Because they're all poor!" Andre yelled, the words bursting accidentally.

The recurring silence was deafening, as if a vacuum had just sucked all the humor and goodwill out of the truck, replacing it with an awkward cautionary quiet.

And then, feeling the need to defend his last comment, he added, "I mean, should we just open up the borders to everyone from Africa and Asia, all the world's poor can come here? I mean, we can barely afford ourselves!"

"The immigrants pay for themselves!" Chrissy replied, cheerfully. "You should be thanking them!"

"There was recently a study down here in Tucson that showed migrants are ten percent of the economy in Arizona, that their contributions offer an economic surplus to the state," Debra lectured, our eyes meeting in the reflection of the rearview mirror. "They're coming here taking jobs that no one wants."

I sighed, cleared my throat, and then replied, "I don't know if that's necessarily true. You're a college professor, it's very easy to say that when no one is going to come and take your job. But when I was out in Campo with the Minutemen, there was this one guy, a construction worker, and he couldn't find work in Vegas anymore because of the migrants taking over the labor force."

"But that's because there's a clandestine work market that's supported by border enforcement. If you let them come in, they'd have to compete on the same terms as everyone else," Chrissy explained.

Andre thought about his next statement long and hard, applying caveats and consideration within his mind before he released it: "But here's the thing, yeah, they act as an economic stimulus because they provide cheap labor for business, but you can't just measure if a positive economic effect exists, you have to measure the cumulative economic effect. Poor people cost the country more money than they provide—it's that way with everyone, your average white hardworking high school dropout has more per capita expenditures spent in his name than he contributes in taxes. They may pay some taxes and provide cheap labor and spend their money, but what's the value of that positive contribution compared to the cost of medical care and education and jails and everything else? We spend so much money in this country that all poor people, white or brown, are subsidized by the wealthy. That's why we have a progressive tax code where the rich have to pay more. The cost of educating one child in school is like seven grand . . . there's no way someone making fifteen thousand a year pays seven grand in taxes."

I nodded as I smiled at Andre.

That seemed like a good argument!

On one side was the humanitarian emotional aspect, the migrants dying in the desert, the struggle for survival here within the United States, but you couldn't feed and clothe a nation on good intentions and feelings of guilt. Ultimately it did seem as simple as he had just described: *We couldn't afford it.*

And why were we obligated to? Regardless of past history, contemplations of lands once conquered, this *was* a nation presently called the United States of America, and it seemed a strange prospect that the idea of controlling our own borders would somehow become a controversial issue.

Chrissy and Jasmine and Debra?

They didn't see it that way.

They were all staring at us now, not even offering the social courtesy of attempting to hide their crimpling looks of contempt: Jasmine from the back seat, Chrissy and Debra both turned around from the front.

I MARKED THE POSITION of the second water point on my GPS as Debra and the others continued to inform us about the ways of the migrant and the ways of the world, all of which had something to do with all acts of security being violence enacted onto the poor migrants who had constitutional rights, what with this being America and all.

"What is an American?" Chrissy asked as she held the hose in place, repeating the question several times, as if its mere utterance had a profound meaning. "What is an American, huh? What is an American? Is it a Mexican? A Native American? Is an anchor baby an American? Is someone born overseas with American parents an American? What about Mexicans, this used to be Mexico!"

I had simply been nodding my head for the last half-hour, pretending to agree fervently with every comment. But some of their comments, dumb and ill-informed though I was, required at least tentative judgment, and as I saw Andre start to speak, I shot him a look—I'd take this one.

And then quietly, and with great timid hesitation I said, "But the Mexicans that are alive now weren't alive when this was Mexico . . ."

"You did not just say that!" Chrissy yelled, holding her hands up in the air and walking away so as to not hit me. "You did not just say that!"

Jasmine and Debra shared another one of their patented looks of incredulousness and slowly moved away from me, shaking their heads in disdain as they went.

"I think you need to do a lot more research on the border before you start making so many conclusions," Debra explained.

I nodded, embarrassed at the audacity of my claim that Mexican nationals did not own at least a minority controlling stake in the United States of America. I certainly did have a lot to learn.

DEBRA CHOSE HER WORDS carefully from the front passenger seat of the van as we drove down the Interstate. "I don't think you're intending to be racist, you may not be racist in your heart, but that's how you're coming across . . . as racist." She bit her lip and winced, as if a symbol of contrition for my benefit, to demonstrate she was being modest about her conclusion that I was racist.

How had this happened? How had I suddenly become a racist?

I laughed. "I can't be racist, it's not possible. I'm a liberal for Christ's sake! I believe in gay marriage! How can I be a racist if I believe in gay marriage?"

"Racism is often very subtle," Debra tenderly explained. "Let me give you a couple of examples. Right after 9/11, there was this wanted poster at this local sheriff's office of the 9/11 hijackers, and all the faces on it were brown and the insinuation was that all the colored people were wanted, were dangerous."

"But all the terrorists *were* colored people," I protested.

"Or another example," Debra continued. "Say you're in town and you have two ATMs equal distance apart. You pick one ATM because it's in a white neighborhood instead of a black neighborhood."

"But sometimes, there's an unfortunate reality that the black neighborhood is going to, statistically speaking not always, but statistically speaking, is more likely to have more crime," I added.

"There you go with the racism again! You're suggesting blacks are inherently more prone to crime than whites!" Debra exclaimed, her mouth agape with another incredulous posture.

"No, I don't think that! I think poor people commit more crimes and more blacks tend to be poor because of years of entrenched racism and subjugation, but that still doesn't mean I'm going to risk getting mugged in a black neighborhood if there's an ATM in a white neighborhood equal distance away! Is that wrong?"

Maybe I was a racist.

Maybe because I didn't want to be mugged, that made me a racist.

I didn't know what to think anymore.

Chrissy turned around in the car and pointed her index finger in my face. "It's racist to only apply border security at the Mexican border. You want to be fair about it? Why not do the same at the Canadian border?"

I squirmed under the question, unable to realize its meaning and consequences.

And then quietly, I risked the response, "But Canadians can enter the country with just a driver's license, so that'd be . . . silly."

"It is racist!" Chrissy hissed. "Right there, you assumed they were all Mexicans. You have Guatemalans, Salvadorans, Hondurans, you have Panamanians crossing the border and no distinction is made. That is racist!"

"What difference does it make? They're all brown," I asked, collapsing into the back seat in defeat.

THEY WERE STILL yelling as we got out of the truck in the church parking lot.

And as we watched the truck drive away, Andre turned to me and asked how many water points I had managed to get.

"Two," I responded as I stared morosely at my GPS.

Andre nodded his understanding. "Well, how many times were you going to fill up on water anyway? Three times, maybe? Two's fine. Nothing wrong with two. Two's very respectable."

"I guess," I responded as I swallowed hard and realized I was very thirsty.

Chapter 10

A VERY FINE AND DANDY BORDER SECURITY APPARATUS
(TUCSON SECTOR)

The control room was filled with rows of blinking screens and the squelch of overlapping radio traffic as National Guard soldiers monitored thermal imaging and motion-sensitive images of illegals crossing somewhere out in the desert. A soldier moved a joystick and a camera rotated, tracking a group of illegals using a ladder to jump over the barbed-wire border fence that cut through downtown Nogales.

"They're about a half-kilometer south of your position," the soldier said into a radio receiver, his voice followed by a blast of static feedback.

"Roger, we're approaching the top of the ridge now," an agent in the field responded.

The city under observation at the moment was Nogales, Arizona, an industrial border town. The intensive surveillance was akin to what I imagined East Berlin had been like during the Soviet occupation of the Cold War—everything filmed, captured by blinking lenses with nothing less than all of the public space within and around the perimeter of the town's boundaries captured forever on digital video files as frowning social monitors observed silently from dark rooms.

The intensive urban surveillance was a key feature of Operation Gatekeeper—an ambitious and long-reaching Border Patrol plan to fortify America's border towns. The theory had been that, by closing off the urban corridors, the Mexicans would be forced into the mountainous and unforgiving stretches of desert, which would be such a deterrent that illegal immigration would grind to a shuddering halt. They had been wrong, of course—there was just as much illegal immigration now as before, except now the Mexicans were spread out in the desert over a much larger commitment of geography and space.

"Tucson Sector is the busiest border in the entire world. At any given time we have two-thousand-plus agents patrolling Tucson Sector, which stretches from Yuma Sector all the way to New Mexico," Agent Thomas said. "We arrest, on average, 300,000 illegals a year. About one in ten will have serious criminal histories. We confiscated 750,000 pounds of dope last year. Nationwide a Border Patrol agent is assaulted, on average, every other day. And eighteen Border Patrol agents have been shot at so far this year."

Andre and I both nodded.

We were told of CIA surveillance drones of the type used in Afghanistan flying across the southern deserts of Arizona. Of Black Hawk helicopters with tactical Special Forces response teams. Of an intricate network of ground motion sensors that were used in a classified cooperation with covert field trackers. We were told of radar and thermal imaging. Of sewer teams that patrol the underground culverts and concealed drainage ditches coming from Mexico. Of undercover operatives pretending to be illegals who fed information to a covert intelligence bureau. Of new recruits being trained and added to the patrol rosters every day. We were told of the pony patrol and the four-wheeler patrol and the aerial patrols.

And then there was the Secure Fence Act of 2006, which called for the creation of seven hundred miles of new fencing within eighteen months.

But better than real fencing was virtual fencing.

"What's virtual fencing?" I asked.

"Virtual fencing is better than real fencing," came the reply.

"But it's not an actual fence?"

"No, it's virtual. Like virtual reality."

"Oh," I responded.

The virtual fence was composed of seismic and infrared sensors, lasers, fiber-optic cables, night-vision cameras, and unmanned aerial vehicles. It was an integrated web of technological prowess and derring-do, a force-multiplier that was both scientific and technological; Americans like that sort of thing.

"Does the virtual fence stop them from crossing?" I asked timidly, imagining robots or cyborgs perhaps, activated by AI computers and running through the desert chasing down undocumented migrants.

"It doesn't stop them from crossing, but it records them crossing. We don't have enough agents to actually stop them all."

I nodded in agreement. It *was* better to know how many were crossing than to actually stop them.

"How does the National Guard being deployed to the border help things out?" Andre asked. "I imagine more boots on the ground means more arrests, yeah?"

"Well," Agent Thomas started, clearing his throat. "They're not allowed to actually apprehend." And then he quickly added, "But they can observe!"

And observing in person was even better than a virtual fence that detected!

"So what do you think about all this?" Agent Thomas asked proudly.

I was crushed. Absolutely crushed. It was a daunting display of defense, one that I had no hopes of circumventing. It seemed impenetrable. I had to remind myself that Mexicans were successfully making it all the time, and that I was surely no worse than a Mexican. It was because I *wasn't* racist that I recognized them as equals, and that meant that it was possible for me too.

"It's a very impressive border security apparatus," I responded, swallowing hard. "It's very fine and dandy."

Agent Thomas buzzed through a series of security doors, as if entering the maximum security wing of a prison, and we found ourselves in a cavernous warehouse split into a labyrinthine division of chain-link holding cells that were accessed by parallel caged hallways labeled with large numbered placards. Inside these cells were a thousand Mexicans lying on the floor and lounging on chipped wooden benches, covering themselves in dull scratchy blankets, the sort you found in the Army. Some were tired, others scared, a few seemed angry. Separation occurred here by age, gender, criminal history, and likely intelligence value. It was like a giant factory sorting the brown M&Ms from the green, efficient and sterile.

The cells were full, hundreds of faces watching us in silence, wondering about the border agent showing around the two battered dignitaries dressed in dirty T-shirts and cargo pants with ratty sneakers.

"Looks like it's been a busy week, what is this a thousand people, yeah?" Andre asked.

Agent Thomas laughed. "Eight hundred. This is just from tonight. Our processing time is three hours. They'll all be out of here by midnight and half of 'em will be back in here again by morning. We do fingerprints, try to find out identities, if they've got a record, we pull 'em and prosecute 'em, but if they don't, or we don't catch it, they get thrown back."

"What do you mean?" I asked, my gaze moving to the floor in defer-
ence to a particularly mean-spirited stare coming from the fellow in cage
number seven.

"Border Patrol is strictly a catch-and-release program," Agent Thomas
answered. "We don't have the resources to prosecute this many people,
so we drive 'em to the border, release 'em onto the pedestrian walk, they
cross back into Mexico."

Releasing Mexicans it seemed was the de facto response to dealing
with illegal immigration. All across the country Immigration and Customs Enforcement (ICE) didn't have the funding or the capacity to hold
anything but what they called mandatory commitments, those suspected
of serious felonies. Assault didn't count as a serious felony; that was
a nonmandatory commitment. Felonious theft and robbery wasn't a
mandatory commitment, either. And so, the assaults and the robberies
were given summonses to appear in court for extradition back to Mexico
using the honor system. No surprise, but most didn't show. ICE
agents could only engage in law enforcement operations if there was
room available for incarceration. All across the country, in places like
Arkansas, Alabama, Louisiana, Tennessee, and Mississippi, they were
releasing undocumented Mexicans back onto the streets of America. No
room to hold them, what else could they do? Constitutional rights, and
all that.

Agent Thomas sighed as he said this next part. "And then after we
release them, they come back over. We see the same people three . . .
four times in the same day sometimes. We try and filter out the dangerous ones, the ones who've committed crimes over here before, but if no
prints come up, there's not much we can do other than hope they give up
their name."

And suddenly, my entire concept of the border security apparatus
shifted slightly off center, became blurred, confusing. Up until this
moment, I had been assuming that each apprehension counted as an
individual statistic, that each illegal stopped at the border was one who
was never to cross again, or at least not for a while; I had assumed that
each immigrant who crossed successfully was one who had never before
been apprehended.

This also meant that every statistical measure we had for guessing
how many were inside the country was virtually useless—we were counting the same people over and over again and in different columns.

Border hopping, it appeared, was a numbers game. You tried until
you made it.

It seemed too easy. The Mexicans should have given themselves a handicap, I decided. Something to balance the game toward the Americans just a bit, give us a fighting chance at competition.

I wondered at how many illegal aliens were actually inside the United States. The Minutemen said the total number of illegal aliens from Mexico was as high as 30 to 40 million. But they, of course, were likely full of shit. But the official number, the one repeatedly cited by reductionist politicians and the U.S. Border Patrol, wasn't any more reliable—the government figure, based off the 2000 Census, had pegged the number at somewhere between 8 and 11 million people of unknown identity and of Mexican origin living inside the United States. The most obvious flaw with this data was that, despite being ten years old, it was strangely locked in and repeatedly quoted as the official figure. I imagined this was because it diverted from the issue, made it more palpable during a time when there were terrorists to fight and countries to invade.

And when asked how many illegal aliens escaped detection, the normative answer by Border Patrol was to respond that they were capturing one out of every three. Yet in 2005 alone, Border Patrol's own statistics, provided by the Department of Homeland Security, stated they had made 1.3 million apprehensions. But if two got through for every one they apprehended, that suggested an additional 2.6 million per year for the last ten years, which necessarily meant that 20 million alone were in the country just within the last decade—a far cry from the stated claim of 8 to 11 million.

But how many returned home and how many stayed?

And that was the problem, no one really knew.

Ghost counting was a difficult business.

My personal guess was that the number of illegal aliens within the United States was double the 10 million number offered by the government but still far below the figure the Minutemen were suggesting. Even still, this meant that one in every fifteen persons within the United States was illicit—a person of unknown criminal background and identity. It also meant that in Mexico, with a population of 109 million this year, as many as one in every five Mexican nationals was now living inside the United States.

I was afraid to ask my next question: "Agent Thomas, how many do you think give up after getting apprehended? Just don't try anymore."

Agent Thomas's voice was quiet as he replied, "I'd assume that number to be extremely low."

I nodded. It was necessarily a somber understanding. The meaning of which was that, for all intents and purposes, the entirety of the Border Patrol security apparatus wasn't one of prevention, but simply one of momentary inconvenience. Anyone could and would get across—they just had to have a little heart, put some elbow grease in it.

"Any other questions?" Agent Thomas asked.

"Yeah," Andre replied. "Do you carry crackers for the illegal aliens? Was talking to someone who said you didn't feed them."

"Yes, we feed them," he answered laughing, leading us toward the pallets of crackers so that we could take a picture.

I STOOD BEHIND ANDRE as he moved behind the Border Patrol agents that were handing out pens and paper to the Mexicans, sitting on the ground, confused and scared. Their faces were gaunt and guarded, but the camera, like a good interrogator, had a way of breaking the truth that was revealed in digital revelation. The camera would flash, a startling momentary incandescent snapshot illuminating the dark like an X-ray in an inky vacuum, and then in the camera's digital playback window, the stern brave faces were transformed to tears and surprised anguish.

Andre smiled wickedly behind his weapon, drunk with power as he moved from one Mexican to another, transforming their steely resolve to tears as he sidestepped knees and hunched bodies, happy in his role as the inquisitor with the magic box that could force-feed revelation: a father holding his two young daughters tight, an old man confused and scared, a young girl alone, they were all stripped naked under the camera's betrayal.

They were dirty and wide-eyed, carrying small meager packs that were, perhaps, most of what they owned. A few of them smirked confidently; it was easy to discern the frequent fliers. But most of them huddled, trapped in a forlorn hesitancy—not knowing they'd soon be released, not knowing border crossing was a numbers game.

I wanted to tell them, cheer them up. Let them know it wasn't that big of a deal, they just had to keep trying. I was subdued by their despondent anxiety, their anxious eyes reflecting shattered hope and dreams. I was embarrassed for them and ashamed of myself. This wasn't a game for them, some silly writing assignment. I wanted to throw myself at their feet and beg their forgiveness for my sarcasm and deliberate irony, for my impish tone. For making fun of the trauma that had cut short so much life and hope. I wanted to apologize for each of my silly literary impulses.

And suddenly, I was concerned that with each picture taken, we were stealing their souls.

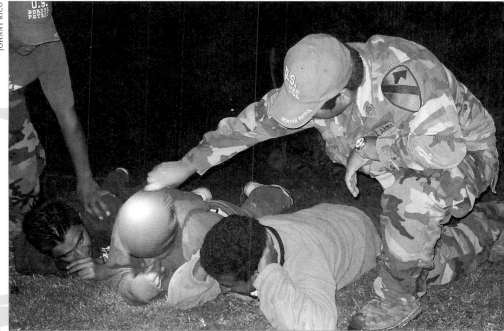

JOHNNY RICO

Caught by a fake Border Patrol at Migrant Mountain.

JOHNNY RICO

Patriot Point.

Little Dog watching for
illegal crossers on the
Tecate Line.

A spare bunk, Patriot Point.

A Migrant Mountain coyote.

Nogales, Mexico.

A paramilitary unit heading for the U.S. border.

Another body in the river.

A Border Patrol checkpoint somewhere deep in Texas.

A Border Patrol detention center, Nogales, Arizona.

Putting water out in the
desert for crossing migrants.

Organ Pipe Cactus National Monument.

A ride-along with the Border Patrol, Tucson sector.

The border fence, southern Arizona.

"Andre, maybe you could stop taking their pictures?" I asked.

"No way, man, these are great shots! Look how sad they are!" he responded, giggling.

"Andre! Will you quit taking their goddamn pictures!" I yelled suddenly, my voice screeching and ragged.

Andre and several Border Patrol agents looked over at me, concerned.

Andre paused, his camera shoved in the face of an old man, as he considered my request. His face stood calm—indecisive—before transforming to an ugly baleful glare. A crack of lightning snapped across the nighttime as Andre took another picture, his face hesitantly hopeful as he looked into the playback window of the camera, and then, delighted by the capture of another soul, he giggled, stepped over the old man, and moved to a small cluster of grade school girls who trembled quietly.

I moved back to the Border Patrol truck where I slumped into the passenger seat as I watched the Border Patrol agents start moving the Mexicans into the back cabs of awaiting trucks—Mexican paddy wagons. The flashes lit up the desert as Andre cackled loudly.

I made a private apology to all the Mexicans in front of me that I didn't know and quietly asked for their forgiveness.

THE DOWNTOWN STREETS of two A.M. Nogales were quiet and desolate, watched by pale haloed cones of illumination from the streetlights as trash and litter stirred in the streets on the back of a light breeze. The shops, all named in Spanish, were shuttered with fierce metal gates, a few shopping carts left abandoned on the sidewalk.

"We don't go over here much," Agent Thomas said, killing the headlights of the truck and pulling forward from the fence just out of rock-throwing range as both of us peered into Mexico, where the crumbling hive of residential houses swarmed up the hillside, one on top of another.

Andre was in the street taking photos, trying desperately for that eerie still-night still shot that he hoped would capture the still stark dichotomy punctuated so dramatically by the border fence between run-down U.S. and regular Mexico, which was still quite a visual distinction.

"See the lights?" Agent Thomas asked. On the Mexican hilltop behind us, house lights started to blink in sequence as they signaled one another. "A lot of drugs come over this border. They have permanent surveillance here, telling each other who's in the area."

"The Mexican government can't seem to get a handle on the goddamn drugs," I replied.

Agent Thomas laughed as he leaned out the truck and asked me for a cigarette. He had dropped the public affairs officer role two hours ago. "Hell, the Mexican government is running it."

"Does the Mexican government cooperate at all with Border Patrol on security?"

"They make an appearance," he said, taking a drag from his cigarette. "But there's a lot of remittance money headed back south. I think it's their number one or two or third biggest source of income. It's not in their best interest." He was quiet for a moment before adding, "And people and countries mostly do what's in their own best interest." He was quiet for a moment before adding: "Mexicans too, you know?"

I smirked. It was a simple yet strangely poignant explanation of the border problem: *People did, as they always did, what was in their best interest*. It was an explanation that made the Minutemen arguments that the Mexicans should refrain from crossing the border because it was an illegal act seem silly. What did Mexicans care about U.S. law when it ran contrary to their own natural interests?

And then there was shouting from the hilltop within Mexico. It sounded angry and derogatory and directed at us. And even though we were still in the United States, and Agent Thomas was an armed federal agent, he seemed nervous. "Come on," he said as he tossed the cigarette and climbed back in the truck, starting the ignition. "We should be going. It's not safe out here at night."

I hoped that later when I crossed the border, Agent Thomas wasn't the one who apprehended me, because that'd just be embarrassing.

Chapter 11

THE WORST SECRET IN THE WORLD
(TUCSON SECTOR)

It was yet one more forlorn motel room somewhere in southern Arizona. Inside, sprawled on shag green carpeting that had still been viable in the late 1970s, while listening to the leaky faucet that dripped as if a countdown timer, Andre and I converged on the map as we planned the following week's battle rhythm.

Altar. I pointed it out on the map several hours south of the Mexican border.

Altar equaled smugglers and badness.

In Altar, I would attempt to hire a coyote.

Andre appeared dubious.

I reminded him that the key word was *attempt*, as in a modest good-faith effort that I would take up to the point of feeling threatened by imminent danger before I abandoned the project.

"That seems pointlessly risky," Andre replied.

"You're probably right, but it's part of the experience," I responded.

At Altar, there would be one of two endings. One, I would feel comfortable and depart with the next wave of outgoing migrants to the border where I would then reevaluate whether to stay with the group or disappear somewhere in the desert on my own because of fears of what the coyote would do to me once alone in the desert. Two, I would leave Altar without a coyote, but at least confident that I had attempted to retain one and I would have Andre drive me to the border where I would attempt a solo crossing along the Amnesty Trail.

During this operation, Andre would move to yet another cheap motel where he could get drunk or jerk off to porn, whatever it was he chose to do, as long as he was ready to receive my phone call that I was ready for a pickup.

I asked Andre if he understood.

Andre nodded his head. He did understand.

Any questions?

Andre raised his hand. He had a question.

"What is it?"

"How are you going to find a coyote?"

"Well, I'm going to ask the Mexicans," I said.

THE DAY LABORERS stood restlessly in the sun, passing the time on the picnic tables with small talk as they leaned over boxes of melting glazed donuts. And with each car that drove down the adjacent road, the conversations would pause ever so slightly, and the faces would all rotate in unison, tinged with a hopeful anticipation. And as the car would pass, driving on toward the main road, the conversations would resume, the faces shifted back, but this time with an increased note of desperation.

There was a lethargic lag to their movements, a slowness of reflex and reaction earned by so many wasted hours at the day labor site. The air percolated with the cumulative tensions and anxieties of a hundred migrants awaiting work that would never arrive. And air fraught with cumulative tension felt oily and toxic.

The center, which wasn't much more than a chain-link fence surrounding a driveway rimmed by picnic tables, had been formed from an unlikely coalition of illegal alien advocates and local businesses in the Phoenix area. For the migrants, it was a solution in the form of a permanent shelter where they would be less likely to be ripped off by the numerous unscrupulous business owners who picked up day laborers and then sometimes refused to pay them. For the business owners it moved the illegal aliens out of their parking lots where they wouldn't dissuade potential business.

But still, despite the unlikely coalition that had birthed the project, it had been controversial, the target of frequent protest by anti–illegal immigration advocates who not only didn't want the illegal aliens to gather on the street corners, but were also upset about the idea of them being given formal approval by the city—an action they viewed as acquiescence.

I walked to the main picnic table where a woman sat with a clipboard and a pen ready to take the information and license plates of business owners. And as I walked, the chatter and speech of one hundred Mexicans quieted as all eyes turned toward me wondering exactly what I was doing here if not offering business.

"Hi," I said loudly, to one and all. "I was wondering if I could talk to someone."

One hundred confused faces looked back at me.

"Anyone speak English? Anyone?"

One hundred confused faces looked back at me.

"I need to speak to a Mexican."

One hundred confused faces looked back at me.

I turned and dejectedly started back to my car.

And then there was a hand on my arm. I turned to see a young man in a muscle shirt with an acne-scarred face and tattoos encircling his arms and upper neck, going all the way up to just below his jawline. He wore baggy shorts and sunglasses atop his head.

"What do you need, bro?" he asked suspiciously.

"I just want to talk."

"You just want to talk?"

"Yeah. To some Mexicans. I want to talk."

He paused, considering my statement. "I'm a Mexican. What do you want to talk about?"

I shrugged. "Life, what's on your mind. Whatever you want to talk about. I'm a writer and I'm doing a story on illegal migration, wanted to get some of the stories of the migrants. You think any of these people would be willing to give me their story? How they got here? What they have to endure and put up with?"

He hissed as he sucked on a breath, contemplating my shitty offer.

"Shit bro, I dunno . . ."

"How about you? You want to give me an interview?"

He thought for a second and then said, "Yeah, why the fuck not. Sure. But if work comes I'm going to have to bail."

We took a seat next to my car on the curb by the parking lot.

"How long do you have to hang out here waiting for work?" I asked as I tapped out two cigarettes, handing him one.

"Depens, sometimes coupla days, at least, bro. Sometimes three or four."

I grimaced. Three or four days for a job?

"Yeah, it's rough, bro," he added as if reading my thoughts. "Three or four days, then you might get work for a day or two. Then sometimes you work for a day or two, and they say, I'll come back and pick ya up tomorrow, I'll pay ya tomorrow. Tomorrow comes, they don't show. How long it takes to get work, it depens on how good your English is. I've been in the U.S. since I was eight years old, so I speak pretty good English, but some of them guys who don't speak English, they can't tell people what they can do, right? A guy might be a painter, right? But he can't fucking tell the guy he knows how to paint. Dude like that will sit here all fucking week."

"That's a lot of people who need work," I observed sullenly.

"Yeah, that's why a lot of people don't stay here. They have to go outside the center. There's too much competition here," he explained. "The police will hassle you out there though, you run the risk of getting arrested. People don't wanna, but dey ain't got no other choice. We got bills to pay, you know?"

"The way it's told, Phoenix is a sanctuary city and the police don't hassle you."

My new friend laughed heartily at this.

That was a good one.

He handed me a card from his wallet. It was a card they were to hand to police if stopped. It informed the police who would read it that they were exercising their right to remain silent, and that they wished to contact some do-gooder attorney whose phone number was listed on the back.

"Marty," he said, holding out his hand.

"What?"

"Call me Marty."

"Nice to meet you, Marty," I said as we shook hands.

Marty was fresh from Los Angeles where he had been a gangbanger, a drug dealer, and a criminal enforcer. But now he had a wife and child in El Paso and was trying to get away from that lifestyle after being released from prison in California. He was slowly working his way east. Making some money, and then when he could afford it, moving on. He liked Phoenix a lot better. The people were nicer and work came easier. There wasn't as much opportunity to get into trouble. Marty had crossed to the United States with his parents as a child and moved back and forth freely across the border because he had a driver's license and spoke American English, despite not being an American citizen.

I asked Marty if he had ever killed anyone, you know, as a gangbanger. He shyly avoided the question but a slight and proud smile broke from his face as if to suggest that, yeah, there might be some confirmed kills to his name, but he wasn't telling. He winked at me as he said it, a gangster's silence, code of the street and all the rest.

"Amen," I replied. I was all about the code of the street.

"Times are getting desperate," Marty explained in reference to the new law that was going into effect at the start of the year, cracking down on employers within the state hiring undocumented workers with the threat of yanking their business license. "Not as many people are coming to pick us up anymore, people can't afford nothing. Some of these fools here ain't even eatin'," he explained, waving to the day laborers. "Not as many jobs, employers are nervous and I don't blame 'em. But what are all these people going to do when no one will come by here anymore? How are they going to survive?" he asked, his voice becoming emotional and upset.

I looked at the one hundred out-of-work Mexicans and wondered at the hundreds of thousands of others within the city, what had to be at least a million throughout the state. It was an excellent question. What *were* they going to do? Some would move to California, or else deeper in the country to other states still friendly to illegal immigrants. Others would return to Mexico. But some wouldn't, some would stay here, survive where their children were, where they were stuck because of economics and pared conditions.

"I don't wanna be a criminal no more or nuttin," Marty explained. "But I got two kids at home. When my kids are telling me, 'Hey Daddy, I ain't got nothing to eat, I ain't gonna let them go hungry. I'm gonna do what I got to do whatever that is an' you can interpret that, I think . . .'"

"Yeah, I can," I replied solemnly. And then after a moment, I asked, "So, when you're in Mexico, like, how do you, get a coyote?"

Marty shrugged and laughed. He reminded me that he came here as a child.

I sighed. "Right, hey would you drive around with me? Interpret for me so I can do more interviews?" Marty's face squirmed apprehensively, so I added, "I'll pay you."

And as soon as I said it, Marty looked hurt.

I winced. I had just inadvertently insulted him.

But then Marty's eyes moved to the long line of waiting workers as he estimated his chances of finding something more lucrative. The economy was playing in my favor.

"Yeah, okay," he replied reluctantly.

"I WANT REALLY bad stories, the worse the better," I informed Marty. We pulled into the rear of a Home Depot parking lot and pulled up next to a group of young men leaning against a streetlight. Marty looked over at me as if to ask if he really had to do this. His face turned sideways and peered out to look at his fellow countrymen and I could palpably feel the shame and embarrassment percolating inside of him as his face betrayed feelings of regret over agreeing to accept my offer.

Marty laughed nervously. "Man, I don't know about this."

"Go on, dammit," I replied. "I'm paying you aren't I? You want the twenty bucks or not?"

Marty sighed and rolled down the passenger window of my truck. He cleared his throat and spoke. The group and Marty conversed back and forth for a minute before Marty turned to me and said, "They don't wanna talk to you. They're embarrassed. They don't want to cause no trouble."

"I'll pay them," I said, my voice frantic and betraying my eager desperation for Mexican horror stories. "I'll pay them for their stories."

Marty's face, already flushed with embarrassment, now looked acutely pained. He sighed and leaned out the window and started translating into Spanish. I immediately regretted what I had suggested. I was the decadent white boy paying poor Mexicans for their sob stories so that I could collect the private shames of people I didn't know.

It was emotional prostitution and I was a pimp.

"How much you paying?" Marty asked, translating for several of them.

I quickly estimated the cash left in my wallet and winced at what I was about to say, wishing I had counted how much I had before I made the offer. Not only was I buying access to their private memories, but I was buying access to their private memories for four dollars.

"Four dollars," I said quietly.

Marty smirked, laughing.

Right. Four dollars. That's fucking funny.

The red-tinged shame on my face told him it was no joke.

Marty shook his head in dismay.

He wanted to tell me to fuck off.

He wanted to ask me who the hell I thought I was?

He wanted to tell me that his people had some pride and that they couldn't be bought for no fucking four dollars.

But times were tough.

"Yeah, okay," Marty said after some brief negotiation. "They'll tell you for four dollars."

THE STORIES CAME OUT in reluctant dribbles, as if being force-fed. They were told with cool indifference, explained in brisk details that, because they were so fractured, were unemotional and cold. I gave eight dollars to two boys from El Salvador who spoke no English and who had journeyed here by themselves at sixteen years of age. They didn't go to school, and they lived in a two-bedroom apartment with seven other people they didn't know. Their eyes maintained a distant look of anxiety at us, at each passing car, as if waiting any moment for police cruisers to pull into the parking lot. They were hungry and most days they felt hopeless. They missed their parents and friends. When I asked if they had dreams for the future, what they wanted to be when they grew up, they didn't understand the question and Marty had to explain to me it wasn't something they had been asked before. They just wanted to get some work standing outside the Dumpster. That was their dream for the future, to find some work for tomorrow so they didn't have to stand outside the Dumpster.

They said they didn't like America and I felt offended.

I had Marty ask them about coyotes and this scared them and they refused to talk any longer.

I had no business asking about such things.

I gave four dollars to a man fresh from Mexico coming to terms with the reality of what constituted begging in America. He was trying to be hopeful, optimistic, explaining about how he had been told about good jobs and he was sure he would find one, they had to be out there somewhere, he just needed a bit more time, but he looked as if he were trying to convince himself more than me. He laughed and half-jokingly suggested that maybe a few more people would come around to pay for his story!

No, I replied, shaking my head decisively.

No, no one else will be paying for your story.

I had Marty tell him he was lucky to even get four dollars, because the truth was his story was worth even less than that. It wasn't anything personal, just the laws of supply and demand: too few dollars, but a lot of Mexicans.

This man suggested that his friend Carlos, still living in Mexico, knew how to obtain a coyote.

I thanked him for the information. Being in the possession of the name Carlos would be very helpful once in Mexico.

I gave another four dollars to another man from Mexico who didn't say much except that he was a good carpenter and no one would hire him to be a carpenter. In Mexico he had been told there was good work for carpenters. Didn't we have carpenters here? I told him I didn't know. I hadn't personally met a carpenter in quite a while. In fact, I didn't even know if carpentry was a viable trade anymore. Engineers and contractors, yes, but carpenters, not so much. He was a great carpenter and wondered if I knew someone who needed one. He didn't elaborate on much more and I wished I hadn't given him four dollars.

When asked about the coyote, he too quieted and quickly walked away.

In the car afterward, as we drove across the street to find some more Mexicans, Marty explained that a lot of them were given false promises, told to expect too much by the coyotes and human smugglers who had taken them across. Some of them knew, but a lot didn't. It was like in California during the Great Depression when pamphlets were distributed across America advertising good wages picking oranges in California, and thousands poured across the country only to arrive to find themselves living in squatter's camps, working for a quarter of what they had been promised.

The only story that mattered, of course, was the worst one that I heard. It belonged to a man we'd found beside a gas station. A man who was thirty-eight years old, thin, wearing a New York City T-shirt and matching baseball cap, something he pointed to often to show that he liked America. His theory was, if you were an American and hiring Mexicans, who would you be more likely to hire? A Mexican wearing a baseball cap with the Mexican flag? Or a Mexican wearing a baseball cap of the New York Yankees?

Clever marketing, that one.

The man had the look of restroom grooming: combed hair, ripped and stained T-shirt tucked in at the waistband without a belt, but his nose hair was trailing out his nostrils, and his fingernails were too long, and he was starting to stink. But still, the demonstrated attempt at cleanliness lent him a modest respectability. I understood the limitations enforced by two-minute incremental grooming in public restrooms.

He was quiet for a long time, saying little. And I had already decided I wasn't even going to give him four dollars when, at the last second, I decided to change tactics and asked about his wife—it seemed the type of thing that would invite emotion.

"Ask him about his wife? Does he have a wife? How often does he get to talk to her? What does he miss about his wife? The smell of her hair? The sound of her voice?"

The man spoke at length with Marty in Spanish, and Marty responded in Spanish, neither one speaking to me, both of their voices elevating in stress and tone.

"What's he saying?" I asked, nudging Marty in the ribs as we all sat huddled, balanced on our ankles and toes, bending our knees behind another Dumpster.

"He wants to know why we were doing this, I told him you worked for a newspaper."

Reluctant timid tears slid down the corner of the man's face as his complexion reddened and his countenance started to tremble and slide toward disaster. He spoke in halting forceful Spanish, strands of spit sticking to his teeth.

Marty cringed at what he was hearing.

"What? What's he saying, Marty . . ." I demanded.

It was the infuriating feeling of missing out on a piece of particularly salacious gossip.

Marty sighed and took off his baseball cap to rub his head as if he'd just received bad news, a death in the family, maybe. "He says, the coyotes, they told him that when he came here, it would be all easy, that he would get a job making lots of money. And he has a wife and two baby girls, right? So he wanted to provide for his wife and his babies, so he came here, but he didn't have the money to pay to come over, so he took out a personal loan with the coyote."

Marty paused and swallowed hard and spoke some more with the man, who was silent now, staring at the ground aimlessly, his gaze locked to a central point of asphalt, unmoving. He wiped away a few tears, his lips pursed together into a steely line.

"The coyote, they say he have to pay, you know. That he's overdue on his loan. But he can't find work, no one will hire him. He doesn't have no food, no money, no place to live. And the coyote said if he doesn't pay, he's going to kill his babies. He's going to kill his wife and babies. He doesn't know what to do. He's desperate. He doesn't know what to do."

The man and Marty both turned to me for answers.

"He doesn't know what to do," Marty repeated. "What should he do?"

I was quiet, unable to speak.

"What should he do?" Marty asked.

"I don't know," I replied quietly, my voice breaking, deciding I wasn't going to ask him how to obtain a coyote and that I didn't want to interview any more Mexicans.

As we stood to leave, I reached into my wallet to pay the man.

All I had left was three dollars and forty-seven cents.

Chapter 12

THE ANGRY CAR DEALER

(TUCSON SECTOR)

The FIRE coalition.
   Civil Homeland Defense Corps.
   Ranch Rescue.
   American Border Patrol.
   WeHireAliens.com.
   Center for Immigration Studies.
   NumbersUSA.
   ReportIllegals.com . . .

Just one more citizen's action committee concerned with the issue of
attempting to control and curb illegal immigration. This one Arizona
local and calling themselves United We Stand and meeting in the lobby
of a cheap car dealership in northern Phoenix.

And boy, were they excited. Governor Janet Napolitano had just
signed legislation that they had nursed from infancy: House Bill 2779—
a piece of employment legislation that gave a single warning to employers caught employing illegal immigrants before yanking their business
license. It was set to go live at the new year.

Arizona, like many other states and cities across the nation, was starting to become proactive, to pass its own legislation within the vacuum of
leadership at the federal level. Joe Arpaio, the sheriff of Maricopa
County, which encompassed Phoenix and the surrounding area, had just
opened a hotline for valley residents to report information on undocumented immigrants. And the hotline was getting thousands of calls a
day. Reports were flooding in on everything from suspected illegal aliens
working at the local fast-food franchise to jilted lovers calling in on each
other. Everyone was reporting everyone else. You had a neighbor who
didn't mow his yard? Hispanic? You called him in on the hotline as an

illegal Mexican. The illegal immigration advocates were even setting up their own hotline, one where you could report Caucasians.

I sat quietly in the back of another room on a folding chair as the storefront filled with retired senior citizens and veterans of the armed forces wearing their caps and T-shirts, and middle-aged homeowners—a packed house, standing room only.

Mark, the owner and acting general manager of the car dealership, thanked everyone for coming, reminding us all of the protest at a local McDonald's that hired illegal immigrants—a new protest every week, this one was to be at McDonald's. He reminded us of the cookies and coffee and turned the podium over to a young and slender pretty attorney who received admiring smiles from the older men in the audience.

The attorney explained the latest on the lawsuit by our opposition meant to stop HB 2779 by having it declared unconstitutional. We, of course, would appeal all the way to the Supreme Court if we had to. A woman in the audience raised her hand, wanting to know about specific tactics. Our pretty attorney demurred, she couldn't give everything away—there might be spies in the audience. Chuckles ensued as the eyes of the audience sought out familiar faces, to see who was new or didn't belong; several gazes ended on me before turning back to the attorney. No worries, she explained, we've got a strategy.

Next up was the battle with a local freebie newspaper that was unapologetically pro-immigrant and had run several disparaging pieces on their organization. A young local college student was spearheading the effort and slammed a pile of newspapers on the counter. Not only was he actively going to businesses and getting them to refuse the newspaper in the free stands at their store's entrance because of some of the racy ads that ran in the back of the paper, but you could also hurt the newspaper by simply grabbing them all up as he had been doing and dumping them in recycle bins where they belonged.

Howls of laughter and terse applause.

A plain middle-aged woman mounted the stage, her face pulled tight in a mask of anger—the Phoenix Art Museum, despite receiving her numerous phone calls, was still running with the exhibit on Mesoamerican art and history. And if we all joined her in the effort by calling and expressing our displeasure, we might be able to get the vaguely Mexican-themed signs advertising the exhibit taken down. She ended by reiterating that she wasn't a racist, but this was the United States of America, dammit. Not some Mesoamerica—whatever the hell that was.

And then it was open business. Volunteers were needed for just about everything. Mail drives, boycotts, phone work, holding up protest signs, setting up meetings at the other location. Stories were swapped about the latest hassles the immigrants had provided them. A landlord was having a helluva time getting rid of his tenants who weren't paying and didn't speak no damn English. A woman's husband was being laid off because the Mexicans would do the job cheaper than he had. Another woman worked at a hospital that was going broke.

Everyone shook their head that it was all indeed terrible.

Afterward, while the crowd milled and made small talk, I moved about the back of the room looking at the various homemade posters showing their rallies, and at poster boards with photographs of misbehaving Mexicans at day labor sites acting rudely to passing motorists.

An elderly man, his Navy cap adorned with military honors and pins and Border Patrol buttons that read "Where's the fence?" set down stacks of pamphlets on a coffee table.

I followed behind and took one.

The pamphlet explained that 95 percent of warrants in Los Angeles were for illegal aliens. That 83 percent of murder warrants in Phoenix were for illegal aliens. That almost 24.9 percent of all inmates in California detention centers were Mexican nationals. That 60 percent of all HUD properties went to illegal aliens. That 34 percent of grade school level students in Phoenix were illegal aliens. That 70 percent of the population growth of the United States was from illegal aliens.

And then there was the anchor baby problem. Anchor babies were children born within the United States to illegal aliens. The parents were undocumented, but their children were U.S. citizens with rights and protections, and that created problems in expelling the parents. This particular piece of literature I was reading suggested that it was the goal of each and every Mexican to cross the border and procreate as quickly as possible: each Mexican needed to get themselves a job and an anchor baby, and if they could do that, they'd do all right. (This piece of literature also went on to state that 380,000 anchor babies were born to Mexican nationals each year and that the hospital bill for this was picked up by U.S. taxpayers. And this was a very terrible thing.)

I immediately assumed a strict methodological accounting during the obtainment of these data sets—statistics weren't the type of thing to be bandied about lightly or manipulated within the United States. Statistics, after all, were always accurate.

Another pamphlet explained that not only were Mexicans ruining everything about this great country of ours, but their IQs were, on average, considerably lower than that of Americans. The pamphlet went on to reference *The Bell Curve* and plot the intelligence levels of the various peoples on the planet. The Asians were first, which really was no surprise, because everyone knew that Asians were really smart. Then came us white Americans, and then at the bottom somewhere blacks and Mexicans.

"Can I help you?" the retired Navy man asked me, appraising me suspiciously.

"I'm just here to listen," I replied politely.

"You the reporter?" he asked through clenched teeth.

I choked on nothing and coughed, feeling an intense and sudden paranoia.

How had they known?

"Uh, yeah, I am the reporter, I guess," I replied with a sigh.

"Mark, he's a reporter!" the Navy man yelled across the room, frowning as he moved away from me, anxious to get some space between us.

"How you doing?" a voice said from behind me. I turned to meet Mark, the franchise owner. "Can I help you?"

"I thought this was a public meeting," I responded.

"You with them?" he asked. He pointed to one of the placards I hadn't gotten to yet, this one framing the large and centered photograph of an overweight man surprised by the sudden taking of his picture at a street festival, a man the meeting's participants were to be on the lookout for, a writer who was pro-immigrant who had apparently infiltrated some of their meetings and was now public enemy number one.

"Um, no, I'm not with them. In fact, I'm on your side. Well, I'm on both sides. I'm trying to be neutral."

"There's no such thing," he replied coolly.

"Yeah, well . . ."

He paused for a moment while studying me and then said, "Well, as long as you're not with the enemy."

"Phhh! Hell, no!" I said harshly.

"Let me round up some people for you to interview," he said as he turned and scanned the still lingering crowd.

C ASSANDRA SAT FACING ME in one of the small cubicles in the back hallway normally reserved for making automotive financing deals as she eyed me seductively, smiling and licking her lips. Cassandra was an aging biker chick, round in the middle, and heavy on top, but she was hoping I'd see past all that to how she used to be as she gently stroked my hand and smirked suggestively at me.

Cassandra: I got really tired fighting for my disability benefits knowing that it seemed like the illegal aliens were getting more money than I could get. That and when they had their major march in the streets and tore down American flags, and ran up their flag with our flag below it. That was it for me. They did it in a high school, ran the American flag upside down underneath theirs. As far as I was ever told, that was an act of war. They should've backed up vans and started loading them up to the border then. People are actually breaking the law, this isn't racial, this is about the letter of the law. If you or I break the law, we get thrown in jail. They get away with it. There's car accidents with them, they have no license, no insurance, and they turn them loose on the streets. The states that are on the border, they know what's going on. The crime rate is out of this world. And because of the threats that are going on, if we persist on, and now that Janet Napolitano finally signed the bill, they started making very loud threats that they'll retaliate. Could all these fires at these construction sites be retaliation? It seems on the news ever since she signed it, there's been a consistency of new homes that are in the process of being built going up in flames.
Me: Maybe it's just global warming. Hot weather?
Cassandra: (Long pause) No, it's Mexicans.

THERE WAS ALBERT, a retired Marine corpsman, cantankerous local Phoenix homeowner, and reluctant Mexican American.

Albert: You were in the Army?
Me: Yeah.
Albert: What was your first general order?
Me: General order? I don't know.
Albert: Sure you do, what was your first general order?
Me: No really, I have no idea.
Albert: (Long pause—agitated glare) You don't leave your post until relieved. Which is what the government has done to us.
Me: Right. Of course.
Albert: I really got involved February 2, I met my neighbor, guy by the name of Jason. A kid who went to Iraq, was a decorated veteran, was

awarded a Bronze Star for manning a machine gun and holding off the Iraqi insurgents while fifteen of his fellow Army Rangers got out. He got out of the military, came and moved here with the promise of a job in the construction field. He moved across the street from me, and it was nice because there was someone I could actually speak to in English. He had a thirty-year-old wife and a nine-month-old baby, a two-year-old baby, and his wife was expecting. Regular all-American. Couldn't find a job, no one would pay him what he was qualified for because of the illegal aliens, he couldn't get into the construction field. On February 3, they were going to move back to Wisconsin, well on February 2 he was stabbed in his front yard trying to protect his daughter from a nut-job illegal alien. He was in a coma for sixteen days. Almost bled out on the way to the hospital. The butcher knife he was stabbed with hit his liver, his heart, his lung. (Pause) You don't remember your first general order?

Me: Yeah, of course. I do now.

AND MARY, ANOTHER MEXICAN AMERICAN, this one a teacher who had been forced into early retirement by the horrendous Mexican school children.

Mary: Other Mexican Americans call me a traitor, they call me the wife of Cortéz.

Me: (Snicker) That's clever!

Mary: (Frowns) I don't think so.

Me: (Serious) Me neither.

Mary: The Mexican kids, they're horrible. They acted up in class, they made no academic effort whatsoever. And the school district is catering to them, classes taught in all Spanish. Well, how are they ever going to integrate if they're going through school never learning English? Why is the school district catering to them when they're bankrupting the school district? All our property taxes are going to pay for all these other children—who behave so horribly.

Me: But white kids behave horribly too, right?

Mary: Sure. But the Mexicans behaved worse.

AND THEN THERE was "Buffalo Bob"—a wounded Vietnam vet who had special knowledge of Mexican counterintelligence agents inside the United States.

Buffalo Bob: I know, at this moment, of dug-in positions in the mountains east of the Indian reservation, just outside of Tucson, of Mexican intelligence agents. They're listening to Border Patrol, observing and acting as eyes and ears and sending these communications back into Mexico.

Me: Wow, that's pretty neat! How do you know this?

Buffalo Bob: I have friends who are investigating the matter and have passed on this information to me.

Me: Would you mind passing that information you were passed on to me?

Buffalo Bob: I don't know you.

Me: Please?

Buffalo Bob: No.

Me: Come on . . .

Buffalo Bob: No.

I WAVED GOODBYE to everyone, lying and saying I'd see them at their next meeting and at the McDonald's protest. I promised to meet Mark the general manager tomorrow for lunch so that he could show me the damaging effect the Mexicans were having on the neighborhood, and exited into the parking lot.

I slept in my truck that night and awoke to mid-morning summer and cars buzzing by on the busy street. I urinated in the parking lot, and reentered the dealership, towel and toiletry bag under one arm as I asked the receptionist about the location of the bathroom. She pointed the way and I entered, laid out my towel and toiletry bag on the counter, moved the trash can in front of the door, and gave myself a sponge bath in the sink.

Afterward, I moved my things back out to the truck and then reentered, handing off the business card and asking for Mark. I stood in the lobby for a few moments, peering into the windows of the show cars when I heard Mark's voice from behind me, "You want to buy a car? I'll give you a good deal."

"I'm okay for the moment," I said smiling, turning and shaking his hand.

We moved out to the parking lot as Mark explained to me that he didn't hire illegal aliens. That it would help his business a lot, he could be saving a lot of money, but there was principle involved. Did I see any illegal aliens around here?

As we walked past the service garage, I had to admit, there were no Mexicans around. I concurred that he probably didn't hire illegal aliens.

"How's business?" I asked, trying to think of something polite and sociable to say.

"Bad," he replied.

He seemed slightly embarrassed about selling such cheap cars. He wanted me to know that he hadn't always done this. He used to be a Chrysler dealer, back just six years ago when this had been a better neighborhood.

"What do you mean by that?" I asked as we reached the parking lot behind the service garage.

"Come on, I'll show you," he replied as he got behind the driver's seat of his Ford F-250 and reached across to unlock the passenger door.

A S MARK DROVE us down the street, he explained that this neighborhood had undergone a face-lift within the last ten years. Would I believe that this used to be a middle-class neighborhood?

And just look at it now.

The restaurants were all Mexican, the people were all brown, and the business signs were all in Spanish.

"There used to be respectable businesses here," he said. "Hardware stores, a few department stores, grocery stores. Now look at it, it's all check cashing and payday loans and rent-a-center furniture and Western Union and Laundromats."

He pointed to the left-hand side of the street.

"That used to be an Osco Drug. They went out of business. You know why?"

I shook my head. I didn't know why. I wasn't very good at business stuff.

"In the last ten years, the illegal Mexican population in this city has skyrocketed, so there always used to be slums, there was always that part of town where it was going to be your colored ghetto, but now it's taking over the city. No one wants to go there if out front there's going to be all these day laborers and litter and police being called, and Mexicans urinating in the parking lot."

"Over there," he pointed to the right-hand side of the street. "That used to be a family-run furniture store. It was there since I was a kid, twenty-five years that store had been there. Then all the day laborers started milling outside and your average Joe Blow starts being afraid to go there, so they start shopping somewhere else. Went from making a tiny profit to complete bankruptcy in a three-month period. We're not talking about rich corporations, we're talking about small businesses just trying to earn enough to make payroll, maybe make a little bit of equity so there's something to leave to the kids someday."

We took a right-hand turn onto a residential street filled with apartments.

"There's 160 apartment complexes now within a small five-square-mile area. One hundred and sixty. And this is all within the last five years. And with these 160 apartment complexes, there's crime, there's kids out causing trouble, there's increased traffic."

I nodded in agreement. "That's a lot of apartments."

"The property values around this place have just plummeted, my dealership used to be worth a lot more. My home used to be worth a lot more. Most people's homes are their single investment, it's what they've worked for over the course of their life to pay off, and it's a real shame when at the end of it all, they end up not being able to sell it for what they paid for it, much less make a profit. It's hard enough for the working man these days, all the production jobs have been outsourced to other countries, most people struggle to get by, and then these illegals come in, they're not even supposed to be here, and they just start taking over the city. It used to be a nice Phoenix neighborhood. Now it's just a conclave, mini-Mexico."

We turned onto another commercial road and he quickly pulled into a parking lot.

"Come on, let's go inside so you can see what I'm talking about," he said as he got out of the truck.

I followed him inside a Laundromat with Spanish signs on its exterior. Inside, a dumpy Hispanic woman looked up at us curiously from behind a cashier's booth. A few other Hispanic women were doing laundry, their kids playing next to them.

"See, this used to be a regular bookstore, I think," Mark angrily proclaimed. "Now it's yet one more damn Laundromat!" he said too loudly, causing everyone to look over at us. He walked to the cashier's window and pointed out all the signs indicating the cost to send money back home to places like Mexico and Nicaragua and El Salvador. Mark pretended as if the cashier wasn't there, pointing all around her, behind her, as if she was invisible.

The cashier looked nervous as she appraised us. I smiled, allowing her to read careful nuance and subtle variations in my smile. My smile was an appeasing grimace, which I was hoping she realized as me communicating to her that I didn't really want to be here and furthermore that I felt bad for being so rude.

She frowned at me. She didn't get me or my covert smile at all.

"They send all their fucking remittance money here, every store's got these. Send it back to Mehiiico and Neeceragggga. Of course, those countries don't want to stop the problem, why are they going to want to stop themselves from receiving all this remittance money? They encourage them in Mexico to cross. Less services they have to provide back home, and now a steady stream of income from up north. You think the Mexicans have the same open border philosophy on their ass? Hell no! They've got border patrol on their southern border, to stop the Salvadorans and Hondurans from crossing into Mexico."

As we left, I attempted one more frantic covert communication with the Hispanic clerk, this one a tense shoulder shrug and a clinched face—body code for duress.

She frowned at me as we left.

I shook my head in disgust at her poor ability to read body language.

Back in his truck, he drove me to the Mexican consulate, just down the street from his dealership.

As we walked through the parking lot, he dug into his wallet and produced an ID card, which he handed over to me. It was a Mexican matricula card, but with Mark's picture. "This is where they get their matricula cards. That's how exacting their standards are, they give them out to anyone. I'm an American and I got one of their cards. You just fill out a form. I've gotten on planes with this card. I've opened bank accounts with this card. The Mexican government should be charged as an enemy of the state for handing these things out. The Mexican government publishes how-to manuals for America, how to cross the border, how to live undetected once in America, how to open bank accounts, it's all about the money. Send home the remittance money."

We moved past a pregnant Hispanic teenager and her large family as we entered the facility. It looked like a DMV, long snaking lines, and a roomful of waiting Mexicans, overcapacity by at least one hundred people with no place to walk—the matricula card business was booming. It was hot and stuffy with a lamely whirring fan with dust-caked blades circulating dry air recycled too many times by the same lungs.

Mark shoved his way rudely through the line until we got to a small desk on which were piles of photocopied forms. He butted into a position around the kiosk and grabbed up the forms the Mexicans were filling out as he loudly yelled, "See! They fill out this form and they get an identification card, it's that easy. Suddenly, they're legitimate, but made legitimate by a foreign government handing them out on U.S. soil!"

The Mexicans all looked at us with fear and apprehension: an elderly grandfather with a Duke hat and two young men in their twenties in ball caps and a middle-aged mother—all hating us silently with their eyes. Just two more racist assholes in a world full of them.

I decided that the Mexicans were, on the whole, a decidedly peaceful people; white people would've kicked someone's ass for doing what we were doing. We shoved through with elbows and arms to the middle of the room as Mark started talking about the Mexicans as if they weren't there, even as he pointed at them. "It's always like this, all day long, they line up here, just like this. Get their ID card and go out into the world legitimized." He looked around him in a circle as the entire room of hundreds silenced, focused only on him. "And they think they belong here! Well they don't!"

I felt my face flush with embarrassment as I looked down and at the floor.

I also had the feeling that *we* didn't belong *here*.

As we started back toward the exit, Mark sidestepped a leak from a pipe in the roof and gave a disgusted glance. Only Mexicans would have a leak in a roof. That just didn't happen with Americans.

We drove in silence back to the showroom, where Mark parked in the spot for the general manager.

"Well, I hope I gave you something you can use?"

"I'm sure you did," I replied. "Thanks again."

I waved and started to leave, walking back to my car.

And then from behind me Mark cried, a bit desperately, "You want to buy a car? I'll make you a good deal."

Business was bad.

You know, what with the Mexicans and all.

Chapter 13

CHASING MEXICANS FOR EXERCISE
(TUCSON SECTOR)

I inched forward in bumper-to-bumper traffic as the 351st vehicle in line for entry into the United States; just some afternoon reconnaissance in Mexico. My present position pushed me out past the intersecting edge of Nogales, Mexico, and fully into the desert. I was pushed fully into the desert because this border with Arizona was the busiest border in the world with millions of furtive souls of varying legal status. Lots of trade too—the Americans sent agriculture and sweatshops south, the Mexicans sent cheap labor and drugs north.

Helicopters thrummed overhead, as thousands of cars and lanes of traffic converged and surged, slowly collapsing toward a small single distressed customs station in Nogales, Arizona, where a handful of officers dealt with thousands of vehicles attempting daily entry—no different from three hundred Spartans at Thermopylae fending off thousands of invading Persians.

Entering Mexico took only seconds, a time limited only by the speedometer and the weight of one's foot on the accelerator, but reentering the United States was an entire afternoon. You had to queue for position twenty miles out like a jet airliner preparing its descent, calculated, time-consuming, and hopefully with a full tank of petrol.

And as the line of cars inched forward in a slow lurching lumbering cadence, bringing us within the outer edge of Nogales's suburban slums, a tall chain-link fence began lining the road on both sides, a man-made protective partition running without break or ending. On the other side of the fence were the insolvent living in cinder block and plywood huts with tin sheeting roofs, the decrepit dwellings stumbling over each other as they clung to the hillside in granulated clusters, and all of it decorated in a sporadic sprinkling of homeless dogs and soil-stained shoeless children.

And this, not the Mexico City high-rises, was the real Mexico—where

80 percent of the population fell under the World Bank's poverty marker, where the hourly wage, when disproportionately weighed with the thin margin elites, was still only two dollars and change.

And as the beggared population on both sides of the road that were trapped by the fence started to grow in both size and bunched frequency, I noticed a hill looming on the horizon, centered perfectly across the road. Except its center was hollowed out, there was a rise on one side, and a rise on the other, but the peak of the hill had been hollowed, the road running at its bottomed center, transforming the hill into two identical cliffs, a chain-link fence demarcating their mirrored edge. And the road continued like this, diving into the earth, built between dug-out entrenchments, the chain-link fence always high above the road with the thin embankment below purposely cleaved and manicured, so as to offer nothing but steep ninety-degree angles and precarious drops to Mexicans with a mind for fence hopping. The earth had been transformed such that jumping the fence was now equivalent to jumping out a third-story window. It felt untoward and rude to be in a foreign country and escorted back to the United States by fortified partitions erected for my benefit.

I moved forward a few more spots as from my side window, on the other side of the fence, the poor side, three Mexican children, dirty with snot-running noses, clung to the fence with tiny curled clawed hands, staring at the line of traffic heading for the United States. The image of the children trapped behind fencing was a striking one, reminiscent of a prison, or a concentration camp maybe—as they looked out onto freedom with what I melodramatically imagined was aspiration and hope.

All of Mexico was like this, militarized and controlled—divided into quadrants and sectors by military and police checkpoints. And also by the toll booths. The toll booths were the most devastating—the charge for using their interstate amounted to eight U.S. dollars an hour. At each toll booth, beggars would wait next to encampments of cars, parking lots transformed into squatter's camps, asking for help to make it just a bit further, presumably to the next toll booth sixty miles on where they'd be forced to beg again. To a Mexican, making eight dollars a day, it was financially impossible.

I assumed that the intention, aside from the obvious purpose of revenue generation, was also one of control—and it was effective in governing the poor masses: the only vehicles on the road had been expensive-model cars with Mexican plates, U.S.-plated cars, or else semis. The poor, it seemed, were not only trapped to stay within the country that they had been born into by the randomization of geographic birthplace, but they were also now trapped within region, like trayed ice cubes, or animals in a zoo.

I sat with my seat reclined strumming the plastic vihuela, a high-pitched five-string guitar used by mariachi bands that I had purchased for sixty pesos, while I crunched on a bag of nuts I had purchased for three. There was a steady revolving rotation of goods being offered out-side my car window, not unlike the sushi restaurants with the conveyor belts built into the counter. Cigarettes, soda, bags of nuts and tlacoyos, maps, shaving mirrors, combs, flags, dolls, medicine, even optometry charts—if it could be carried, lifted, or stolen, it was for sale a half-mile out from the border.

I waved at the gape-mouthed children as I moved forward a few more spots.

The children didn't return the wave.

I silently cursed them for their unfriendly ways.

MY TRUCK CAME to a screeching halt in the gravel parking lot of the gas station, sending a spray of rocks onto the shoulder of the highway. I was traveling at speeds that were faster than necessary because I was playing a game, and games demanded a rapid temperament. As per my directions, I jumped out and ran to the pay phone where I made my next phone call. I rapidly scribbled the directions to the next location and raced back to my truck.

As I pulled back onto the highway and built my velocity, I pulled out my audio recorder and offered some explanative narrative to accompany my actions: "I'm in southern Arizona, Tucson Sector, the busiest illicit border crossing in the world. I'm here for my next attempt at the border, which is the money shot, where everyone crosses. And I'm hoping every-one crosses here for a reason, and, maybe, if I'm lucky, that reason is because it's easy."

Ten minutes later and I was at a small desolate highway diner out on Highway 86, just west of Tucson.

From the diner parking lot, I made another call, this time on my cell phone.

Where to now, Gus?

"Step out of your car," Gus responded into my cell phone.

I stepped out of the car and whirled around in a 360-degree spin, try-ing to see if I could find where he was calling from. A dirt mound on the other side of the highway certainly looked suspicious.

"Step forward four steps and let me get a look at you," Gus said.

I stepped forward four steps.

"All right, now come on inside the diner," Gus said before hanging up.

I entered the diner—nondescript with a small handful of checked-cloth-covered tables at its center, the daily specials written on a chalk board above a simple Formica counter with a cash register. Along each wall were two rows of booths, old, the seats ripped with cotton peering through, the tables marked in pen and pencil. The diner was sparsely populated, a few people finishing lunch, and in the back booth sitting alone with a single cup of coffee, nearest the window, was Gus.

Gus was a big man, his pockmarked face and large ruddy nose mostly concealed by an embellished and exaggerated mustache. Gus was dressed in hunter's camouflage, looking as if he should be out in the forest hunting pheasants, not hiding out looking nervous inside a roadside diner in the desert.

Gus eyed me suspiciously as I approached and took a seat opposite him.

"I apologize for the cloak-and-dagger," Gus said, "but these are dangerous times and it's been explained to me that the cartels have put a price on my head."

"And who was it who explained this to you?" I asked.

"Border Patrol. We had a surveillance operation going up north of here, Border Patrol agents rode into camp, said we needed to clear out, that they had intercepted intel that said we had disrupted a million-dollar drug deal and they wanted us dead. I've been getting calls, people hanging up, heavy breathing; veiled threats."

Gus took a sip of his coffee.

And then suddenly he pointed out the window, excitedly. "Right there! That was a smuggler's truck!"

I stood slowly and peered curiously out the window. "Where? Which one?"

"You just missed it. It just passed on the highway."

"Are you sure? I don't see anything," I replied, a bit agitated that I had missed seeing the cartel truck.

"You just missed it, I'm telling you." Sip. Good coffee.

I reluctantly sat back down into my seat.

"Shit, there's four Mexicans right now!" Gus said.

I stood back up. On the other side of the highway, four Mexicans waited for a pause in traffic before darting across, running through the diner's parking lot and out of view.

"You going to call them in?" I asked, pointing to his cell phone on the table next to him.

Gus offered a limp defeated wave. He didn't have time to worry about four Mexicans. He was on a coffee break. Sip.

"What can I help you with?" he asked as he slurped heavily from his mug.

I interlaced my fingers solemnly as I spoke: "It's been explained to me that you're a man who knows this area better than anyone else. That you know every culvert and gully, and are a tracker of sorts. That you know where the immigrants cross and where they don't. That you've mapped out the trails they use and that you know how to cross the border in these parts?"

Gus nodded with a heavy heart and a lead-filled sigh.

Yes, this was all true.

He did happen to be just that sort of man.

WE DROVE SOUTH DOWN Highway 286 as Gus popped some pills for the pain and pointed out his various physical scars and imperfections courtesy of Vietnam, where he had been a machine gunner: shrapnel in the abdomen, the leg, the back. And then, of course, the Agent Orange exposure, which had melted some of his insides. "I could die any day now," Gus explained matter-of-factly.

But full-time disability had ancillary benefits, like being able to commit himself to the cause. "I've got no problems with Mexicans, my wife is Mexican. The real reason I patrol out here is to save lives as much as report them to Border Patrol. I've saved five so far this summer! Five!" Gus beamed at his five saved lives as he paraded five proud fingers. "It just breaks my heart, these poor people who have nothing coming over here and dying in the desert, I think we have an obligation to find them and stop them from killing themselves, and if they get sent back to Mexico in doing so, well, so be it. The Southern Poverty Law Center says I'm a hate group, do I look like a hate group to you? I'm a cripple driving around the desert in his truck with cookies and water for God's sake."

"No, sir, cookies and water surely doesn't sound hateful."

Gus smiled as he turned off the highway onto a dirt road and held up a single finger motioning for me to be quiet as he monitored the CB radio, the Border Patrol band.

"I want to find out who's working today," he explained as he let up on the gas and cocked one ear to the radio as he listened to the voices talking back and forth, before, satisfied with his listen, he sped forward again and turned to me to explain. "We have a varying relationship with different Border Patrol officers, some of them like us, some of them don't. I try to stay clear of the ones who don't like us, just don't see any reason for a confrontation. One of 'em's working down south across the 306 marker, so we'll just stay north of there."

"Well, that sounds just fine," I replied.

"This whole valley here is the Amnesty Trail, Refuge Land, the Cocaine Valley," Gus explained, referring to the sixty miles south of Highway 86 before the U.S. ran up against Mexico. "There's a story to this," Gus stated, signal for me to shut up and pay attention. "In 2004, our esteemed commander-in-chief floated the idea of the temporary guest worker program where they'd all get amnesty. Well, down south, they all heard 'amnesty' and suddenly there was a huge surge in illegal immigrants coming north, and when they surveyed the ones that got caught, they said they were crossing to get Bush's amnesty. And when they came they made all these trails through the national park . . . two thousand miles worth of 'em."

Gus brought the truck to a halt as he pointed into a trash-filled ravine. "See, that's a trailhead right there." Gus started forward again, this time pointing to the other side of the truck. "Found a dead body over there just last week."

And as Gus drove me around the desert, he told me of the Amnesty Trail.

Highway 86, which ran west into the Tohono O'odham Indian Reservation and east into Tucson, was the demarcation line. If you made it the sixty or so miles past Highway 86—you got amnesty, you were in the "safe zone," outside the custody and care of Border Patrol. And it was only past Highway 86 that the orchestrated fleets of pickup vehicles, vans, semis, late-model cars, pulled over onto the shoulder of the back roads and rural corridors to make a pickup of product in the form of Mexican persons and disseminate them to various points across the nation. Everything south of Highway 86 was a free-for-all.

And throughout were hundreds of small snaking trails of smashed plants and worn grass and ripped branches, some small and meek like deer trails, others large and obvious like a thoroughfare, and all of it consisting of thousands of miles, each step echoing with the phantom footprints of millions of anxious sweaty Mexican feet. And the trails were littered with the remnants of their passing—discarded clothes and backpacks and plastic water jugs—lines of trash that stretched for miles, because when you crossed, you needed to travel light, reduce your weight as you went.

The routes and the trails inside the United States were the intellectual and physical property of highly organized criminal enterprises within northern Mexico who depended on these trails as their lifeline to continued revenue, no different from cell phone service providers that owned the airwaves and cell towers. Spies, surveillance units, spotter teams, and yes, covert operatives within the United States fed counterintelligence on the movements of Border Patrol, on the opening and closing of new routes and trails, all of which was processed at communication centers within Mexico, not unlike a Special Forces command center.

The routes had been divided and partitioned by business models. They were scouted by recon units and adjusted to compensate for U.S. security strategies. Nothing was permanent, not routes, not timetables, not prices, not staffing levels. Everything was fluid and fluctuating, subject to change, to market conditions. Effective counterinsurgency was flexible counterinsurgency.

Gus lived out here, and he told me of his neighbors, local ranchers who were prisoners in their own homes, unable to leave without their houses immediately being burglarized within mere minutes of their departure. Of families waking up in the morning to find Mexicans rummaging through their kitchen pantry, hungry for food, or of walking out the front door to get the paper to find a group of twenty rifling through the garage. He told me of another rancher whose home had been broken into sixteen times. He reached into the dashboard and produced an article written by a Leo Banks for a local paper, as positive proof of his claims.

He continued, telling me of personally encountering drug runners armed with machine guns and men of Arabic descent, of tens of thousands marching through the desert daily. And then there was the rape tree, where the young and oh so very dead woman with her clothes half-ripped off had been found and where also too frequently he found during his routine patrols panties and bras, hung up in the branches like Christmas ornaments by the human smuggling coyotes as a symbol of conquest.

North of Highway 86, he drove me into the "safe zone," the area outside Border Patrol's reach, where I was taken to a trash field: an unending stretch of discarded clothes and backpacks and bottles and shoes and toiletries. There were syringe needles and used diapers. Children's underwear and smeared toilet paper. This was the unloading point where, once safe, the final dissolution of material possessions occurred.

I kicked a Disney backpack still in good condition with the toe of my boot.

"Why do they dump everything? This backpack seems still in good condition."

"To make room. Gotta push 'em into the cargo vans like cattle. No room for stuff."

We moved about the trash, hands on our hips, surveying the carnage.

"So, you want to see base camp?" Gus asked.

BASE CAMP WAS a collection of RVs and campers, encircled like old wagons in the Wild West with a few large blue tents, one as an impromptu meeting area and mess hall, the other a makeshift barracks with cots for the volunteers who didn't own RVs. Base camp was also thirty miles out from the border. It was early afternoon and most were still sleeping: hunting illegal aliens worked best during the evening, swing, and late shifts. Above us, the sun screamed in a furious tantrum. We sweated it out below, mopping brows and aching in the heat until it felt as if we would glow long into the night, burning as individual illuminated candles within the dark.

Gus left his camper as he adjusted an antenna and then leaned back inside to send an e-mail to his forward-positioned reconnaissance team, currently in camouflage and hiding within the brush surveying and tracking the popular trailheads of the moment. They'd then report the information over the radio and sometimes over e-mail back to Gus, who would disseminate the information to his team of volunteers, who would then take up position thirty miles out in preparation of nocturnal interception as the illegals raced toward Highway 86 and amnesty.

"We think they're changing trails, traffic's dying out on the twelve," Gus explained as he studied a topography map, trying to guess where the migratory paths of the moment had shifted to as he prepared for the upcoming evening's battle.

Gus made some circles on a laminated map with a marker, tossing me a soda before he popped his own. He sighed with sipping satisfaction as his wife, short, stout, and full-blooded Mexican, exited the RV behind him, smiling at me as she moved to the makeshift kitchen and began to set up for the evening meal of franks 'n' beans—this was a sophisticated operation on a shoestring budget.

Gus pointed to a distant electrical pole that ran through the desert.

"See that? Some groups follow the electrical lines because they can see them and they know they'll eventually get somewhere if they stay on them. Those are green groups; don't really know what they're doing. That might be a new coyote, a group that somehow managed to cross without being detected by the smugglers who decided to go solo. Other groups follow naturally occurring steams, gives them a last opportunity to fill up on water before the streams die out up here in the desert. But these days, most of the coyotes have GPS so they're increasingly moving off trail, but then of course, enough of them cross through and they end up making a trail. I've got two guys sniffing out a new route we think they're using right now."

"So you do this full-time?" I asked as I pulled out my GPS and locked in the location of the camp as a waypoint.

"Oh yeah, this is it, full-time job. I'm out here every day, every evening. Caught twenty last night, twenty-nine the day before. My government's not going to do it, so someone's got to pick up the slack. But tell you what, I'm getting worn out. María and I are thinking of retiring soon." Behind him María hugged him briefly before moving back inside the RV.

"Where you going to retire to?"

"Mexico!" Gus replied laughing.

"You're joking!"

"No, sir! Things are just too damn expensive in this country anymore. We've got a little RV park picked out just across from the Pacific Ocean. Going to rent out the house, move down in the RV. Practicing my Spanish every day, got me one of them tapes, learn language while you sleep." Gus took a step back from the map to assess his predictions and then, satisfied, he smiled securely, folding his arms.

"Are those the positions of your men?" I asked, pointing to the map.

"They're variable, changing," Gus responded.

"Uh-huh," I responded, moving up from my chair and leaning over the map. "But say you had to give me a range that your men would be placed within, say from like here to here, or there to there, where, how far would you say your men were spread out?"

Gus pointed at two points on the map. "Oh, I'd say from the cattle guard out to the ten-mile marker."

"Right, right," I responded, as I quickly attempted to plot those positions into my GPS. The last thing I wanted to do was get caught by Gus's men when I attempted my own crossing. As I struggled to assign positions on a gridded map to my GPS, the camp started to awaken, as if programmed like an alarm clock, and in a shared sequencing rotation, doors opened and tent flaps were lifted. Gus's soldiers arrived for a late lunch, still yawning and wiping the sleep from their eyes.

They carried sidearms and wore hats marking them as military veterans and T-shirts that asked where the fence was. There was a group of men who had traveled all the way from Kentucky, and a Black Hawk pilot still in the Army. They were a motley collection of races: Hispanic and Indian and white. There was a retired judge from the Midwest whose new Ford pickup was adorned in "Dixie Pride" bumper stickers and clever euphemisms in support of the Second Amendment. He proudly proclaimed that he had never made his decisions on the bench based on the rule of law but on the only law that ever truly mattered, that fine and decent book of the Lord. King James edition, if you wanted to know and even if you didn't. Too old to go out on patrol, but still able to provide moral support, as he cackled with Mexican jokes and commented on the moral decline of the country as he continually reminded me that these Mexican hunters were the salt of the earth—hardworking and God-fearing.

I smirked silently as he said this. He could just as easily have been talking about Mexican Catholics.

I sat with them as they made small talk as they popped the tops of soda cans and lit up cigarettes and lounged lazily, relaxing before the upcoming evening shift. The big topic of conversation for the afternoon was the drug mules who had almost been intercepted last night, a group of Mexican soldiers moving in disciplined sequence through the brush in full camouflage, carrying identical backpacks that were used to transport drugs. They argued over whether or not assault rifles had been seen on them and whether or not they'd use the same route taking over the next shipment tonight.

And after they finished talking about the drug mules, they talked about the upcoming election and made jokes about Barack Obama being a Muslim. They complained about corporations and the rich cheaters one moment, the socialist agenda the next, and how socialism was ruining the country. And then they discussed the new toys they were going to buy when their next government pension and disability checks arrived. A local rancher brought the conversation back around to Obama and how horrible it would be if his socialized medicine plan was pushed through, before going on to explain that Medicaid suited him just fine. Another concurred, socialized medicine was no damn good, the Veterans' hospital was all that he needed, and he didn't need it socialized.

A retired Navy man explained to me that in Vietnam, he had been on a top secret mission he couldn't explain, where he'd learned, through means unarticulated, that the entire world was controlled by a small handful of men called the Bilderberg Group—and they were in charge of starting the wars and the problems of the world, occupying the people while they conspired to increase their profits. Jews, maybe. Although he quickly added that he had no problem with Jews, his sister-in-law was a Jew, it was just that he heard they were Jewish is all.

They complained bitterly about the Minutemen and a competing operation by the Minuteman Civil Defense Corps occurring parallel to their position on the other side of Highway 286—and goddamn they hated it when people called them Minutemen. They weren't Minutemen, just concerned citizens.

"John!" Gus yelled out from the other side of the RV.

I jumped up, vacating my lawn chair for a retired Native American police officer, and moved over to Gus's position where he introduced me to Duke, a dashing commando in brown camouflage fatigues with a prestigious mustache, thick and curled, his assessing eyes peeking under orange reflective Ray Ban wraparound sunglasses.

"John, Duke here's going out to see if he can intercept the drug smugglers tonight. You want to go?"

I considered the proposition carefully.

Did I want to go out and attempt to intercept drug mules?

I asked Duke if he thought the drug mules last night had carried assault rifles.

Duke didn't know.

I nodded before saying, "Yes. Yes, I will go with you to attempt to intercept the drug mules."

A wicked smile came to the corner of Duke's mouth as he appraised me.

"I was in the Army, infantry. I've been shot at. I've shot at people. I know what I'm doing."

Duke nodded, my qualifications were good enough for him.

"You got a weapon?"

As a matter of fact, I did.

AS DARKNESS DESCENDED we packed the truck as the others argued and bickered over who was going to take which route and how so-and-so was on the wrong radio frequency and David, shit, he hadn't even bothered to get suited up yet and we were supposed to have left five minutes ago. And how come the Minuteman Civil Defense Corps on the other side of the highway got to take credit for their captures, but they didn't give so much as a good golly goddamn thank-you when traffic was diverted to them. Hell, the next time an illegal was spotted heading toward MCDC, they wouldn't even call them up and the illegal could just get on through to America, that's how pissed off they were.

Duke closed up the back of his Isuzu and stared at the squabbling group, smirking silently before he nodded at me, cocking his head toward the truck. Duke didn't have much patience for this type of infighting; he had a job to do. I decided then and there that I liked him very much.

DUKE SAT BEHIND the steering wheel of his Isuzu, driving with one casual crotch-perched hand as he led us away from camp and across the burnt mauve gravel that cut a ragged swath through the desert—the road was a visible alteration to the landscape even from a distance, a delineated fiercely patrolled boundary.

Duke freed a contagious twitching smile from stern lips as the road began to slide beneath us and he emerged into his element—it was the only facial feature visible under a wide-brimmed cowboy hat and thick mustache, but his minimalist expression was suggestive and empowering like the devil's grin; his smile made me want to smile. With his free hand, he meticulously performed a last-minute check of his mirrors and then the M4 semiautomatic rifle suspended between us by a web of green Army 550 cord. He was dressed in a dashing demonstration of auburn camouflage, a sidearm strapped to his hip, and I realized that he looked exceedingly cooler than I did in my adventure tourist's cargo pants and golfer's pastel blue windbreaker, completely unprepared for a fight save for the firearm in my backpack, the model and make of which I was unsure.

Outside the truck, the desert was having a Cinderella moment with a final exhilarating burst of predusk delight before nocturnal transformation into a cold and dangerous place of cacti and shadows. It was at this moment, during the brief flash revealed by the twice-a-day time-lock of dusk and dawn, that the rich crimson and apricot textures of the rock and gravel revealed themselves in celebrated distinguishment from their daytime muted ashen grays. It was at this moment that the proletariat plant life, typically dismissed as feeder shrub and thistle, conceded the affluent jade and lime of its fingered leaves, normally made invisible by the bleaching glare of the day and the vacuous dark of night. It was a hidden beauty that begged to be appreciated, and because of the time-sensitive rarity of this visage, it was a memory that the heart quickly enveloped as a precious secret.

Wink and you missed it.

The radio between us barked with the chatter of last-minute preparations:

Duke this is Dog Base, copy . . .

Tac on line?

Roger that.

Cisco Kid, how about moving your squad down around the curve where you can see the other way over?

What way are you talking about?

Go back east to the curve.

What's he calling himself? Butch? Ranger Butch?

Duke, Duke, where the hell are you, Duke?

"Who's calling Duke? Go for Duke," Duke barked into the hand mike of his truck's radio as he sighed, a careening squelch of feedback following his voice.

"Duke, this is Dog Base, you in position, over?"

"Ahh, negatory, we're still out by the two-seven cattle guard, over." Duke shook his head and sighed—I didn't understand the reason for the sigh, but I recognized it as the universal sigh offered when routine actions were made unnecessarily complicated.

The radio screamed with static feedback.

Open mike! Open mike!

Who's got the open mike.

Okay, Duke, you copy, Dog Base. Who's got the open mike? Very bad interference. Dog Base, this is Duke, there's some very bad interference coming over the airwaves, open mike or something.

We pulled up next to another man in camouflage, this one on the side of the road on a 4x4 ATV and waving his arms for us to stop. The window slid down in a dragging electric purr.

"Duke, you guys going out to the cattle guard? I'm wondering if I shouldn't reposition myself if you're going out to the cattle guard."

Duke looked out at the sky, now dark, and shook his head with another sigh. "Do what you want."

And then he pulled forward, leaving the man on the ATV scowling.

"Should've thought about that a half-hour ago," Duke quietly cursed under his breath. "Sorry about that," Duke said to me, his face offering another contagious smile as apology. "Where were we?"

He drove slowly, keeping the Isuzu to the edge of the road, a custom-mounted searchlight on the side of his vehicle breaking the predusk haze as he scanned for human tracks.

"You were telling me what you liked about being out here looking for illegal aliens and how you got started."

"Right, uh, Kim and I used to do a lot of pig hunting out around the Tohono O'odham Reservation, and I guess that's when we had our first encounter with armed drug smugglers. You know, it was pretty scary stuff and after that we decided to get involved, and hell, we've been doing this about three years now."

I nodded appropriately as I tried to think of another question to ask. I was holding the tape recorder up to him, pretending. It wasn't even turned on.

Duke started to speak and then laughed, his giggles unknowingly prefacing his statement as one of interest. I decided to turn on the tape recorder . . .

"Don't take this the wrong way, but searching for illegals . . . it's a lot like hunting. I haven't done any actual animal hunting for three years, but I'll tell you what, I'm getting lots of tracking experience. It's a chance to do something for my country and maybe save a life. And I get to spend quality time out here with Kim and get exercise and I get to be in the outdoors, and hell, you even get a chance to see wildlife out here. Being a tracker is really like combining the best of all worlds: hunting, being in the great outdoors, exercise, and spending time with loved ones. Kim and I both really enjoy it."

WE SAT NEXT to the Isuzu in the dark, behind a clustered clove of cacti at a point where we could observe the trail briefly ending to cross the dirt access road before picking up again on the other side. The desert was alive with an orchestra of noise, buzzing insects, and blowing wind, the screech of distant animals, the burning buzz of the stars, humming like radioactive lightbulbs suspended in the heavens.

"Liz and I are big environmentalists, you know? So we really hate what's happening here," Duke explained in a hushed whisper as he dropped to his heels. Being a desert vigilante wasn't all sexy fun time, it was mostly boring and monotonous as you watched the clock waiting for your shift to be over—same as being on guard duty in Afghanistan. "There's this annual volunteer cleanup and last year they took five hundred tons of trash just out of this valley right here, in one year, I shit you not. But where's the Sierra Club on the issue of illegal immigration? They'll happily sue to stop a new barrier fence going in on the border because it's disrupting the habitat of some goddamn wild chipmunk or whatever, but they don't care that animals out here in the desert are dying eating the trash, that endangered plant life is being trampled on."

"Do you think we'll intercept anyone tonight?" I asked.

"Probably . . . it just takes a while. It's like fishing, you know? Might not be until early morning, you'll be bored playing with some rock with your boot, not paying attention. That's when it happens, you know? "

"Yeah."

We were both quiet for a moment.

"Duke?"

"Yeah?"

"What do we do when we intercept them? I mean, is there some SOP I should be following?" I was suddenly concerned about what I would do exactly when forced to intercept a group of possibly armed drug smugglers.

"All we can do is call Border Patrol and hope they stop on their own accord."

"Why can't we physically stop them? Citizen's arrest, no?"

"They got groups trying to sue us for stopping them."

"But if we don't care about getting sued? We can stop them, no? We're witnessing the violation of a law, that's covered under the citizen's arrest statutes, isn't it? By law isn't it covered?"

Duke sighed, looking slightly embarrassed.

"Well, you'd think it might work that way. But Border Patrol won't let us. So we just . . ."

". . . let them go?" I asked, my whispered voice pitched and incredulous.

"Let them go. Catch and release. Like I said, it's a lot like fishing."

"So if you call Border Patrol, how often do they respond and actually catch the guys?"

Duke looked embarrassed again, and I imagined that I could almost see him flush within the darkness. "Not often," he replied, quietly, painfully, as he was forced to admit that all this surveillance and the entirety of this complex operation and interception was ultimately for nothing. "Basically, it's like this—private citizens aren't allowed to stop them even though they're catching them breaking the law. Police officers even aren't really allowed in most jurisdictions to arrest because they're not properly trained. The only people who can stop and arrest them are Border Patrol agents, and there's just not enough of them. It's like the federal government said, no one can do this job but us, and then the federal government turns around and doesn't do their job, so they just come on in." He was quiet for a moment before adding, "I think Border Patrol's just afraid of lawsuits, to be honest." He was quiet for another moment before also adding, "Did you know that the city of Tucson got sued by an illegal because one of the water points wasn't full when he arrived at it while crossing illegally into the country?"

No, I replied. I hadn't know that.

Duke shook his head at this crazy strange world of ours.

And then with another hushed whisper, I asked, "Duke, hey, how many guns you got at home? You strike me as the type of guy that might have a couple of firearms back at the house."

Duke laughed quietly. "Thirty-seven. I own thirty-seven guns."

I T WAS TWO A.M. and the wear and drag of time had played hell on my sensibilities. I wasn't even paying attention to the trail. I was just staring at my feet, seeing how many rocks I could flip over my other foot within thirty-second intervals.

I felt a tapping at my shoulder. I started to speak when I saw Duke put a finger to his mouth as he stared further down the road. And then I saw it too.

It was a line of men dressed in black, moving silently and in formation through the brush, just a hundred meters away from us as they crossed the road, each carrying packs, unaware of our presence. They weren't a motley crew of migrants, they were fit and young and lean and mean—soldiers.

I saw Duke's hand move silently to his sidearm, which he unsheathed, gripping it with both hands as he flicked off the safety. I remembered that I too had a gun and reached through the darkness for my rucksack and carefully sorted through the mess of clothes wondering where the hell I had placed that stupid gun.

Duke silently pulled out his handheld radio and explained our situation to Dog Base in hushed barely audible whispers.

Excitement stole over me as I produced the firearm from the bottom of my pack. I flipped off the safety and modeled Duke's ready tiger crouch, quietly cursing him for looking exceedingly cooler than I did while attempting the same pose.

"WHAT DO WE DO NOW?" I yelled in the form of a muted excited whisper.

Duke looked at me strangely.

Nothing.

We did nothing.

We weren't allowed to do anything except call Border Patrol.

Hadn't he already explained that to me?

Chapter 14

SEARCHING FOR COYOTE
(ALTAR SECTOR)

Who is this trickster archetype, the one who inspires such mixed feelings and brouhaha? Trickster has been with us from the beginning. Trickster will be there at the ending.

—"The Riddle of the Trickster"

It was the day of my crossing and we were moving, freely, inside Mexico. No passport required.

The shift from Arizona was startling with the world suddenly compressed into narrow streets and buildings, and all of it adorned in a carnival aesthetic of loud noise and street performers who begged at each intersection for spare change. And the wires—telephone and electric—crisscrossed the street in a jangled mess of intersecting and bisecting confusion—as if its intention was to block out the sun itself.

At an intersection, survivalist capitalists swarmed our car offering a variety of services. One squeegeed our windshield, while another offered to sell us miniaturized knockoff Mexican piñatas. A mime covered in face paint moved in front of our vehicle with that old trapped-in-a-box trick.

"Run over the mime!" Andre giggled.

I smiled as I revved the engine of the car we had rented after deciding we didn't want to be in northern Mexico in a truck plastered with Minuteman stickers.

"Time for some tunes," I said as we raced forward, navigating a considerably more liberal traffic system where cars no longer adhered strictly to their lanes. Behind us, our windshield cleaner cursed us as we left him without either pennies or pesos.

Mariachi music poured from the radio as Andre nodded his head, searching out the beat before he found it and exclaimed, "I know this one! I downloaded their whole album off of iTunes!"

"Yeah, I think they played at the MTV Music Awards," I replied smirking. "You ever been to Mexico before?"

"Never," he responded. "You?"

"Well, besides for my recon work, just Cancun." And then, as an afterthought, "And my training camp, of course."

"You speak any Spanish?" he asked.

"Not a lick. You?"

"Nada," he replied.

We both nodded silently at our cumulative qualifications.

"Well, I think we'll be fine," I replied meekly to a question not asked, trying to inspire a tepid courage. "We're both," I paused, trying to find the appropriate word, ". . . plucky individuals."

Twenty minutes later, approaching the town's edge, we broke into the countryside. We drove slowly in the right lane with our emergency lights on as we sought out the right-hand turn that would take us parallel to the international border along Mexico's rural roads where we would then find a left-hand turn and head south to Altar.

"Andre?" I asked softly, noticing it for the first time.

"Yeah?"

"Change out of that Minuteman T-shirt, please."

THE BOTTOM OF the Ford Focus tore against another rock; it was the screaming scrape of steel against concrete. I cringed and applied the brake as we crested the hill and saw the road ahead curving slowly back and forth down the mountain and then moving onto the next, the space between them choked with cacti and lean desert forest and sagebrush.

Andre bit his lower lip as he turned to me apologetically. "In the United States a squiggly dotted line means gravel . . . I didn't know it was going to be like this."

We'd been driving for two hours, attempting to cover a meager forty-mile distance. And for two hours, we'd been playing that game of assumption. Where you assumed that it'd get better just ahead so why then would you want to turn back? The further we went, the more we became committed to our errant decision.

We passed a cinder-block ranchito, its owner gazing curiously from horseback at the two gringos behind the border, bouncing along the ragged rural back roads in a Ford Focus.

I held my GPS out the window to get a reading.

Six miles inside Mexico and six miles from the U.S. border.

Six miles inside the most crime-ridden precinct of the North

American continent—an area firmly under the control of the cartels, which governed like warlords in Afghanistan.

It occurred to me, with a horrible understanding, what would eventually be required of me. To cross the border at a point where I hoped to have any probability of success, I was going to have to cross *here* in no-man's-land, in the barren frontier, the only place where I could hope to cross into the American desert undetected.

I already knew crossing in a populated border town wasn't going to be feasible. It was realization suddenly pregnant with undesirable consequences. It meant I'd have to be alone, trespassing in this mountainous terrain where cartels and criminal syndicates had divided routes and allocated territory to their various franchises. It meant I wouldn't have a retreat, no path of escape to evacuate to should an exit become necessary. We were deep in cartel territory and if we got into trouble, there would be nothing we'd be able to do about it: there were simply no trusted authorities to be called and no working cell phones to call them.

I lowered the window and stuck my hand outside the air-conditioning and immediately felt my arm begin to broil. I peered up through the windshield and squinted as I appraised the sun. It was glistening with sweat.

Ahead of me, the road wrapped and curled with no end in sight.

ANDRE LOOKED BEHIND us through the rear windshield to see if we were still being followed. We'd just left the small mountain hamlet of Saric, where we had drawn the attention of several angry-looking Mexicans in pickup trucks that had seemed to be following us. But for the moment, we seemed to be free. And, most importantly, we were on smooth road now, Mexican Highway 64.

My eyes focused on the broken yellow median line as I took in deep breaths and built up the courage to turn around. I needed some excuse besides cowardice as a proper reason why we should be heading in any direction but toward Altar.

I eyed the road, looking for a place to turn around as I started to slow down. I was about ready to offer some lame excuse to Andre about not being ready, about needing more intelligence, more training, about not having enough time and Altar being too far even though it was only twenty miles away, when my dashboard lit up—two emergency lights, one yellow, one red.

The red one had an exclamation mark at its center—never a good thing.

The steering became sticky, as if lubricated in molasses.

"Shit! Shit! Shit!" I screamed as I struggled with the wheel.

"What?" Andre yelled, upset because I was upset.

"Something's wrong with the car!"

"Pull over to the side of the road," Andre replied evenly, attempting a cool and even-keeled tone, taking charge of the situation.

I pulled over in a spray of gravel and we both jumped out and crouched down, looking under the bottom of the car.

Underneath the car, it was raining—a downpour of sticky oils and black fluids that popped and hissed upon contact with the gravel.

My first and only thought was to wonder how much this was going to cost me and to curse myself for lying and saying that I had rental insurance in order to save costs. My second thought was that we'd be lucky if we could make it to Altar.

AFTER VISITING ALTAR and the desert surrounding it, one thinks, "Well, yeah, that makes sense now."

The two seemed an appropriate coupling of residence and geography. The Sonoran desert here was fierce and barren and lacking even in the slight aesthetic of a feeble forestry or a cloudy but cool watering hole, and it wasn't kind enough to compensate with either good humor or a mild manner. Some cacti, and that was about the size of it. You could go blind staring into the bleached auburn landscape, the sun reflecting simultaneously off of all known points. It was a goddamn stove here; you could incinerate in these parts.

And beneath the clouds broiling in the sun, between the trembling mirages that project on the horizon like gasoline fumes whispering secrets, there was Altar, all pockmarked motorway and abandoned crumbling village, but set to the aesthetic and tempo of a gas station, of a truck stop sickly incensed with diesel fumes.

The industry economy was mostly gone now, though the remnants of carved earth and mining still scarred the landscape. No, the economy that had taken its place was more covert, not one powered by mammoth machines, but by desperation and faint tendrils of hope.

Altar, frontier settlement, and last stop for civilization, the bastion of the great northern desert. Altar was a product of September 11, 2001, a nowhere nothing desert town lost to history, transformed by the militarization of the border that pushed the immigrants into the desert to cross. Half a million transitioned through each year now, and like any barter town, here you could get what you needed, and most everything was for sale: sex, drugs, and weapons.

In the grocery stores, the shelves were stocked with beans and tortillas, tins of tuna, and Red Bull and other assorted energy drinks used in the assembly of protein packs. For a little more kick, the farmacia sold electrolyte solutions, caffeine pills, and ephedrine stimulants.

Water bottles were on sale on each corner because it was important to hydrate—the Egyptians lost their war with Israel because their soldiers didn't hydrate. A bank and Western Union did a steady business as remittance money came from the north to assist the next wave. And an International Red Cross aid station offered free outgoing medical check-ups, advice about how to cope with chafing, muscle burns, and sprains.

In Altar, there were buses and pickup trucks that would transport you, motels that would house you, prostitutes that would fuck you, and coyotes that would smuggle you.

Everything was for sale in Altar, the gateway to hell.

I FOLLOWED THE MECHANIC through a junkyard of disassembled automobiles, past a ratty torn couch, and in through a gate where a fierce and angry dog barked furiously, straining its chain as I jumped backward.

"No, no, no!" the mechanic said, followed by more rapid-fire Spanish. It was Spanish that sounded annoyed and bothered. He motioned for me to leave, as if he was squatting at a fly.

Shoo, go away fly.

"Lo siento, no español. I'm sorry I don't speak Spanish," I replied desperately. I quickly pulled out my wallet and grabbed all of my money and waved a stack of twenty-dollar bills. "I'll make it worth your while. Fix my car . . . my coche . . ." I pantomimed a wrench tightening something I didn't know how to fix.

The mechanic wiped greasy hands on a filthy rag and made a joke to his partner. Shoo, go away fly. They both laughed.

I moved dejectedly back to the road, defeated, blinded in my walk back to the car by the sun's gripping reflection in my driver's side mirror. Andre leaned against the car smoking as behind him the city hustled at a confirmed and steady tempo carrying out a brisk smuggling business, the Mexicans on both sides of the street pointing to us and smirking.

I slouched against the side of the car, scrunching my face and blowing hot air out my nostrils as I wiped a sheen of sweat from my face. I could feel the heat wafting up from the asphalt, the concrete itself made almost malleable. A few more minutes and I'd be able to go swimming in it, diving into the tar and surfacing through liquid concrete.

Andre peered under the hood one more time, this time with optimism, and this time with feeling. "I think I can probably fix it," he said despite having just told me he had never worked on a car in his entire life. "I think it's just the transmission that's shot. We just need to get tools somehow. Or if we can figure out where to put in the transmission fluid, we can just buy a bunch of it, and keep filling it up as we head back to the border, yeah?"

"What if they make me pay for the entire cost of the car because I brought it into Mexico? You're not supposed to bring rental cars to Mexico. They specifically asked me if I was going to take it into Mexico and I said no."

Andre shrugged. "Do what I would do, don't even worry about it."

And then the mechanic, who had just dismissed me, came back, disgusted pity on his face as he motioned for us to follow him as he got in a rusty pickup truck and it coughed to life, spewing pungent black smoke over us. We both jumped in the car and turned over the engine, which grinded alive, metal against metal, without the benefit of hydration.

We followed him down a central avenue until he turned off onto a gravel road, driving past a series of carnival rides, long ago disassembled, with weeds growing around them. The road got progressively narrower and increasingly rough as he turned into a small side street of broken and shuttered homes, abandoned properties dutifully declared derelict within the exacting standards of Mexico. He pointed to a large garage surrounded by a yard of weeds, encircled by a ripped chain-link fence, and then drove off.

Andre and I shared a concerned look. This is the part where they lead us out of sight of the city's main avenue and deliver us to human traffickers who would rob, rape, and kill us.

I was sure of it.

Andre and I shrugged at each other and got out of the car, walking onto the property. Confronting human traffickers was a risk we were willing to take. Behind an empty garage, there was a cavernous cement wall, shielded from above by a rusty sheet metal canopy. Three blackened grease-stained Mexicans slowly raised from the ground as they somberly appraised us. They wanted to know what we were doing here, why we were intruding in their private space.

I pulled a wad of bills from my wallet, flapping and waving them.

"Will you fix my car, please?"

I RODE THROUGH TOWN in the back of a pickup truck with two ripped tires and loose Pepsi bottles that rolled back and forth, glass sliding over metal. We were shopping for transmission fluid so that the grease-stained Mexicans could fix my car.

And with the immediate worries of my car responded to, I'd diverted my attention to at *least* inquiring about a coyote. I was in town, after all. It wasn't something I wanted to do, but some things, like crossing the border illegally, you didn't get to just quit because it was hard.

I scanned the roadside taco bars and grocery storefronts, trying to decide where would be a good place to go shopping for a coyote. I was clueless and naive, the equivalent of a Mexican illegal wandering the downtown streets of Phoenix hoping to bump into an immigration lawyer in an alley. But clueless and naive was all I had.

At a traffic light, another pickup truck pulled next to us, filled in back with eight or so tired peasants in cowboy hats and cloth trousers. The proud ones wore blue jeans. They wore glowering exhausted faces that told me everything I needed to know, they'd taken a long journey to get here, and they were also uneasy about the future—they were immigrants in waiting, potential illegals not yet ripe.

"Hi," I said.

I waved.

They stared at me, offering nothing in return but vacant inquisitive gazes.

The light turned green and both trucks started forward, ours going straight as they made a right-hand turn. As we pulled into the parking lot of the automobile parts store, I saw their truck come to a stop at a motel set back from the main avenue.

And as we left the auto parts store a moment later and drove back toward my broken Ford Focus, I memorized the turns, capturing the images of landmarks at each intersection, leaving a trail of mental bread crumbs that would lead me back to the not-quite-yet immigrants, and their hotel, and just possibly, a coyote.

A NDRE MUNCHED ON Doritos and Pepsi as he arched his eyebrows at my approach, smiled amicably, and said, "They're really taking your car apart."

I appraised the various parts of my engine and transmission lying around the floor of the makeshift shop with a studious knowing look of examination—as if I had the slightest idea what I was evaluating.

Eduardo, the shop's owner, who had taken me to get the transmission fluid, gave me a suggestive thumbs-up. I nodded and returned the thumbs-up. Yes, I've decided that your work is satisfactory.

Eduardo asked me something in Spanish slowly, accentuating each word.

I shrugged. Sorry, I have no idea what you're saying.

"Cuando horas por el coche?" Andre asked, pointing to his watch and the car.

Eduardo replied, "Dos horas." He thought for a second and then said, "Two hours."

Andre and I both nodded. Communication was a good thing.

I sat down on a broken stool that long ago lost its swivel and nervously tapped my feet.

Andre nodded his head out toward the city and I pretended not to understand him.

"Well?" Andre asked.

"Well, what?" I replied, feigning dumb.

"WHAT THE HELL DID WE COME HERE FOR?" he yelled, causing two of the Mexicans to look over at us curiously.

"Just give me a moment, okay?" I replied, suddenly realizing that my neck was full of kinks, and that I felt tired and hungry. And these facts of condition I immediately assumed as proper excuse to delay the operation—you couldn't do a border crossing tired and hungry.

I pulled out my Spanish-English handbook as I tried to piece a question together to ask our mechanic, my mind blistering with thoughts of the *mala prohibita* variety, just sitting and waiting for the courage as I contemplated the form and function of coyotes.

IN ANCIENT MEXICO, coyotes were thought to have diabolical powers. The Navajo associated such bad luck with the coyote that they sometimes called off war parties upon simply sighting one. The Hopi associated the coyote's howls as a premonition of bad tidings moving on down the line. Throughout all of Mesoamerican history, the coyote had been an archetypal mythical figure—the trickster, disobedient and mischievous.

It wasn't an accident then that the human smugglers, those paid to take the Mexicans across, had assumed the name of the coyote; it was a frightening title, one impregnated with historical and cultural meaning. It was like becoming the boogeyman, or a vampire, maybe. But one with heroic undertones—the coyote, after all, was leading the people through the valley of darkness, acting as both spirit guide and savior as they made a midnight crossing toward the Promised Land.

And because of this, the coyote was a modern-day gunslinger, a romanticized rogue, a lovable scoundrel on the wrong side of the law for the right reasons. At least, that's how they were sometimes portrayed in modern Mexican folklore. In the daytime soap operas and the comic books, in the Mexican rap songs.

It started with recruiters scouring rural Mexico as drifting slinking snake-oil salesmen, offering big dreams in exchange for cash up-front. No money? Buy today, pay tomorrow! There was credit financing and graduated payment plans. It was like buying a car. And like any huckster or con artist, the dream was always better than the ride. Immigrants were lied to about how few days it would take to cross the desert, about how easy the crossing would be, and about how much money they would make when they got to America.

The immigrants were herded to northern Mexico where they shored up in derelict motels in squatting border towns as they waited for an opening in the schedule, like waiting stand-by at the airport on an outward-bound flight.

You didn't cross anymore without a coyote. In the old days, maybe, but not anymore. It was like paying protection money to the Mafia, it was obligatory nonoptional insurance. The smugglers owned the corridors and if you wanted to travel, you had to pay the maintenance toll.

And it was the smuggler that was the most important part of the operation. The coyote, the one who charged the border like a combat infantryman. In military terms, he was the trigger puller, the one who got shit done and made it happen.

But in real life, coyotes were gangsters—miserable teenage boys and young men in their early twenties—low-level organized crime enforcers who had dealt both drugs and death. They had tattoos and colors and flashed gang signs.

And once in the vacant desert, anything went. There were no rules. There was no authority. Those who couldn't keep up, who were felled by dehydration or sickness, were left behind because there was a schedule to maintain, this wasn't a humanitarian gesture. Sometimes the immigrants were robbed and abandoned by the coyote. Sometimes they were raped. Sometimes they were murdered.

The coyote had total power because it was only the coyote who had crossed back and forth into America fifty-six times. It was only the coyote who knew the American desert better than the American Border Patrol. Who knew, even in the vacuous dark, the position of the water points, the familiar patterns of the security patrols, the time of night that the suburban residents of Agua Linda went to bed so that they could pass quietly through their backyards.

For this service, the immigrants paid up to three to five thousand dollars, almost a year's salary. Less if they carried drugs.

The coyote got two hundred dollars.

Two hundred dollars for the entire group.

The immigrants delivered, the coyote headed back for the next load, but while he was gone, another was in the pipeline. Multiple coyotes were assigned to each route, to keep things moving, to keep things . . . perpetual.

To maintain this relentless pace the coyote intoxicated himself— drugs, lots of drugs—methamphetamine, speed, uppers, cocaine. And because they *would* eventually get caught, they couldn't be intimately involved in the operations. So they were made disposable, like paper plates. To get a new one all you had to do was travel to the slums and flash some cash. The kids would come calling, never knowing they were expendable, no different from fourteen-year-old corner crack dealers, low man on the totem pole, managing and dealing bodies instead of rocks.

And also like low-level Detroit crack dealers, the coyotes sparred and fought with one another, contesting and conceding and encroaching and impeding over routes and rates. Murdering each other and their clients. To be a coyote meant to be involved in organized crime, it meant having ten other young men waiting to take your position, which required viciousness and fierce territoriality.

Coyote life expectancy was low.

But damn, it felt good to be a gangster.

I SURMISED THE benefits of my condition in order to bolster a meager confidence: I knew the location of at least two water points, I knew the location of the Minutemen, the methods of the Border Patrol, I had driven incessantly around the U.S. side of the border taking GPS readings— there was nothing else I could add to my inventory except courage.

And so I stood, inhaling a deep breath as my mind began to replay my memorized directions backward, to lead me from *here* to *there*.

"Andre, I'm going out for a walk, I'll be back in an hour . . . I hope."

No guts, no glory, as they say.

Andre clapped, cheerfully excited regarding my imminent demise.

As I went to leave, I paused, moved to Eduardo and asked, "Dónde está . . . el coyote en un hotel? Sí, en un hotel?"

Eduardo laughed nervously.

Coyote? For you? He pointed at me. Speaking half in broken English, half in Spanish and acting out the rest.

I nodded in the affirmative.

Petting coyote or killer coyote?

Eduardo pantomimed petting a dog and then a chest-out young angry male.

Killer type.

Eduardo shrugged and pointed out toward town.

Sí. Coyote *is* possible. Are we from the United States?

Yes, we are.

We're going back to the United States, yes?

Yes, we are.

Eduardo was going back soon too.

To Phoenix. For work. He'd been there before. He liked Phoenix.

Are we going back to the United States with coyote?

Over the border, over the fence?

Me, not him. But yes, if possible.

Is expensive. Coyote is expensive.

Yes, I have money. Not a lot, but I have some.

Eduardo sighed and moved to me. He put one hand on my shoulder. It was an intimacy that caused me to look up, to look him in his eyes, which were studying me carefully, with . . . tenderness, maybe.

No coyote for you, he said.

And then, he moved his finger across his throat. It was a clean slice. He winked.

I trembled silently as I sat back down.

And I was quiet for a long moment.

And then I stood and pushed my phrase book into Eduardo's hands.

It's a gift, from me.

For Phoenix, I said.

THREE HOURS LATER and we were driving back toward the border as daylight shriveled on the horizon. The car was running smoothly now, our tires humming over clean-running asphalt. Eduardo had only asked for fifty dollars—a price I assumed was simultaneously inflated for gringos but still given a kindness discount. I gave him one hundred.

Andre angrily berated me for my lack of conviction and courage, my weak-willed integrity, as I silently assumed his detrimental slurs against my character.

"Look, I'm sorry," I replied sullenly. "I'm sorry I didn't get the coyote and risk dying for your amusement." Despite the sarcasm, I sincerely meant it. I was sorry. "Where's our map at?"

Andre reached into the back seat and grabbed the map, flipping it back and forth, and folding it until it was manageably readable.

"What am I doing?" he asked.

"You pick a spot, any spot you want," I said.

"We're still doing this?"

"Yeah, we're still doing this. We get a motel for the night, we try again tomorrow. This isn't a deviation from plan. The plan always was to call abort with the coyote if I felt threatened and then move on to the border. I felt threatened and we're moving on to the border. Nothing's changed."

Andre smiled as he examined the map to pick out a spot. His smile lasted for a minute before inverting into a frown.

"Infrastructure," he said.

"What?"

"Infrastructure. Mexico's not as developed as the United States. There's no roads."

"What do you mean there's no roads?" I yelled as I attempted to yank the map from him with one free hand while I drove with the other.

"There's no roads," he repeated as he pulled the map back. "There's Sasabe and Nogales, and that's it. Two cities, two roads. The roads dead-end at the cities. There's no side roads that we can drive off onto."

THE NEXT MORNING I sat nervously in a cloistered ravine peering up and down the brick terra-cotta valley. Just a half-mile from the United States. Every few seconds I looked at my watch, to see how much longer I had before Andre left and I'd be alone.

We had moved east of Nogales, on a dirt artery that extended from Naco, Mexico, just south of Sierra Vista and the Coronado National Forest. I wasn't sure if this longitude east of Interstate 19 counted as a part of the Amnesty Trail, but it was still a part of the harried central Arizona migration route. It counted. But it also wasn't what I had prepared for. I had no idea about the territory on the other side, which, technically, made it a more accurate experiment but did nothing for my self-confidence.

I looked at my watch.

I sat breathing in long pregnant cycles as I clapped my hands together in preparation for an imminent departure that never came. I willed myself to stand only to find that I suffered from an obscure form of paralysis.

And I knew the reason.

It was all just too much. Everything up until this moment had been theoretical, talked about in abstract terms and owned by indefinite future moments. But at this very sudden and abrupt point in time, I was finally considering all that I should have contemplated long ago before I had accepted the assignment and signed off on the book contract.

What if I got caught by Border Patrol?

My mind attempted to run some scenarios, theoretical excuses that could be offered to the authorities. I tried to frame stories of justification for mental consideration, but every cycle of thoughts self-destructed and erased before they reached the part of my brain that was responsible for examination. And in its place, my mind kept coming back to the single foreboding question: *What if I got caught by the Border Patrol?*

I was on a nature hike and got lost.

I was camping in Mexico and was assaulted by thugs and the only place I knew to run was back to America.

I'm a journalist conducting an experiment.

They all failed my own litmus test, which I knew to be considerably less stringent than the one that would be applied by the Border Patrol.

I looked at my watch.

And it wasn't just the Border Patrol. It was the fear of running into coyotes in the desert who would think I was tracking them or that I would alert the authorities. It was the fear of stepping on a rattlesnake and dying because I couldn't cut open my own wound and suck out the venom properly. It was the fear of getting lost, of falling and breaking a leg.

And then there was Andre. It was just the goddamn pressure he was suddenly applying onto me. He seemed to be eagerly anticipating, not just my crossing, but my demise. I didn't perform well under pressure. Hell, I couldn't even piss in a urinal when someone was standing next to me.

And then, of course, there were the Minutemen. The Coronado National Forest was rife with Minutemen. Minutemen I hadn't spent time with. I had spent time with the California Minutemen. I had spent time with the Amnesty Trail surrogate Minutemen. But I hadn't spent time with the Coronado National Forest Minutemen.

It wasn't the fear of what I could see; it was the fear of what I *couldn't see.*

And the desert loomed large with potential threats, imaginary and otherwise.

And then I laughed, because this was part of the experience that I had wanted to capture, the feeling of what it felt like. Maybe, I didn't need to actually perform the crossing, I could just sit in the dirt and contemplate it, pretend that I was going to and see what that felt like.

So? How was it that I felt?

I felt uninvited. I felt like a bank robber fugitive. I felt paranoid.

I felt scared.

I looked at my watch.

DRAGGING UNDER THE WEIGHT of my pack laden with water and food, I returned to find Andre smoking in the rental car, an act I had strictly forbidden. When you returned it at the airport they charged you extra for that nicotine incense.

"I was just about to leave," Andre stated, not bothering to start the car and instead just staring over at me as I tossed my rucksack in the trunk and climbed in the passenger seat.

I looked at my watch. Even if I hadn't returned, he wasn't supposed to have left for his position for another fifteen minutes. "You've still got fifteen minutes."

"You want to sit here for fifteen minutes?"

"No we can go," I replied evenly, buckling my seat belt and lowering the window to light a cigarette as I took in the beauty of the mauve valley of thinly sparse trees, mountains, and cacti, avoiding the one question that hadn't been asked.

The one question that hadn't been asked: "I thought you were going to cross the border?"

Andre pulled forward onto the dirt road, the Focus bouncing and jostling again as I prayed our repairs would hold.

I sighed, and then speaking too defensively, I yelled, "They had a . . . a spotter . . . a what do you call it? A spotter thing. You know, a crane, lifted up and a little booth looking into Mexico. There was a bunch of 'em, all up and down the border."

"So?"

"So! I'm not going to cross when they have a spotter thing!"

"We could look for another spot," he replied evenly.

I glanced at my watch for the second time. "It's too late. There's nothing to do but turn back now."

"It's not even noon!" Andre yelled.

I sighed, exasperated as hell. Andre didn't understand a single thing about illicit border crossing.

"I *said* it's too late!"

"So we're going back to the States?" Andre said slowly, appalled.

"Yes, we're going back."

Andre glared at me. "Dude, we spent a week planning this thing. You could at least try."

"I did! I did try. Didn't take."

I could feel Andre quietly judging me.

"Look, I don't want to!" I replied defensively. "I'm just being smart about it is all. When you're robbing a bank, do you go forward with it regardless? Or do you do it smart and know when to call abort? We got weeks left, so it didn't happen today, big deal."

And I meant it. It wasn't a big deal. There was lots of time left. It was a process of acclimation. Sometimes you just needed to perform border crossings in baby steps.

Baby step to the border.

Baby step to the fence.

Baby step over the fence.

Andre hadn't said anything when I blurted out, "I don't see how they do it. I really don't. The fucking spotters are right there, how the hell are they all getting over the border without getting caught, there's a fucking shitload of towers!"

"Maybe they're crossing somewhere else," Andre suggested, ignoring the fact that this was purportedly the busiest section of the U.S. border for illicit crossing.

"I mean, I'm not dumb! I've got two master's degrees for Christ's sake! Two!" I held up two fingers. That was how many two was. "How come I can't figure out how they're getting past the spotter cranes?"

"They're probably just crossing at another spot," Andre replied, patting my leg reassuringly.

Part Four

THE DEVIL'S HIGHWAY

If the Tecate Line is a migrant freeway, heavy with traffic and commerce, the Devil's Highway is a backwoods dirt road to nowhere—a veritable death march. Whereas in California migrants need only to manage a sprint to the highway, here it is forty miles to the first minuscule offering of civilization in the form of Why, Arizona, which really isn't much more than a gas station and an abandoned motel. Getting somewhere useful means Ajo, a small village of two thousand souls heavily patrolled by Border Patrol fifty miles to the north of Mexico. And getting somewhere really useful means the Interstate at Gila Bend almost one hundred miles off.

For crossing illegals, there is no civilization to fall back to in case of a mistake, nowhere to give up and surrender. Not like Tucson with its sprawling suburban forts and forward-positioned residential settlements with a golf course at the center that pace the Interstate every couple of miles to the border.

But it is also less crowded, not as many crossers. There are only a handful of park rangers and Border Patrol agents and thousands of square miles of room to navigate, to maneuver, and to get lost. For the illegal aliens, this is what in skiing terms is considered a diamond run, a black trail; for serious contenders only.

And for some, it is worth the risk.

Chapter 15
THE TERRIBLE,
HORRIBLE INDIAN RESERVATION
(TUCSON SECTOR)

All the problems we face in the United States today can be traced to an
unenlightened immigration policy on the part of the American Indian.
—Pat Paulsen

Sundown in Why, Arizona—a tiny serving of civilization in the form of
a gas station run by Indians, a hotel that looked promising in the early
1970s, a diner, and a small unhygienic trailer park. A right-hand turn
here took you into Injun country. A left turn took you back to Ajo.

Andre was running around the parking lot, rolling onto his side in
the middle of the highway—all to get that perfect photographic imprint
of dying light. Photographers loved sunsets. I leaned against the truck
smoking a cigarette, studying the desert as the sun dropped, wholly
bathing the desert in an ashen umbrage.

Andre ran up beside me, winded from his photographic acrobatics.
"So where we going?"

"Ali Chuk," I replied, my finger moving through the complex hive of
small Indian villages accessible only on dirt roads, eventually ending on
a small dot that saddled the demarcation line between the United States
and Mexico. "Ali Chuk looks to be about a mile from the border. And it's
only five miles or so from a back road in Mexico. I say we drive to Ali
Chuk and investigate it for potential. If we like it, we could drive into
Mexico, wait for there to be no traffic, pull over to the side of the road,
and I'll run off. You drive back over to this side and drive back to Ali
Chuk to pick me up. It's only six or so miles. I can do this by morning."

"How am I going to know when to pick you up?" Andre asked.

"Well, I'll call you on my cell phone."

"Is this the official border crossing plan, yeah?"

"Best plan evolving," I replied as a chill charged my body and my eyes studied the map. I had a good feeling about this plan. The idea to cross on the reservation had been sudden and almost overlooked, but after looking at the map I had realized there was a plethora of small Indian villages, many of them close to the border. And the one I had chosen was only six miles. Six miles could be crossed in the cool of night in just a few hours. Six miles was worth a little westward backtracking across Arizona toward California.

And there wasn't supposed to be much border patrol, Minutemen weren't allowed on the Indian reservation, and there was no fence on the reservation. I tossed my cigarette to the side of the road as I pulled out my GPS to mark our current position. "Let's go see some Indians."

IN 1776, the same year that give birth to the United States of America, a Shawnee chief named Cornstalk led a delegation from the northern tribes of the Delaware, the Iroquois, and the Ottawa to meet with the southern tribes of the Cherokee, the Muskogee, and the Chickasaw. The central issue before the intertribal confederacy was simple: what was to be done about the white migrants?

The white migrants who kept spilling into the Kain-tuck-ee and the Tennessee Valley? The white migrants with the exploding population. The white migrants who were changing the culture of the border.

And 231 years later, our headlights broke over the silently suffering village, illuminating momentary snapshots of disheveled poverty like a flashlight waved through an abandoned building, or a haunted house maybe. The houses were the sort born not from some coherent original architectural plan, but by the piecemeal appropriation of tin sheeting and plywood additions. There were bedraggled grubby trailer homes with broken windows and misshapen huts with doors that didn't fit and porches held up by cinder blocks. Sheets of plastic vinyl, duct-taped at the corners, acted as walls; just another impoverished desert civilization, a sight that was becoming familiar and routine.

There were telltale signs of residency, the occasional aging pickup truck in the driveway, but not a soul on the city's main street and no lights emanating from inside the buildings. No shops, no businesses. A local school, modern and new, the village's one concession to modern life, seemed out of place and corrupt.

Ali Chuk had all the warmth and feeling of a ghost town.

The reservation was a nation divided by the border of another. Half the people of this tribe lived in Mexico, dating from a time before the U.S. existed. And now, with their movements restricted by the international recognition of certain nation-states, families were divided, and many of the people were cut off from basic tribal services and holy sites.

Andre clipped his Motorola radio to the visor of the truck and set it to scan for activity. "Jesus, I didn't know this is how they lived," he said as he stared out the window, somewhat surprised to find a Third World enclave buried in the rear-ass of the United States. "Man, we really fucked the Indians, huh?"

I stared quietly out the window and thought back to an Indigenous Studies class I had taken in graduate school. The Native American professor had been vehemently anti-American, still raging on about his peoples and the harm that had been bestowed on them by the Europeans and their progeny. My professor had been actively engaged in legal action against the United States for violation of hundred-year-old treaties, which, if he was successful, ostensibly meant nothing less than the return of millions of square miles of occupied U.S.-controlled territory currently leased to Burger Kings and Starbucks to the collective ownership of Native Americans.

His moods in class would be dictated by the progress or lack thereof with the lawsuit, which, after many years of quiet waiting, was starting to feel a tug of activity and examination within the judiciary. On the good days, he was smiling, *actually believing* that millions of Americans would ever shrug their shoulders and give up their houses and businesses and move back to Europe from which they had never personally come. On bad days, he reminded us how we and our forefathers had engaged in nothing less than cultural genocide.

And when he spoke of the genocide, he always used "we," including himself as one of the victimized. Meanwhile, "us" the students, despite being mostly white and middle-class, fervently agreed that we were indeed evil, if for no other reason than it cost us nothing to do so and alleviated some mild historical guilt that we felt. After all, we had seen *Dances with Wolves.*

But I had resisted the urge of sentimental acquiescence. I had resisted because I had never taken control of anybody; I could barely take care of myself. And I had resisted because my professor had been born in Wisconsin in the 1960s and had never actually seen his people murdered and pushed back across their lands to inhabit these feeble desert settlements.

At the time, it had felt to me that it was blatantly unfair to assign present-day blame based on the behavior of genetic ancestors I had neither known nor cared about. And it had also seemed a bit self-righteous to claim victimization that had occurred to the dearly departed a hundred years prior. It was my belief that my dear old grandmother who was sixty-five years old had more of a claim to American land than he did, if for no other reason than she had been living on the land a quarter of a century longer.

But now as I saw the village, I understood. The distinctive division between life in the United States and life on the reservation was all too apparent. Life on the reservation where teen suicide was 150 percent higher, and unemployment was rife, and infant mortality was five times the U.S. average.

There was an identity and culture within their shared suffering, in growing up on a reservation, that, after all the thousands of years, was the only real inheritance to be passed along. They couldn't escape the past because it was all around them.

And I realized that objectivity on the border issue was impossible. That *all of it*, I was only seeing from one cultural perspective, my own. That I'd never be able to understand the Mexican perspective. The cultural shame and embarrassment they likely felt at being the butt of so many American jokes. The struggle they endured to "make it" in Mexico and the courage that was needed to risk everything to go to the United States where they had to be keenly aware of the resistance against them. In their own way, the Mexicans were heroic.

For my class final, I had submitted a paper that argued that, as horrible as the Native American genocide had been, the unfortunate reality was that it was a natural phenomenon for populations to migrate as the Europeans had. My theorem was proved, I had argued, by simply picking up a historical atlas and rapidly flipping through the pages, thereby transforming the book into a crude animation. Besides the entire history of human civilization from early birth in Mesopotamia to the present day elapsing in seconds, what you saw was the fragile tenuous state of borders as the land encapsulated within national boundaries grew and shrank as territory was both conquered and conceded. As borders changed color altogether after being rebirthed as a new nation, later divided yet again through revolution or cessation, and sometimes, as is the case with those indigenous to the American continents, almost entirely died out all together from both warring conquest and the all-consuming momentum of invading cultures. From this perspective, history began to take on the attributes and character of cells and bacteria, perpetually at war with each other as they struggled for co-option and division.

My conclusion, as stupid as it had been, as if murder would have been justified simply because it was a behavioral norm throughout history, had been an attempt to absolve myself of the blame I felt from my white ancestors.

"Hey Andre," I said, turning to him in the darkened interior of the truck. "What do you think of Mexicans who have babies here? Should they be forced to go back? This is really all they've ever known."

"Yeah, they're called American citizens, yeah?" Andre responded, giggling silently.

"Yeah, I guess so," I responded, feeling quite stupid. "Hmm . . . what about this? Everyone pretty much admits that we stole the land from the Indians, but no one admits to stealing the land from Mexico. Why is that?"

"Yeah, we only do that to the Native Americans because they're a conquered people, down for the count, out of the game," Andre replied. "If they were feisty like the Mexicans we wouldn't feel the same way. It's easier to be nicer and feel bad for people when they're conquered."

"And another thing," I added. "How come when we took the land over from the Indians, we just came in and started breeding like the Mexicans are doing. But then when the Mexicans do it, we're like, 'Uh-uh, boundary! You just crossed an international boundary!' Gotta play fair! You're breaking the rules!"

Andre and I both broke up laughing as through the passenger-side window I saw a black SUV with tinted windows hiding behind a rickety trailer home pull into position just behind us.

I abruptly stopped laughing and adjusted my rearview mirror.

Its dark grille was suddenly a mess of swirling crimson strobes.

I pulled to the side of the road and killed the engine, turning on all the dome lights in the truck, and moving my hands to the top of the steering wheel where they could be easily seen. I did all this because I took great pride in making the officer pulling me over feel secure in knowing that he could see both my hands and the interior of the vehicle. It had the secondary effect of making the officer typically more appreciative of my efforts and more likely to be kind in his approach.

Click. Click. Boots on the pavement. The window slid down in jerking cranks.

"Did I tell you I have a kilo of cocaine in my backpack?" Andre asked quickly.

I turned to him, flushed with panic as a beam of light hit me in the face. Andre broke up at his own joke.

I stuck my head out of the car to see a Native American in a bullet-proof vest thrown over a T-shirt with his badge hanging on a chain around his neck like they always had in the movies. He was muscular and suave, cowboy boots and jeans, a real tough guy.

"What are you guys doing out here?" he asked, one hand on his gun, ready to perform a quick-draw kill if needed.

"Um, uh . . ." I started, once again not being fast enough to respond to even basic questions. Indian reservation or not, we *were* in the United States and we hadn't broken any laws. "We're journalists and we just wanted to see what it was like back here."

He paused for a second and then asked, "What does that mean?"

"Well, we're journalists and we're writing about illegal immigration so we needed to see what the Indian reservation was like."

He stared at me for a moment, his eyes blinking, confused and unsure. "But I don't know what that means."

"Um," I replied, finger to my lip, unsure of what to say next. "Well, we're doing research for a book on illegal immigration and lots of illegal immigrants come out here, so we just felt it was necessary to get a feel for the environment that I'd be writing about."

"Uh-huh," the officer replied, his flashlight flickering around the interior of the truck before the light ended on Andre's smirking grimacing face where it held.

"Well, what's your opinion about it?" the officer asked.

I turned to Andre, unsure of what to say next.

"It's not good," Andre said, still squinting under the light's glare.

"No, it's not good," I concurred. "Yeah, it's bad. We're against it."

"Uh-huh," the officer replied. "How'd you get out here?"

I felt the sweat rise to my forehead. I didn't understand any of his questions.

"On the highway? Yeah, we were on the highway, then we weren't on the highway, and we drove . . ." I pantomimed driving with an invisible steering wheel two inches above the real one in case he was unfamiliar with this driving reference. ". . . and then we were here."

"Uh-huh," the officer replied.

The Motorola radio from the visor chirped as garbled Spanish flooded the interior of the truck. Andre scrambled to turn down the volume just in time to catch a beam of light back in the face.

"WHAT THE HELL IS THAT?" the officer yelled.

"It's a radio!" I yelled back. "It's just a radio."

"WHY THE HELL DO YOU HAVE A RADIO? ARE YOU MONITORING TRAFFIC?"

"No!" I replied, wishing he'd stop screaming at me.

"Yes!" Andre said.

The flashlight pivoted to catch me in the eyes. I could feel myself melting under its watchful scrutiny.

The officer leaned forward, his head inside my driver's side window to get a better look.

"You're not drug traffickers are you?"

"No! Look, I have a book I wrote! I have papers!" I cried as I grabbed my satchel bag in a quick movement that dropped the officer's hand to his pistol as he took a step back ready to shoot me in the head. I started handing items out the window. Itineraries and copies of articles I had written for magazines and my passport and all the contents of my wallet including my library card.

The officer was quiet as he browsed my recommended selection of reading materials and started handing them back to me one by one.

"You can't be out here," he said finally, offering my passport back, still gripping it and not letting me take it. "This is Native American land and unless you have written permission to be out here, I can arrest you for trespassing. Besides, you guys don't want to be out here at night, it's too dangerous. You've got drug runners that go through all the time, and they are armed. You're gonna get yourself killed out here and, frankly, I have better things to do than worry about two journalists with their thumbs stuck up their ass." He studied me for a moment to make sure I got it before releasing his hold on my passport.

"I'm taking the thumb out of my ass and we're leaving, Officer."

"Have a nice evening," he replied, retreating to his vehicle.

"Thank you!" Andre called out after him in his best manufactured gay voice before erupting in a fit of giggles.

WE KEPT THE TRUCK idling on the side of the road as Andre turned on the dome light to study the map. "Drive north to a place called Gu Vo, then take a right-hand turn . . . there's another place called San Miguel on the other side of the reservation."

"How far away is it from the border?" I asked. "We're looking for easy spots, no long walks, nothing too physical."

"It's pretty close to the border, a few miles," Andre replied shrugging, indifferent to my desire for physical conservation.

"Who do you think that guy was? DEA?" I asked as I pulled back onto the road and started driving.

"Nah, man, he was a fucking Shadow Wolf!"

"What the hell is a Shadow Wolf?" I asked, noticing distant head-lights far behind us in my rearview mirror.

"They're like Indian Special Forces, I read about 'em," Andre explained. "The drug runners are always paying off the Indians since they're all poor and shit, so the Shadow Wolves is this elite group of trackers that does counternarco stuff on the reservation. They're trackers, so they get out in the brush and chase the drug traffickers. They even went to Afghanistan to track al Qaeda and shit."

"Wow, that's pretty cool . . ." I said quietly as I contemplated attempt-ing to cross the border here and being tracked and caught out in the desert by a Shadow Wolf. And suddenly, I longed desperately to be cap-tured by a Shadow Wolf. No one else I knew had ever been tracked and captured by a Shadow Wolf. I would be the first one and that meant something.

Behind me the headlights were getting closer and gaining fast.

"What the fuck?" I yelled. "What's this asshole want? Do I speed up?"

"Probably a drunk Indian," Andre said, his voice slightly alarmed as the headlights flooded our rear window, just a foot off our bumper as we traveled down the gravel road at fifty miles per hour, spewing a cloud of dust behind us. "You should probably try and outrun him. I've had prob-lems with drunk Indians in the past, it never ends well."

And then, the two bulbs erupted into a red and blue rotating flash.

I sighed as I pulled over to the side of the road.

I watched in my side mirror as the Border Patrol agent moved toward us, his hand on his pistol. "Do you have this weird feeling that he's going to shoot us? I do. I have this weird feeling that he's going to shoot us."

"Good evening, gentlemen, what are you doing out here?" the Border Patrol agent asked, his face hidden behind the blinding light of his flash-light, which, in a repeat of the Shadow Wolf, peered into the interior of the vehicle.

"We know! We know! We're leaving, we're trying to drive north to get out of here," I said defensively before deciding I came on too harsh and I erupted in an awkward blush of uncomfortable halting laughter.

The Border Patrol agent stared at me as he moved the flashlight to my eyes. "You're not on anything tonight are you? You taken something tonight, maybe? On a little rush to LaLa Land?"

Cops out here in the wastelands of the nation had a real way with words.

"No, no, not at all. Never. I don't do drugs," I replied. "No LaLa Land."

"We don't do drugs," Andre added firmly, leaning across my seat and offering a friendly wave.

"One of your buddies just pulled us over told us to get lost so we're trying to get out of here," I explained, a bit irritated as I pointed back south toward the Indian policeman.

The Border Patrol agent looked back the way we came. "You don't say? Is that a fact?"

"Yes, sir, it is a fact."

"Where you boys coming from?"

Andre and I looked at each other, not quite understanding the question.

"Do you mean like, recently? Or do you mean, originally?" I asked.

"Originally."

"Philadelphia," Andre replied at the same time I said, "San Diego."

"You a teleporter?" the Border Patrol agent asked. "Able to come from two places at once?"

"No, sir, I'm not a teleporter."

"Why don't you go ahead and step on out of that vehicle?"

THE BORDER PATROL AGENT handed me back my passport as he gave a quick two friendly knocks to the hood of my truck, "You boys get on out of here now, ya here? This ain't no place to be at night."

"Yes, sir," I said taking back my passport.

"Do you catch many teleporters around here?" Andre asked, leaning in across my lap, his tone earnest and sincere.

"What?" the Border Patrol agent asked.

"I was just wondering if you catch many teleporters around here?" he asked again, his face giving no hint of amusement.

The Border Patrol agent studied us for a moment, as if deciding our fate, before replying, "Well, hell, they're everywhere. One minute they're in Mexico, next minute they're ten miles in-country."

Andre and I were both quiet while the agent studied us again, giving his flashlight one quick final scan around the interior of my truck before he retreated to his own vehicle, smirking as he went.

I punched Andre in the arm as Andre erupted into a raucous fit of giggles.

WE DROVE FOR another twenty minutes before we came to Gu Vo where I stopped at the town's edge at a desolate intersection. Left took us back to the highway that led to Tucson and right took us deeper into the Indian reservation.

"I say we try for it, yeah?" Andre said.

I examined the map. "We can also get to San Miguel on the highway by getting off at Sells. Kinda shortcut through the Indian reservation."

Andre considered this. "Yes, this is true. But what if you can't get to San Miguel, what if you need to quit being so damn lazy and maybe walk to one of the villages not right on the border, someplace a little further away but not as heavily patrolled. Might make sense to check some of them out in the interior, not on the edge."

I nodded. This made sense.

"Yeah, okay," I replied as I put my turn signal on to blink silently alone in the desert and I moved deeper into the reservation.

I sighed, adjusted my seat to make myself comfortable, rolled down the window, and lit a cigarette. It was going to be an hour or so before we made it to the other side of the reservation.

Behind us, red and blue lights flashed silently.

"OH, JESUS CHRIST!" I screamed. "ARE YOU FUCKING KIDDING ME?"

Andre erupted into another fit of giggles.

I craned my head out the window to see this time that it was a local sheriff.

I got out of the vehicle, a big phony fake smile plastered on my face as I started to walk toward the officer and said, "Officer, we're just trying to figure out how to get out of here and I think I took a wrong—"

"GET BACK IN YOUR VEHICLE!" the sherriff's deputy yelled as his hand moved to his pistol and he took cover behind his open driver's side door.

"Getting back in the vehicle!" I replied as I slumped into the driver's seat.

The sheriff approached and another flashlight beam hit me in the side of the face.

"I'm just trying to get out of here, we've already been pulled over, we were told to leave, we're trying to leave, we just got lost, I took a wrong turn," I said.

"It's true, we're lost," Andre added helpfully from his passenger seat.

The sheriff studied us for a long moment and then said, "I'm going to need you to step out of your vehicle."

AND THEN, BACK in Why, Arizona.
Was that a song somewhere?
Why again?

I had firmly decided that any crossing I subjected myself to would not, under any circumstances, be instigated on reservation land. Andre held firm in the passenger seat of my truck, offering me contemptuous glares for my continued cowardice before he got out and moved to his own Taurus.

It was time to go our separate ways for a while. I was headed to New Mexico while Andre was heading to the dog track to take photos of the handlers, regarding whom, he had heard it rumored, they were all Mexicans. Different approaches to the same story, I suppose.

"See you in what? Three or four days?" Andre said.

I nodded, grunting my approval, as Andre waved goodbye and drove off, leaving me alone. I stared into the horizon toward New Mexico and sighed.

It was a hell of a long haul.

And then, there was an itching sensation along the edge of my back.

I turned slightly to face south into the Organ Pipe Cactus National Monument.

Toward the Devil's Highway.

Chapter 16

THE DEVIL'S HIGHWAY
(YUMA SECTOR)

The drive south from Why, Arizona, to Sasabe, Mexico, was a straight-shooting artery, nothing but flat asphalt—no turns, no curves, no intersections, no traffic. Flat rolling dust-caked sepia prairie on both sides of the road as far as the eye could see, and everywhere throughout, emerald saguaro cactus herded into long lingering parallel rows, standing with arms held high as if suggesting surrender. The flat was broken only in random and irregular intervals by single-serving mountains, giant jagged granite sheer-faced monstrosities.

Going the other direction, from Why, Arizona, it was another ten miles to Ajo, the local urban metropolis with a population of three thousand. From Ajo, it was another fifty to the Interstate. And all of it connected on a single unused mostly abandoned highway, numero ochenta y cinco with no turn-offs, no side avenues, no roadside service stations—this was just, perhaps, the most remote region of the nation for the southern forty-eight states.

The land south of Ajo was the Organ Pipe Cactus National Monument, sandwiched between the Barry Goldwater bombing range and the mountainous Indian reservation—it was federally protected land for the recreational use of Americans everywhere. There was wildlife like the Sonoran pronghorn deer and nature trails. The type of place where there was supposed to be Frisbee and barbecues, screaming babies, fighting children, and barking dogs tied up on leashes beside the picnic table.

But the parking lots were mostly empty, the gravel normally displaced by parked tires, flat and smooth. And throughout the monument, vehicle barriers up everywhere, blocking trails and access roads on the Pozo Nuevo, the Camino de Dos Republicas, North Puerto Blanco, and South Puerto Blanco Drive. The Dripping Springs was also closed, just as was the Sweetwater Pass. And there was no camping anymore, and no entry after dark, although the park rangers estimated there were a thousand people inside the park every night, what with smugglers and illegals pouring through the holes in the border fence. A third of all the drugs confiscated in all the national parks and monuments across the nation was right here at the Organ Pipe. Here, the small handful of existing park rangers snuck up on visitors with their guns drawn and for good reason; the United States Park Ranger Lodge of the Fraternal Order of Police called it the most dangerous national park in America.

Partly, it was dangerous because of the drugs, but it was also that everything out here wanted to tear and cut. There were bats and snakes and scorpions. The plant life was vicious too: needled cacti, barbed chollas, and lime mesquite trees with eye-level thorns. The temperature, at this time of the summer, dropped to 97 degrees at night; 120 or more during the day. There were no creeks here, no rivers, no ponds—water didn't exist here. It might as well be the moon, or Mercury.

The Mexican migrants didn't call it the Organ Pipe Cactus National Monument. They called it the Devil's Highway. Because out here in the desert, el diablo whispered to you, walking you through one bad turn after another as you slowly got lost, teasing your eyes with deceptively nearby mirages that lingered playfully on the horizon just long enough to entice and distract.

In May of 2001, twenty-six men entered the desert and were abandoned by their coyote. They were left to wander for days on end as they slowly went mad, imagining whispering devils that led them deeper into the desert. Mummified corpses kept turning up all summer, picked over by vultures, partially devoured by wild animals.

As Luis Alberto Urrea wrote in a book documenting the tragedy, "Desert spirits of a dark and mysterious nature have always traveled these trails. From the beginning, the highway has always lacked grace— those who worship desert gods know them to favor retribution over the tender dove of forgiveness. In Desolation, doves are at the bottom of the food chain."

IT WAS STILL early morning dark when I awoke at the motel. The motel was freaky in the way that desert dwellings had a tendency to be: pink cinder blocks, a blinking neon sign undecided whether to be on or off, gravel parking lot, and a blue-tiled swimming pool filled with aquamarine water—a septic tank of squirming bacteria and suntanned parasites. I climbed the waist-high locked gate detailing the pool's hours of operations and went for a long and relaxing swim.

I dried off, turned on my GPS, locked in the coordinate of the motel as a waypoint, and then went into my motel room and got on my laptop.

We were serious now.

No more fucking around.

This was go time.

I moved about the room trying to hook the faint edge of a fading wireless Internet signal. I managed to reel it in from the motel office and make a tenuous connection in the bathroom with my laptop hanging half out the window while I stood on the toilet.

I used Google Earth to zoom in on my present position. I peered out the window into the dawning pale blue sky, imagining that I could see the satellite as I waved at myself, purposely forgetting that these were long-ago recorded images. It was funnier to believe it was live television.

I needed to see the fence, to see the extent of border security in place out here. And then, I saw the border fence, an intense blank line against shaded desert—like an erased middle in a flurry of graphite pencil scratch. I zoomed in and Google told me the particular level of surveillance I was requesting was unavailable.

I moved back to the bed and studied my North American road atlas.

Here, at the Devil's Highway, getting somewhere useful after crossing the border meant my current position at Ajo, for all intents and purposes a Mexican village inside the United States, fifty miles from the border. And from here it was still another fifty to the Interstate, which was still a gazillion miles from civilization.

It was one hell of an unforgiving nature hike.

But the Mexican side was sitting pretty. Sonoyta, just on the other side of the border, had Mexican Highway 2 running firmly parallel to the U.S. border all the way west to Tijuana, and Highway 2 was only a few miles set back from the border. I wouldn't have to spend long in Mexico, which was half my worry.

But this was the bitch—fifty miles to Ajo, forty if I did her at a straight angle.

Three miles an hour, that's what I had done in the Army. And with distance lost to circumventing mountains and climbing elevated positions, I was estimating twenty hours. That's all it was, just one day, which was nothing really. Concentration camp survivors had endured years of days a hundred times worse. Afghanistan had owned more than a couple of really bad days, and that was while taking enemy fire. Hell, the contestants on the show *Survivor* had to endure thirty days. I just had one day—just one.

I APPROACHED THE checkout counter of Ajo's single grocery, a small multi-purpose convenience store, and slammed the four baskets filled with Gatorade and water and iced tea onto the counter. The Hispanic woman behind the desk looked at me strangely.

"I'm a little thirsty," I replied, grinning sheepishly.

What I was about to attempt would require perpetual and constant hydration. Under these conditions, the body excreted fluids as fast as they were consumed, like a backyard fountain in some garden, spraying out of the concrete penis into the basin, and then being recycled by underground pumps to be expunged all over again.

I hoisted up another two baskets, these ones filled with PowerBars and chips and cookies and candy, anything with sugar and energy. In the Army when we had done thirty-mile movements, the full extent of what I had been capable of at a time when I had been both conditioned and in good shape, we had also along the way consumed two, sometimes three MREs, meals ready to eat, that had three thousand calories each. Thirty miles through the desert with a weighted backpack in the height of summer, your body didn't just burn calories, it exploded them in mass genocide like an atom bomb in the nervous system. Your body actually felt tingly as it burned like an industrial furnace. Fat people could lose pounds in a single day doing this. Skinny people like myself without fat to lose just started emanating a curious stench of nail polish remover—cannibalized muscle being devoured for energy.

Eighty-six dollars was the total.

I handed her my blue Citibank card.

She started to hand it back a moment later.

No good, she said.

I stared at the card in her hands for a long horrifying moment, refusing to take it back. I winced, realizing I was burning through my credit reserves on this trip faster than I had anticipated. I sighed and pulled my wallet back out—staring at my two remaining credit cards, my hand lingering over the selection. Was it to be the pretty one with the mountains, or my esteemed Fozzie the Bear MasterCard?

I handed her the pretty one with the mountains.

I RANG THE BELL in the front office and a few moments later from a back room where a small black-and-white television played, a smiling Hispanic man emerged.

"I'm going to need to reserve the room for the next three days," I replied.

My plan was to drive tomorrow to Sonoyta, Mexico, tomorrow morning, where I would park my truck. I would take a taxi out on Mexico Highway 2, stop the driver on the side of the road to take a piss, never to return. It would be only a few miles to the border where I'd survey the other side, and then, assuming all was safe, I'd hop the fence, or if there was no fence, simply walk to the other side.

It would, of course, be the hottest part of the day. Hovering around 120 degrees, with the desert absorbing half of the heat, and reflecting the other half back upward so that it would also be like walking on a frying pan, the air pungent with a stinging sizzle. But I would also at this point be fresh, well rested, hydrated, and with three good meals under my belt. I needed to start at this moment because as the day wore on and I got progressively more tired, the temperature would also be cooling—first into evening, then night, and then morning. If all went according to plan, I would finish before lunch the following day, right before the heat became blistery again.

Then, I would retreat to my motel room, where I would have both snacks and water in the room's tiny refrigerator waiting for me and I would eat, hydrate, and sleep. Heal myself for a full day, doing nothing but resting. Then, the next morning, I'd worry about how to get back to Sonoyta to get my truck. There were no taxi services out here, but there had to be a bus that passed through on its way to the border, or a local I could talk to at a bar whom I could pay to drive me, so I could then pick up a taxi in Sonoyta to take me the rest of the way to whatever safe spot I had found to park my truck. Then, I'd drive back to the motel, pick up my things, and I'd be off, and my mission would be complete.

IT WASN'T EVEN yet lunch as I sat on the bed watching daytime soaps with nothing left to do but wait for tomorrow. I turned my GPS on and off, just to make sure it was still working. I counted and recounted the AA batteries in the plastic Baggie next to me, more than enough to last several days. I laid out what I was going to carry on the bed, and then on the floor, and then on the opposite bed: binoculars, first-aid kit, audio recorder, a map sealed in a Ziploc Baggie, sunglasses, baseball cap (New York Yankees, not the Minutemen), an extra pair of socks, a sweatshirt and light jacket for the nighttime, and all the batteries and food and liquids that I could carry. I unloaded the pistol, put it on safe, and tucked it under the mattress, and then I repeated this process every half-hour, wondering if I had indeed put the pistol on safe or if I had just imagined doing so.

I decided to get in some last-minute training: five hundred push-ups over the course of the next hour. And I was also giving up smoking, from this very moment forward, I would never have another cigarette, give my lungs a chance to heal while I was still relatively young. I slid off the bed with a sigh and positioned my body parallel to the shag-carpeted floor as, behind me on the television, Maury revealed the results of the blood paternity test. I pushed myself up with my arms, locking them out, and took a deep breath.

A few minutes later, after I had managed a compromise with myself of forty-five push-ups, but no soda with dinner tonight as punishment, I climbed back up on the bed and debated whether to jerk off. Whether to keep the sexual frustration around, some potential backup reservoir of energy for the body to feed off of later, or whether to dispel the frustrations, go in relaxed with a happy state of mind. It may have seemed like an inconsequential decision of little relative importance, but everything at this point mattered. Small dietary mistakes the day before could end up being catastrophic; a single unfinished dinner salad could have been another survivable hour in the desert. Slight abrasions on the toe today, by the end of the trek tomorrow could be pulsating puss-oozing festering open sores. The desert had a way of exaggerating things.

I decided not to jerk off.

I needed it there in reserve.

Everything helped.

I STUMBLED THROUGH the desert, keeping to the dusty road, one heavy foot after another as I wheezed for breath. I leaned forward and paused, resting my hands on my knees as I peered up at the sun, which, even under the shading of darkened sunglasses, burned furiously like the heart of a bomb, its color that of pure snow, so hot it had consumed all color. Even from this distance I could hear the cataclysmic explosions of each sunspot exploding forth with a rippling roar stretching like some cosmic lava Slinky, before being pulled back in by gravity and slamming into the sun's molten nuclear core.

This was what was known as High Noon—showdown time in the old Westerns. And I understood now why it was called that. If midnight was where you ran and hid from monsters hiding under the bed, it was High Noon where you made your stand and confronted them.

And I also knew why this was called the Devil's Highway—because this was surely hell.

Every few moments, my hand reflexively shot up and wiped a sticky glistening sheen of sweat from my face as if it were the windshield wiper of a car in the middle of a rainstorm. My left arm strained as I reached backward into my pack to grab another Gatorade. I stumbled to a stop and twisted the top—gurgling, the whole thing in one gigantic swallow. I looked at the ground and contemplated whether to toss this one as I had the last. I considered myself an environmentalist, someone who didn't appreciate litter as a sacred archaeological discovery waiting to be discovered by future generations who would learn about us from our garbage. But I also had to make the pack lighter. It was only an empty bottle, but every bit counted. It wasn't just the weight of the empty plastic bottle; it was also the weight of the slight few drips of red Gatorade at its bottom, and the weight of its accompanying shadow. I could afford none of it. So I kicked it into the desert where it would slowly recycle for the next thousand years.

I could afford no more weight because it was my pack that was doing me in. Fifty miles was a tricky thing to explain to some people. Some people, fit people, not myself, but other people, had done marathons, for God's sake. Fifty miles wasn't going to get any sympathy from them. But it wasn't just fifty miles, it was fifty miles with this cursed heat, but mostly, it was fifty miles with this horrible terrible god-awful pack.

The first half-hour wasn't bad. The first half-hour felt good, even. It felt solid, masculine, the strain pleasurable. But heavy packs that one is unaccustomed to carrying after a few years have a secret way about them of growing increasingly heavier and with little patience for negotiation. One minute after the thirty-minute marker, the feeling quickly transformed to one of severe irritation and resolute discomfort. An hour in and it felt like I was slogging an anvil through the desert. An hour in, it made the small of my back throb and pulsate with pain, as if ripping and tearing muscle tissue, as if I had stood gritting my teeth, bracing myself against a brick wall as I was repeatedly sucker-punched by a heavyweight boxing champion. The real bitch of it though was the straps that cut into my shoulders like two sharp-edged knives slowly whittling their way into the interior of my body cavity where, once inside, I imagined they'd simply melt through my innards like butter until they fell to my feet. I kept readjusting the straps, sliding them additional inches left and right of my neck just to feel those few seconds of tear-inducing relief before the burn started up again.

The desert burnt, mama. The desert burnt.

I wiped another sheet of sweat from my face, my palm now permanently sticky.

"Jesus," I said quietly to myself. "Did someone drop a nuclear bomb around here?" I stumbled to a stop and rotated in a circle, my hands acting as a visor over my sunglasses as I peered into the horizon looking for a mushroom cloud. I didn't see a mushroom cloud, but that didn't mean one hadn't gone off, that its billowing cratered cloud wasn't hiding behind one of the distant mountains that dotted the landscape. Maybe, one had been accidentally dropped next door at the Goldwater jet bombing range. Maybe, they had thought they loaded a training dummy and had accidentally loaded a real one. No different from mixing up a few rounds of live ammo in a clip full of blanks on the firing range, really. That sort of shit happened all the time.

And as I felt my neck redden, as if exposed to an openly lit match, I looked up into the sky and realized the problem. After I had left my hotel, there had been some type of cosmic accident. Global climate change must have had unforeseen effects that had more quickly dissolved the atmosphere in a sudden climatic moment, or maybe a distant star had exploded, sending spiraling microwave emissions across our planet that had peeled back the atmosphere like a leaf of crispy peeling sunburnt skin, a blowtorch to the retina of an eyeball.

Whatever the cause, our ozone layer was gone and I was being bombarded with deadly radiation and *that* was the reason for my physical struggle. I laughed sadly at my situation. The universe hadn't planned this to occur simultaneously, of course, the universe cared too little for me or anyone else to start looking at one's calendar; it was just the bad luck of statistical inevitability and the errant timing that strangely seemed to pervade so much of this life.

And then I decided that if my radiological death was imminent, there was no reason to continue hiking. I wanted to spend my final moments doing something important, like thinking deep thoughts, or thinking of my friends and family, or getting in one good moment of last masturbation, before the foreskin started sloughing off in my hand from the radiation poisoning.

I stumbled forward off the dirt road to a small alcove of shade under a cluster of cacti and behind a boulder the size of a Volkswagen Beetle and collapsed onto the ground and took off my pack as I oohhed and ahhed, in tender relief at being rid of the pack, the blood refilling my shoulders feeling like a cheap two-dollar massage in Thailand—brisk, rough, and oh so good. I peeled my shirt off my chest, it ripped like duct tape. My thinness felt more severe, more acute—bone segregated from sinewy muscle. The shade was only a ten-degree drop in temperature, and a cactus thorn was pinching the back of my neck, but it felt like poolside at the cabana, Bahama Mama in hand.

I peered out the delineated edge of the cactus's cover where shadow abruptly transformed into light as I reevaluated the sun one last time, cursing it silently.

Why did the sun hate me so?

What had I ever done to the sun?

And then as I peeked at the sky, drinking Gatorade, an epiphany hit me. And it occurred as all good epiphanies should—like a startling smack across the face that left you seeing stars. The only thing missing was the music in the background, swelling into crescendo.

This was what the Mexicans were willing to endure to come here. No, not all of them knew what they were getting into; some were lied to and suddenly confronted with the stark reality. And had they known, they surely wouldn't have come. But some of them, half maybe to apply a completely artificial unsubstantiated number, had to have known. They had family who had crossed, they had done it before, they had heard stories. And still, they were willing to risk it all, and to endure *this*! That was how bad they wanted it!

The joke in middle America was that it was easy to cross the border. That the Mexicans did it almost as an afterthought—for a few extra bucks, for the opportunity to stand outside Home Depot. And no one in America could imagine that being worth this. So they assumed the trek to be slight and casual. It made them feel better about feeling tough against illegal immigration and it made the Mexicans who crossed criminal and arbitrary.

Or they assumed that not everyone was crossing in the desert, but they were, of course, wrong. Almost all the Mexicans crossed in the desert now, away from the cities and the motion-sensitive thermal-imaging night-vision cameras and the five layers of barbed wire in El Paso and the floodlights and the intensive Border Patrol that pervaded like a swarm of locusts; they crossed in the desert where they would have a fighting chance. And this wasn't something you did for a few extra dollars an hour. This was something you did for your children, or your dreams, maybe.

This was something you did for survival.

I looked at my watch wondering how long I had been out on my trial test run before tomorrow's big event.

Four and a half hours. I had been out only four and a half hours.

I ENTERED MY motel room as evening began to shade the sky, stumbled to the air conditioner and turned it on full blast as I dropped my rucksack to the floor, and collapsed on the bed, exhausted. Four and a half hours I had been out on my test run. And four and a half hours was the full extent of my capabilities. I tried to sit up and found I was stuck to the bed, unable to move, without even the energy for a single struggling tummy crunch.

My body felt weak, dehydrated, my throat was parched, and my muscles throbbed. Even with constantly consuming both food and liquids during my four hours, it still hadn't been enough. To run the Devil's Highway properly would also require an additional mouth. I thought about how I would manage this, an IV feeding me nutrients as I went, maybe?

I briefly contemplated whether I still remembered how to insert an IV and whether one could purchase a saline drip at a Walgreens in Tucson. But then I had always had problems sticking my partner in my combat first-aid course. There had been considerable gushing and blood spurting into the air from numerous veins before I had actually plugged one correctly. And the image of mutilating myself in the bathroom, puncturing myself with one hole after another with forearms covered in blood, seemed unsightly. And if nothing else, I didn't want my border crossing to be unsightly.

I managed to roll over onto my side into a slight fetal position as I felt myself nod off toward sleep. I performed some quick math while I calculated the distance I had crossed during my practice run and correlated it with the time it had taken me. I frowned slightly, eight miles in four hours, that wasn't good. At that pace, it would take me a day and a half, two days, maybe. Of course, that had also been with a couple of breaks. I wasn't going to be taking any breaks tomorrow, fifteen minutes for tea. That was it.

I decided to take a quick nap, go out and get some dinner, and then head back to the motel for a full night of sleep. I would feel better by morning, and with a little rest, my muscles would bounce back, and they would be glad they got some exercise, and because of it, they would perform better tomorrow. And also tomorrow, I would have a different attitude about it all. You took it seriously, pushed yourself further when it was real. No more breaks. You didn't try as hard when you were just a few miles away from your motel on a practice run.

I wasn't giving up. I was just taking a nap.

Everything was still on for tomorrow.

The failure of my test run had changed nothing.

IT WAS TWO in the morning when I was outside the darkened motel, yawning from having just woken up as I banged on the screen door to the motel office, illuminated in the headlights of my idling truck, my rucksack packed and in the cab, my Gatorades rolling loosely in the truck's bed.

I banged on the screen door harder as I covered my hands and peered in through a small window into the darkness inside before I noticed the sign that said "Closed." Apparently, there was so little traffic, motels closed around these parts. I banged louder, angrier this time. I needed a refund on the additional three days I had reserved. That was a hundred and fifty bucks.

Nothing. For all I knew the motel proprietor didn't even live on premises.

I sighed as I climbed into my truck and pulled out onto the main road and started down the highway toward the Interstate.

Part Five

TEXAS TWO-STEP

The coyotes wail, along the trail,
deep in the heart of Texas . . .

Chapter 17
HATCH, NEW MEXICO
(EL PASO SECTOR)

Deming, New Mexico, just an hour shy of the Texas border, was a single strip of truck stops, fast food, and cantankerous drinking establishments of the sort where you expected Friday nights to be filled with tattoo-adorned bikers of nefarious character.

Deming was also the epicenter of what Democratic governor Bill Richardson had declared a state of emergency, saying that the region "has been devastated by the ravages and terror of human smuggling, drug smuggling, kidnapping, murder, destruction of property and the death of livestock." Six months after we'd leave, the police chief of Palomas, Mexico, his deputies having abandoned him, and fearing for his life, would stop at the port of entry asking for political asylum.

It was for all these reasons that Andre and I had made Deming our new base of operations while in New Mexico. We had spent the last week visiting local hospitals that were going broke and farmers who were struggling to find enough migrant workers, their respective conflicting conclusions leaving us with no clearer understanding of the border.

We slid the two chairs in our ailing motel room outside to the empty parking lot and swallowed hard on gas station beer while we stared into the distant desert horizon, which flashed with splintering cackles of radiated lightning behind a yellow-storm-tinted horizon. From the far side of the parking lot, I could catch the faint edge of a wireless signal and check e-mail. Andre ate gas station burritos, the bear spray by his side in case of attack by the local drug dealers who were also using our motel as a base of operations. Beside us semis pummeled past on the Interstate, pushing up a fine breeze as we quietly listened to the radio.

"Why am I hearing two different stories," the man being interviewed on the radio said. "One from Washington, D.C., another from West Texas. Unfortunately, the situation on the border is worse than people have read or heard. You don't need to go to Iraq to see the War on Terror, all you need to do is go to Laredo, Texas, and drive to the border with a deputy in a marked sheriff's vehicle where you will probably be machine-gunned immediately."

"Storm's a-coming," Andre replied defensively even though I hadn't said anything.

"Yep," I said quietly, appraising the storm's distant latitude. The storm felt thick with unintended metaphorical meaning and menacing value.

"You want to cross here in New Mexico?" he asked. "That guy at the bar told me there's lots of coyotes in Palomas."

I winced as I turned into the horizon, the wind kissing my face. "Nah, doesn't feel right."

"How do you know if it feels right?"

"Just do."

"And you couldn't cross on the Tecate Line?"

"No, too crowded."

"And you couldn't cross on the Devil's Highway?"

"No, too far and too hot."

"And you couldn't cross on the reservation?"

"No, too many police."

"And you couldn't cross on the Amnesty Trail?"

"No, too dangerous. And too far." And then as an afterthought: "And they had those spotter things."

A confused bubble of forced sarcastic laughter burst from Andre's lips. "So, where exactly do you want to cross at?"

With a mouth full of gargling beer, I explained. It was an explanation I knew by heart, as each failure I had endured had sharpened my shopping from one of vagueness to one of specificity. "I want someplace where I don't have to walk too far, you know? Someplace where roads are just on the other side of the border like it was in California. But also, no Border Patrol, or not that much Border Patrol anyway." I paused as I considered what else it was that I was looking for. "And another thing, on the Mexican side, I also want it to be at least relatively safe, no cartels, no coyotes—someplace like that."

I was supposed to be doing formal migratory trails. I was supposed to be doing the tried-and-true routes because the border crossing experience was only necessary so that I could better empathize with the Mexican crossers. But somewhere along the way, my mission had changed. I no longer cared about emulating the path and processes of crossing migrants—now I just wanted to cross the fucking border.

Andre rolled his eyes. "Don't you think if such a place existed, all the illegal aliens would be using that point and therefore, by paradox, it would no longer be the place you wanted because of all the illegal aliens using it?"

I shrugged. "Dunno. It's a big border. There could be some singular point along it that's easy. And maybe it was never discovered because people are herd animals, pack mentality, you know? No one looking systematically for the holes like I'm doing, they're just following the crowd. Look, I still got three weeks left, I got plenty of time."

"What about just going back to the Tecate Line? I know some of the guys, I could talk to them, they could turn the other way, you slip in . . ."

"No," I stated firmly as I took another swallow. "I will not accept charity. Besides, it'd feel funny going backward, we need to keep the momentum on our side. Keep moving forward."

"Momentum!" Andre laughed. "So . . . where then?"

"Maybe, the ol' Texas Two-Step?"

"What, the dance?"

"Maybe it is. I heard it used in a joke about illegal immigration."

"You'll do this in Texas." He said it as a command, not a question.

"Sure, I feel confident about Texas," I explained. "There's just a little river too. Should be easy."

"You a good swimmer?"

"No, but I'll use a floatie. Those little floatie things you put on your arms. We can stop at a Kmart and I'll buy some arm floaties."

Chapter 18

ANOTHER BODY IN THE RIVER
(EL PASO SECTOR)

Blacker than night were the eyes of Felina,
Wicked and evil while casting a spell.

—Marty Robbins

From orbit at the atmosphere's edge, it's difficult to distinguish El Paso from Ciudad Juárez, each crowding the Rio Grande, polluted and murky from the upstream factories. It's the perennial tale of two cities. Conjoined twins separated after birth by the creation of the border: Romulus and Remus, Cain and Abel. One sibling under the possession of the economic American powerhouse, the other owned by a late-developing nation with rampant crime, corruption, and triple the murder rate of the other.

Consequently, it's impossible to tell the story of El Paso without explaining Juárez.

And it helps to explain Ciudad Juárez to mention that a tiger was discovered roaming the streets in the mid-1990s.

Juárez doesn't have a zoo.

Explaining the tiger doesn't explain anything except to say, that's just the type of place that Juárez is. The type of place that births brand-new subsets of homicide. Juárez is the type of place that creates words like femicide, the systematic killing of women; almost four hundred rapes and murders by strangulation in the last two decades, systematic and continuous, and not a one of them solved.

And explaining that serial killers who prey on women have run freely for twenty years without investigation also doesn't explain anything except, that's just the type of place that Juárez is. The type of place where the federal authorities are forced into large-scale public works projects, like exhuming mass graves where they retroactively attempt to identify the four thousand buried inside, no different from Iraq, or Cambodia under the rule of Pol Pot.

And if you understand this, then perhaps you do understand the type of place that Juárez is.

Of course, the Mexicans have a different understanding of Juárez. For them, Juárez is as California was for the Americans during the Great Depression, a mythologized refuge for the economically disenfranchised from across the country, lured north by far-flung recruiters who aided flight with the luminous slippery promises of steady employment. And from all across Mexico they come, thousands each year, flooding into Juárez where they find work at the maquiladoras, hundreds of international sweatshops set up around the city's edge, and almost all of them owned by U.S. corporations anxious for cheap labor.

Maquiladoras flourished after the North American Free Trade Agreement was signed and they exemplified everything that was hated about outsourcing because that's all they were: the parts were shipped in from the United States, assembled into products in Mexico, and then shipped back to the United States for consumption.

And when the migrants arrived in Juárez, living in slum shantytown colonias that crowded the border with no planning for water or electricity or waste disposal, they were offered fifty dollars a week for six days of work within the factories; it also helps to explain Juárez to say that the cost of living in Juárez is 80 percent of that in El Paso.

And so, because the cost of living is 80 percent that of El Paso, but wages are only 20 percent, they head across the river, and they head north, despite the Minutemen and despite the Border Patrol and despite it being illegal, because this whole living thing?

It demanded survival in a way that could almost be called a genetic predisposition.

WITH JUÁREZ JUST on the other side of the river, I decided to go on a ride-along with El Paso PD, to see the impact that the direct importation of the crime and gangs and drugs of Juárez was having on a major U.S. city geographically tied to the border.

We were parked behind the central district police headquarters, running late, all the other officers having already started their shift when Officer Robert kicked the side panel on the driver's side of his squad car until the panel settled back in place, broken but deceiving. "You have to pay for damage to the cars," he explained, critiquing the side panel to see if it gave the appearance of passing muster.

The interior of the patrol car was filthy. Seats soiled with spilled drinks and sweat, the floorboards covered in cracker crumbs and dirt. The small computer at the patrol car's center console appeared to be a Commodore 64, or an early-generation Apple, ancient—black screen with basic green frost font. No windows and double-clicking, instead it was Alt + Ctrl + F1 for this and Alt + Ctrl + F7 for that. Central District covered downtown El Paso, the river, and most of the border with Mexico, he explained, as he smiled.

Officer Robert was twenty-eight years old, handsome with a shyly flirtatious smile, proudly Mexican American but the sort that Minutemen loved, with marginal Spanish skills, the type of guy who got excited when hearing Toby Keith sing about soldiers and who worshipped at the altar of the Dallas Cowboys; just another red, white, and blue American.

We weren't even out of the parking lot behind the El Paso PD Central Command but two minutes when the calls for service started flooding in, backing up in queue on the small impaired laptop. Officer Robert explained that this was a normative routine, and within the hour, we'd be twenty to thirty calls deep, some of the older nonpriority calls in queue were already five hours old. He repeatedly hit F7 to rotate through the already existing calls for service: a drunk old man outside a 7-Eleven, a body lying in an alleyway, a property damage report, and on it went.

Officer Robert stared at the computer, his fingers F7-ing through the queue, and announced that instead of taking care of the calls for service, we were going to be driving to his house to retrieve his cell phone. He needed to call his wife, see if she could get tickets for a sporting event this weekend. He looked over at me from the driver's seat, wondering if I was judging his dereliction of duty.

I told him that I wasn't.

"CAN YOU FIND a body?" Officer Robert asked.

I shook my head, I didn't see a body.

"If you don't see a body, and I don't see a body, then I'm going to say there's no body. That sound fair to you?"

"Sure."

Officer Robert giggled at my monotone indifference and grabbed up the radio to call the dispatcher. There was no body in the 1800 block, either someone moved it or it got up and moved on, and if they got another call for a body, don't call, just place it at the bottom of queue, someone else will get to it.

Officer Robert guided the cruiser to the side of the road in front of a row of lower-income houses as he continuously pressed F7, advancing through the queue as he sighed, staring at the computer.

He turned to me and asked, "All right by you if we just sit here for a while?"

"That'll be fine," I replied.

Officer Robert explained that there was really no incentive to go out and actually *respond* to calls for service. For one, it was getting ridiculously dangerous. You know the Wild Wild West, right? He pointed at his feet. The Wild Wild West, that was here, in El Paso. People used to think twice about killing a cop. That used to be bad form. Rude, you know? Nowadays, it wasn't nothing and he had two little girls he damn well wanted to see grow up and get married off to some decent men, he couldn't afford to die young.

For another, the country was lawsuit crazy. Police officers were starting to be sued in civil court and the city wasn't defending them, cost too much. And gangbangers were suing all the time now, just to fuck with the cops. And administration was expecting reports on every possibly contentious thought that passed through an officer's head. Mistakes happened, but now you got sued after the fact for them.

For risking life, limb, and civil liability, he made $2,500 a month. He worked on the weekends and days as a security guard at the hospital to make extra money. He emphasized that he really couldn't afford to be sued.

So instead, sometimes he hid out from calls for service.

"That all right with you?" he asked me.

"I ain't got no problems with that," I responded.

We were both quiet for a moment. Officer Robert made a loud slurping sound as he sucked on his soda's straw.

"How'd it get like this?" I asked. "You know, all crazy-like?"

"We're short 350 officers," he explained.

"But how'd it get like that? Being short 350 officers?"

Officer Robert smiled and pointed. From our vantage point on the hill, we could see off across the downtown and the train tracks and the river and all the way into Juárez on the other side.

"Meh-ico," he explained.

El Paso had struggled ever since the Treaty of Guadalupe Hidalgo in

1848, which pushed Mexico south of the river. El Paso was an example of what happened to property values when crack dealers moved into the neighborhood. And the years of economic attrition were showing. North of the city, the Rio Grande was lined with the remnants of a mostly evacuated fragile and dirty industrial endowment. Downtown El Paso was vacant and underdeveloped, mostly abandoned to pawnshops and throngs of Spanish-speaking illegal aliens.

And with no real corporations that called El Paso home, there were no jobs. Why should business bother when Juárez was just across the river? And with all the Mexicans here illegally and the sluggish economy, the government was breaking. No money. The reason they were 350 cops short was the same reason they were short on teachers.

"How's the crime?" I asked.

Officer Robert laughed. "Wild Wild West," he explained. "Gangs, thugs, and drugs, what else do you need to know?"

"And how much of it comes from illegal aliens?" I asked.

He pointed at his computer with the thirty calls in queue.

FOR THE NEXT four hours, we took calls. A domestic dispute between a Fort Bliss soldier recently returned from Iraq to find his marriage ruined in his absence by another man. Graffiti over the windows of the Guitar Warehouse. And always, Officer Robert was exemplary, the perfect cop, kind and generous to the citizens, genuinely concerned about their welfare, dutiful as he promised follow-up visits to investigate on his own time, off shift once he got done at the hospital working as a security guard.

It was midnight when Officer Robert pointed to the right as we drove down the street. I looked to see a parking lot filled with wrecked police cars replete with smashed fenders and crumpled hoods and bullet holes. Dozens of them, one after the other, locked up behind barbed wire.

"We're running out of police cars," he explained. "We don't have the money to fix these old cars that get wrecked or to replace them."

"People want to know why you don't investigate immigration status," I said. "When you encounter someone, and you have reasonable suspicion that they're not an American citizen or a lawfully resident alien, why don't you inquire, investigate further?"

Officer Robert winced at the very idea of such a responsibility.

"How?" he asked.

It was a strange statement coming from a position of authority. In the United States we assumed the ability of each public servant and government entity to be able to adhere to whatever regulation, judicial ruling, or additional encumbrance we threw at them, finite budgets and resources be damned.

We expected our soldiers to fiercely defend us on the battlefield—but not too fiercely lest they accidentally kill an innocent indigenous person. We expected our police to protect us from those who would do us harm, as long as they didn't make the wrong choice in that split second when real-world decisions were made. We expected our Border Patrol to secure our nation's borders, but goddamn, couldn't they do it more humanely?

We didn't realize, and rarely stopped to remember, that at the bottom, underneath the thirty calls in queue we'd lined up for them to deal with, sometimes it became too much and they were forced to start sitting in their patrol cars.

The radio barked alive with the dispatcher offering numbers in progress—secret police code.

Officer Robert put the car in gear and started to pull forward out of our parking spot as he turned to me behind a smile and translated, "Another body in the river."

THE POLICE OFFICERS lined up on the bridge staring into the Rio Grande. They did this every time a Mexican turned up in the river, which was often. The border and the river was fiercely defended with a series of depressed canals big enough to support an Interstate and reaching spiraling stretched barbed-wire fencing and floodlights everywhere.

For the officers, it was an informal meeting, a coffee break, a call to service that they couldn't do anything about since they were patrol officers and not river divers. So instead they watched the boats and rescue personnel below and took a breather.

After all, there were thirty calls in queue.

Chapter 19

THE PRICE OF THE RAIN IN BOLIVIA
(EL PASO SECTOR)

The building we were looking for was located in an epicenter of poverty: a downtown El Paso neighborhood flooded with a parasitic industry of cash advance loan stores, pawnshops, and deteriorated strip clubs where obese aging women gloriously strutted. At the gas station just around the corner, it's nine in the morning when toothless spandex-clad welfare mamas push past Spanish-speaking illegals to buy lottery tickets and beer, counting out the total from a large jar of coins—their own twisted stab at the American Dream. The building itself was crumbly and red-bricked, rough and unseemly, invisible.

"Check it out," Andre said, nudging me as we walked from across the adjacent parking lot. I looked up, following Andre's gaze to the roof where our approach was being watched by two figures. "Spotters, you think?"

"Don't know, guess we'll find out."

We knocked on the door as we stood in the street, waiting patiently.

It was forty-eight hours after our El Paso PD ride-along. We had spent the previous day driving along the Rio Grande where I had refused one opportunity after another to cross into Mexico. Somewhere along the way, we had given up and abandoned entering the U.S. from Mexico; now the goal was simply to cross into Mexico.

I had refused, citing arguments of irreducible logic that I quickly forgot after their delivery.

And after we had been pulled over by Border Patrol and told we needed to evacuate the area as quick as possible due to a Mexican Humvee with a mounted .50 caliber machine gun straddling the border and peering curiously into the United States, we had driven back to our El Paso motel room.

It was then that I told Andre that my attempt at a border crossing had been reduced to necessarily finding a route that was chaperoned by angels; I would accept nothing more difficult. Fortuitous then that our next stop was an underground railroad of sorts operated under the guise of Catholic protection. And we assumed it was an underground railroad because the Catholic organization that managed this particular safe house had sister houses in Juárez. Sister houses where the immigrants started from before ending up here on the U.S. side where they were then sheltered and clothed, fed and offered assistance before dissemination into the country's interior.

As Andre had put it, if I couldn't cross here, with the Catholic Church, free of coyotes and with both a known starting point and a known ending point, all while under the protection of saints, I simply couldn't cross the border.

From the other side of the door, there were the sounds of rapid movement. It took minutes though before the door was opened by a young and blond college-aged girl who peered at us anxiously through a crack.

"Can I help you?"

"Yes, we're journalists, we're here to see your facility."

"Do you have an appointment?" she asked.

"Yes, we do," I responded.

The door closed again as a chain was heard unhinging from its other side.

"Last chance," Andre whispered to me. "Don't fuck it up."

All I had to do was ingratiate myself with our hosts, find out the address of their sister houses in Juárez, make an appointment to visit, and then wait for the next group to leave and hitch a ride.

THE BUILDING WAS one of those that had been brought to full life through years of addendum additions, assimilating what already existed as they went, so that the final structure was a curious hybrid of past architectural vision with new floors and added wings, each cheaply constructed, but homely and personable. The front room was for reception and community gathering, a few ratty couches and cork boards. The back room where the staff congregated was part office, part kitchen, part living room. A sign on the refrigerator, which did not work, reminded not to put meat inside, "or the blood will be on your hands!" Stuffed animals were gathered atop the fridge. Signs carried inspiringly insipid messages like, "If you want peace, work for justice." A painted picture of Che Guevara looked down on us from the wall.

The facility was managed by a full-time staff of volunteers who lived on the premises in exchange for free room and board. They earned ten dollars a month in spending money, which was the only gratuity the foundation could afford. Each managed a caseload of illegal immigrant clients they counseled on how to operate within America, on how to maneuver within the system.

Dan, a former school bus driver from Colorado who had been inspired by the hardworking but poor migrants he had driven to school day after day, and who was delaying law school to be here, was also responsible for food. As he explained this, Dan sat on a broken office chair as he sorted peppers into two buckets—one for the dearly departed and expired, another for the still questionably consumable.

A man named William explained that he had worked at a Fortune 500 company, making six figures in Silicon Valley, an important type of person. Until one day he realized it was all fucking meaningless and had given away everything, quit his job, and moved down here to the border where he now wore secondhand T-shirts and pedaled a used old-fashioned ten-speed bike around town. He explained this as the best decision he had ever made. The people here, the Mexicans, were the best human beings he had ever met, hardworking and helpful; the facility practically ran itself. Everyone here was conjoined by the feeling of being a fugitive, you never had to ask for help with dinner, it was offered by too many willing to lend a hand.

Lucy had graduated from Georgetown University, prestigious, you know? Could've done anything she wanted, was choosing between Harvard and Princeton for graduate school. Good family, rich too. But she also had chosen a life of destitute humanitarianism for the next few years.

Good for the soul and all that.

THEY CALLED HIM SALVADOR, probably because that's where he came from. Salvador was afraid to leave the facility now. He was nervous and fidgety, anxious as he simply hovered around the windows, peering outside at the big ol' USA, intimidated as hell. Salvador had almost been picked up by Border Patrol who had been driving the street outside. When he had been approached by the officers, he had run inside. The officers had knocked on the door, a break in the "no questions asked" detente between the facility and Border Patrol. The volunteers had asked the officers if they had a warrant. Safe house, right? Border Patrol had relented and Salvador had avoided a return trip to Latin America. Filled with gratitude, and to become useful, Salvador had placed himself in charge of cooking the evening meal. Rumor had it, he cooked a mean tamale.

As Salvador explained in the day room through his translator, another migrant of considerable English skill named Juan, it took him a month to get here. And everything was riding on Salvador's success—and by that he meant literally everything. Back home were his mother and his grandmother and his cousins and his father, all hungry and hopeful, who had sent Salvador north with the grand collective investment of twenty dollars, which was all that could be afforded. They needed Salvador to do well, to start sending back that remittance. Hell, back home, you made five dollars in a single day, which was the cost of a single meal. It took Salvador three tries to make it across. He knew it was a numbers game. He had been handcuffed and beaten when caught by the Mexican border patrol during the previous two attempts.

"Twenty dollars," I replied. "That's not a lot of money."

Salvador's eyes narrowed as his face trimmed and he explained this next part seriously.

Juan laughed. "He say, uh, he say he didn't steal once." Juan waved away Salvador's righteous claims with a flippant wave. "He's lying! He's a fucking goddamn thief."

Salvador beamed, thinking he was earning praise.

"What's he want to do now that he's in America?" I asked.

Juan translated, listened to the response, and then sighed heavily. "He say he wants to make bread. He wants to be a bread maker, a, uh, a baker." Juan allowed Salvador a few seconds of his happy dumb puppy beaming smiles before he added. "He's dumb, dude! He don't fucking know what it's like, you know? He's just a dummy!"

I nodded. Perhaps he was a dummy. Perhaps he was.

We didn't have no room for no more bakers in these here United States, I was pretty sure of it.

THE CHURCH MEMBERS sat around the table listening intently, patting the man from Mexico on the back, coaxing him to reveal his soul's every jagged fear for our collective good-natured liberal enlightenment.

"Go on, tell them," the young blond college coed volunteer chided the Mexican, who frowned reluctantly.

The Mexican mumbled in Spanish.

The blond volunteer smiled and patted him on the back again. Good Mexican! That was such a good Mexican!

She turned to myself, Andre, and the church group, who, just maybe, if they were adequately impressed, would donate some money, maybe some groceries or rotten peppers.

"He says, in Chihuahua, he ran a taco stand!"

The church members applauded, their faces alit with dewy comfortable smiles.

Well, a taco stand! Well, that was just fine! Just fine, indeed! No harm in a taco stand, no, sir.

The man mumbled in Spanish.

The blond volunteer smiled, and once more patted him on the back, as she translated, "But he couldn't make his taco stand work, not enough customers."

The church members sighed and shook their heads with angry indignation. What was the world coming to when you couldn't make a proper go of it with an honest taco stand?

The man mumbled in Spanish.

The blond volunteer smiled, and patted him on the back, as she translated, "He would like, if the Lord's willing, to open a taco stand here in the United States."

The Mexican said something else, mumbling, of course.

The blond volunteer laughed as she added his footnote: "But only, that is, if Americans like tacos!"

The church members all laughed. Well, he was in luck, because, as it turned out, Americans did like tacos very much!

Everyone smiled at everyone else, beaming with agreeability.

Everyone, that is, except the Mexican, who frowned.

ISAAC SAT IN the rocking chair sipping an herbal tea as he gently rocked back and forth. Everything about him was minimalistic and deliberately austere, from his hair, which was cropped short, to his clothes, which were casual and secondhand. His house, a block away from the safe house, was subsistent only, which was the way he liked it, the porch creaking with rotted floorboards, the paint peeling and stripped, not because of an imminent renovation, but because it was only paint, an aesthetic and unimportant. His facial expressions were minimalist, his smile subdued, subsistent, yet still pleasant and unforced, and the volume of his voice that of an admonished whisper—you actually had to listen when he spoke.

"We've been around since the late 1970s, it was formed by a group of young Catholic adults. It originally belonged to the diocese and then it got donated to us. We call it hospitality for migrants and refugees and we have actually five houses in our safe zone, three shelters. We have two shelters in El Paso and we have one shelter in Juárez. The border enforcement in this area really started to crank up in the 1990s with Operation Hold the Line . . . and that was when we started to see a decline in the number of people coming here. When the border enforcement started, it started pushing them out to the Arizona desert. Crossing here had dropped by half while Tucson had gone up four times. The rationale of Operations Gatekeeper and Hold the Line is that we won't let them cross here in the cities and it'll be a deterrent since they'll have to cross in the desert. But it's completely failed. They continue to cross in the desert. Ten years ago, up and down the border about a million people were detained each year, and presently, it's about ten million a year. But when you look at the budget, it's increased exponentially. One of the things I've learned is that people don't leave their country on a whim, most people stay in their country even if they're earning quite a bit less. If people are able to provide for their families, they'll stay in their own countries."

Isaac seemed like a smart fellow, the type of guy who just might know the answers to this whole immigration mess, the reason behind it all.

So I asked him.

And he told me.

And the answer to everything had something to do with the dollar's worthless international value and OPEC trading in euros. And this was the answer because war in Iraq and Afghanistan was expensive. And war purchased on the credit of future generations was even more expensive and countries like the OPEC nations preferred trading in stable currencies. The British pound was strong and the dollar was oh so very weak because the British had the backing of the European Union and access to so many low-wage workers of Eastern Europe who were now a part of the European Union. And, to even hope to compete, the U.S. needed low-wage workers too. And that is why they would never completely seal off the Mexican border.

Isaac pointed out to the horizon into Mexico. "Drive to the outskirts of Juárez and you'll find hundreds of American factories, jobs that in Ohio were unionized, where they had to pay forty and fifty thousand dollars a year. They pay a dollar fifty an hour over there, the Mexicans can't sustain themselves, so they come across. And this also fills a need for low-wage workers over here. The only concerns being met are the concerns of the corporations, because that's capitalism, our American free market. You want to know who's to blame for the border crisis? For Mexicans rushing the fence, pull into a Wal-Mart parking lot and watch the people rush the doors to satiate their desire for so much cheap crap, and that is your answer."

"Do you ever fear being raided?" I asked, trying to avoid asking the one question I was supposed to ask, the question about visiting their sister house in Juárez, the question that would move me incrementally closer to being able to cross with their organization.

There was a long moment before he responded: "The fear is constant."

Isaac cocked his head, noticing in me the unborn question that I grappled with.

But I couldn't get it out.

I couldn't get it out because he and all the rest of them were too decent. I couldn't get the question out, because I didn't want to piggyback on their sincere efforts for the personal profit of my book. I felt shamed, confronted with the collective nobility of the Mexicans and for attempting the same experience for what amounted to nothing more than a personal adventure by one who didn't need to.

So instead I said nothing.

ANDRE AND I lay in our respective beds within the darkness of our El Paso motel room listening to the radio. Sean Hannity was interviewing Asa Hutchinson, the former director of the DEA, as they discussed a confidential 2005 internal government warning of tenuous cooperation between terrorists and drug cartels.

"So what state are we waiting for you to do your crossing in now?" Andre asked. "Louisiana? Arkansas? Oh wait, there aren't any more states with a Mexican border!"

I didn't respond.

"You know what you should call your book?" Andre asked from his bed.

"What?" I asked, my voice breaking in the darkness.

"*Waiting for Rico*. Like *Waiting for Godot*, yeah?"

"What's that mean?"

"It means you wait and wait and plan and plan, but you never cross the border."

I sat up in bed and turned to him in the darkness. "I *am* going to do it, I just don't want to do it half-assed."

"Okay . . . sure," Andre replied, smirking silently as he rolled over.

I reached beside me and turned on the lamp, flooding the room with light, causing Andre to sit forward with bleary eyes and look over at me.

"What do you mean by that?" I asked, my voice trembling.

"It means you're a coward, dude," Andre replied calmly. "No offense. I don't think I'd cross the border either, but everywhere we go all you do is come up with excuses for not crossing the damn border."

"Because everywhere we go, there's border security!" I replied, exasperated.

"Yeah! It's the border!" Andre laughed. "You're going to find border security on the border, yeah? At a certain point in time though you just have to jump. Do the damn thing already, brother."

I turned the light back off and shrank into my blankets.

"Well, I'll tell you what I don't need is you pressuring me, you building it up into this big thing and making it difficult."

"No, you're doing that yourself," Andre replied, turning in his blankets away from me.

We both pretended to sleep as I contemplated his criticisms.

So what if I didn't end up crossing the border? That would make for a funny book. The protagonist would plan for it and then never actually do it—that would be entertaining.

Right?

Entertaining?

No, that would suck.

I frowned in the darkness, suddenly consumed by my fears and failings.

He was right, of course. I *was* stalling. I was stalling because it had been a big joke when I had submitted the idea to the publisher, something theoretically envisioned from my home in Europe without ever having seen the border. And now here, faced with the *real* border, I had become scared and was trying to avoid the one thing I had been assigned to do.

But the border was, in many ways, very much like a war zone—contested territory in a battle with men with guns and bad intentions on both sides. Trying to cross the border as myself seemed akin to running back and forth naked with flapping arms between the trenches of dug-in soldiers of the First World War and hoping for survival. It seemed suicidal and stupid.

I swung my legs over the side of the bed and was quiet as I studied him.

And then, I silently dressed and put on my shoes.

I gathered my things, packing my rucksack and my man-purse limply in the dark.

I moved to the door and cracked it open slowly, cringing as the door squeaked in protest, appalled at my imminent departure. I offered one last look back in on Andre and started to move through the door.

And then Andre's voice from behind me: "Where you going, dude?"

"Uh, tacos. Taco Bell is open twenty-four hours. You want one?"

"Yeah, sure. Bring me a taco," he replied with a yawn before turning into his pillow and becoming indecipherable.

I closed the door.

Andre never got his taco.

I WAS SITTING in my truck silently observing one of the many maquiladora sweatshops that ran along the periphery of Juárez. I watched the buses pull up and the workers trudge out, passing the outgoing shift and everyone listless and dead, the minutes and seconds of their lives sacrificed to the industrial machine that ran around the clock.

I knew certain things but I didn't know enough. My tracts of knowledge were clouded, obscured by my own ignorance. I didn't know how to make sense of them or how to parse the propaganda from the facts. I didn't know how to do this because it was economics and complex and I wasn't that smart. I felt helpless recognizing the shadow of some giant leviathan passing overhead, influencing events outside of media awareness and the normative fact-sets that were required for day-to-day living.

For instance, I knew that the corporations, which started their plundering centuries ago with names like the Dutch West India Company, which pilfered newly discovered lands of the Western Hemisphere for riches despite already existing indigenous peoples, hadn't really changed all that much. The primary difference being that now instead of being owned by monarchs and kings, they were transnational, country-hopping the globe for desperate Third World economies that would provide perpetual tax-free holidays without environmental regulation in exchange for a meager sliver of poor-paying jobs. First World working-class jobs got outsourced and the poor people who assumed them earned a third of 1 percent of the cost of the garments they manufactured.

I knew of CIA action against the Sandinistas in Nicaragua, and U.S. Marines enforcing corporate profits in Honduras, and democratically elected socialist leaders in places like Guatemala being replaced by ruthless American-backed dictators. Ostensibly, this had all been done to stop communism, but the secondary effect had been to allow U.S. corporations to continue their ownership of the natural resources and wealth in faraway countries where they were not based.

I knew that development loans given out by the World Bank and the International Monetary Fund came with fine-print obligations to contract out infrastructure projects to large, already rich First World corporations and forced accession to shitty trade policies that benefited few, like in Bolivia with the rain. When Bolivia sought to refinance the public water service of its third largest city, the World Bank offered the loan with the requirement that the public water be privatized. The San Francisco–based Bechtel Corporation won the contract and started charging the local population, most of whom subsisted on two dollars a day, up to a quarter of their earnings for access to fresh water. In collusion with the government, it became illegal to gather runoff from precipitation, which is, after all, how a corporation came to control the rain.

I knew of discovered lobbyist disclosure forms filed with the U.S. House of Representatives I had found online that listed page after page of U.S. corporations making millions of dollars in donations in an attempt to influence Latin American foreign policy; billions of dollars secretly being funneled for covert influence in countries where the contributors did not live.

These were the things I knew, but they were simply pieces of a larger story, the details of which I was ignorant of. So instead of being outraged, I mused contemplatively. And as I watched the Mexicans enter the maquiladora, the hours and years of their lives traded for pennies on the dollar, the profit being pocketed somewhere further up the food chain, I felt a strong kinship in our shared victimization to policies and forces we knew nothing about. We were pathetic in our common helplessness, and it was within this shared idiocy that I felt an emerging brotherhood that defied language and cultural barriers.

And suddenly, I felt as if I didn't want to learn any more about the border; I was too afraid of what else I'd discover.

My investigation felt complete.

I simply didn't know what else I could expect to find except more frustration.

And, consequently, there was nothing left to do but cross the border.

Chapter 20

NO MORE BORDER
(McALLEN SECTOR)

I spit back the bugs attempting entry into my mouth as I lay on the dirt mound, shrugging away the scratchy antenna end of too many weeds brushing my face as I watched the dubious conglomeration of men in the pickup trucks just south of the U.S. border through my binoculars as they, in turn, watched the U.S. border with their own binoculars. I looked at my watch, and sighed; they looked to be planning something and unlikely to leave anytime soon.

I climbed up off the hill and dusted myself off as I slid down the slight embankment back to the rental car I had crossed the border to acquire in Juárez, then driven back to the States before departing for Mexico. I grabbed the map off the passenger seat and looked for my next spot. The problem with the portion of Mexico across from Texas is that there is a dearth of easily accessible towns on both sides of the border.

And at each point of failure, from Ojinaga to Piedras Negras, I felt the anxiety within me broaden and steady its center. It was because I had given up and retreated in the past that it became easier to give up and retreat now. The contemplation time between serious consideration and actual evacuation was irreducibly growing smaller with each passing hour. Like a seasoned legal counselor with well-rehearsed arguments, my mind already knew the evidence to be presented; it was simply a matter of rapidly flashing through the exhibits and then leaving.

I had become conditioned to the peculiar paralysis that took hold at every potential crossing site like Pavlov's dog. I had rewired myself physiologically to resist actually crossing the border. Yet just as I was more easily conceding failure, there was also a correlating increase in despondency with each assumed border crossing abort. Just as the Mexican migrants who crossed were desperate, so now was I. I no longer knew anything of journalistic literary assignments or of attempting to re-create the experiences of migrants. All I knew was that I yearned to reach that northern border, difficult and unobtainable.

The migrants and I, we had become one and the same.

I yawned and felt the pull of gravity on my eyelids as I struggled against the urge to nap. It was a new self-imposed handicap—I wouldn't sleep until I crossed, and I hadn't been sleeping for two days now. I cursed myself for another failure as I started the car's engine and attempted to think of another handicap to apply to myself. That's how it worked, the more you failed, the more handicaps you applied. It was a treasonous form of self-motivation, the hope being that eventually the fear of imminent application of yet another handicap would force me to say to hell with it and cross despite the dangers and excuses I found at each spot I investigated.

I wished I hadn't left the gun with the truck in America so that I could shoot myself in the foot—because that would be a real handicap. Surely knowing that the next time I failed to cross the border I was going to necessarily have to shoot myself in the foot would be the type of proper motivation to instigate a reluctant individual such as myself into daring action.

And then, I started laughing crazily.

What did I intend to do with my rental car?

Even if I had found a spot, what was my intention, to abandon the rental and come back for it later? And if somewhere in the back of my mind I knew I was trapped, tethered by my responsibility to the rental car, what did that mean about my border surveillance?

Was I seriously assessing the border for the feasibility of crossing or simply stalking it like a deranged obsessive jilted lover?

A ND THEN, JUST like that, I ran out of border.

Late afternoon outside Matamoros, Mexico.

Above me, the fractal reflection of a fat tawny honeyed ball of light descended onto the Gulf of Mexico as I sat on the beach. The waves cresting as a preening green fan before merging imperceptibly with the deep blue further out.

I snickered quietly as I looked over the map, this couldn't be right. All of Texas, which loomed long and large across the continental United States, and there had only been a meager handful of opportunities.

And why the hell didn't Mexico build more access roads anyway?

Didn't they know that there were folks who needed to escape?

I set the map down beside me as I basked in the euphoria of prolonged sleep deprivation.

Andre had been right.

I had run out of border.

Part Six
DESPERADO

Desperado,
why don't you come to your senses?

—*Eagles, "Desperado"*

Chapter 21

A LONG, DANGEROUS DRAG THROUGH TEXAS
(LAREDO SECTOR)

The world is full o' complainers. An' the fact is, nothin' comes with a guarantee. Now, I don't care if you're the Pope of Rome, President of the United States or Man of the Year; somethin' can all go wrong. Now go on ahead, y'know, complain, tell your problems to your neighbor, ask for help, 'n watch him fly. Now, in Russia, they got it mapped out so that everyone pulls for everyone else . . . that's the theory, anyway. But what I know about is Texas, an' down here . . . you're on your own.

—*Blood Simple*

It was eleven at night, and going on to my third day of no sleep, as I pulled into line at the rear of the vehicle queue for entry back into the United States at Laredo. My present plan was to reenter at Laredo, and then cut across Texas backcountry to El Paso where I'd cross the bridge, return my rental car in Juárez, and pick up my truck. And after that, I was heading home to Denver to return the truck and the gun.

I was done with the border.

I realized, somewhere behind my conscious mind, that I was quite high, my mood buoyed and inebriated by a straining adrenal gland forced into overtime by my perpetual lack of sleep. Sleep deprivation was a funny thing, because if you could carry it past the exhaustion, you found a hidden reservoir, that second wind which burned like incense-flavored caffeine. The problem with the second wind, of course, was that when it finished, it crumbled like an imploding building and you crashed hard. But if you soldiered onward, straining the eyeballs to stay open as the blood capillaries burst inside, offering the retina a little crimson splash of flavoring, then you found the third wind. And the third wind was rapturous, a tingling relaxation, as if taking ecstasy. The problem with the third wind was that the inevitable crash was like jump-ing out of a plane without a parachute—it was a full-velocity plummet.

I PULLED FORWARD and smiled delicately, presenting my passport as my dewy forehead became heavy with perspiration. The terse frowning Hispanic officer with the crew cut reached for my passport and swiped it through his machine as I sighed heavily, too loudly, worried about imag-ined and imminent blinking messages on his screen that I couldn't see but knew would bleep in a flashing sharp robin-red boldface font fol-lowed by too many exclamation points, stating that I was to be refused entry.

His face darted up from my passport, studying my sigh. I noticed his terrible scrutiny and forcibly transformed my face to a practiced arti-ficial gaze I liked to call "relaxed ambience." And then I wondered if my facial transformation had been performed too rapidly. I wondered if my facial transformation had appeared unduly unnatural. As I pon-dered these questions, I was quite sure it was perceived by the customs agent as one of mental preoccupation by one who was worriedly attempt-ing to conceal important facts.

Which, actually, I was.

The truth of the matter was that I felt as if I had a helluva lot to declare.

He studied me.

He studied my passport.

He studied me, again.

"Why are you coming to the United States today?"

The question took me off guard, I wasn't a visitor. I may not have been living in the States, but America would be my home until the day I died. It was like arriving at your mom's for Christmas dinner and having her ask why you had come.

"It's my home," I replied uncomfortably, unsure of the reason for his question.

"You live in Europe? Why are you coming back?" he asked, glaring just a bit.

And suddenly, it seemed as if he knew the true purpose for my visit.

He was only waiting for me to admit it.

"Uh, I'm here on work," I replied, trying very hard to be casual, my face flushing guiltily.

"And what do you do for work?" he asked.

"Uh, I'm a journalist, I guess," I said as I averted my eyes.

"A journalist you guess?"

"Yeah."

"What type of stories do you guess you write?"

"Uh, people that aren't supposed to be in the United States, I guess."

"Uh-huh."

"And you're driving a car with Mexican plates?" he asked.

"Well, I was driving in Mexico," I replied, an answer that was no good whatsoever.

"And why were you driving through Mexico?" he asked.

I paused for an inordinately long period of time as I struggled to think of a proper response. "I don't know."

"Where are you supposed to return your car at?"

"Ciudad Juárez."

"You're a long way from Ciudad Juárez."

"Yeah, well, I thought I could just zip through Texas to El Paso, and then return it."

"Just going to zip across Texas, huh? Texas is a big place."

"Yeah, but it's still drivable."

"Where are you coming from?"

"Uh, Ciudad Juárez."

He frowned.

"And where's your final destination?"

I paused as I stumbled over the question, "You mean, like, ultimately in an existential sense, or just like—"

"I mean, after Juárez, where are you headed?"

"Uh, Denver."

The perspiration on my brow, which had been holding steady at contemplation, began to drip in a regular rhythm as I saw the customs agent become increasingly confused at my schizophrenic itinerary.

I giggled nervously.

The stern Hispanic officer frowned at the giggles.

Giggles were no damn good.

You weren't supposed to giggle guiltily when going through Immigration.

"I'm going to need you to go park in spot number five," he replied, with a frowning unhappy grimace.

AN OFFICER SQUATTED to his heels as he began pounding on the passenger door panels below the window as two additional officers sorted through the inventory of my rucksack that was spread out over the sterile metal table I was standing behind, lifting underwear on the tips of ball-point pens, their noses smelling shampoo for malfeasant motive.

"Pound away, Officer, you won't find anything," I replied, cocksure and arrogant from behind the metal table.

The officer sighed and replied, "Well, I wouldn't be too sure about that."

"Yeah, why is that?" I asked, smirking quietly, chomping some gum.

"Well, for one, this car has been used for drug smuggling."

"Eh? What's that?" I replied, my gum bubble bursting onto my nose and lips as I nervously shoved my hands in my pockets.

"SIR, HANDS OUT OF THE POCKETS!" yelled the second agent who was sorting through my clothes.

I removed my hands from my pockets and displayed them prominently in the air for inspection.

"Yeah, these side panels," the first agent explained, pointing to the car. "The screws aren't in all the way. And up underneath the dashboard, the carpet's been removed. The back seat comes out too easily . . ." He continued to walk around the car, pointing out the vehicle's checkered criminal past.

And as the officers continued to search the car, using various devices to scan its metal interior, examining the engine and the trunk, I started to feel that bite of distant encroaching anxiety. "I wouldn't know anything about that. It's a rental you understand."

I started to move around the table toward the glove box, which held my rental paperwork.

"SIR, BACK BEHIND THE TABLE!" the second officer yelled.

I moved back behind the table as my mouth went dry and I began to wonder if the smugglers who had rented the car before me had accidentally left something deep inside the car's metal bowels, a little present for the next person in line. And try explaining that in federal court.

I watched with bated breath as a new female officer brought in a German shepherd to sniff the exterior of my car. I had been living in the car while in Mexico and, consequently, my car had been compiling numerous strange odors: cigarettes and body odor and fast food. It wasn't a clean car; it was the type of car that would give a nose hound an orgasm. Consequently, it seemed unfair to have my fate decided by a dog. Dogs didn't know anything. Dogs humped your leg and pulled on the leash to be able to smell a pile of shit. I tried reminding myself that these were professional dogs. Dogs that were well trained, disciplined.

The dog began to excitedly bark.

"He's picking up something!" his female handler yelled.

"All right, break her down!" the first officer yelled, twirling his fingers in the air, which I interpreted as the signal to dismantle my car.

A moment later and two officers carried my back seat and set it down beside me.

"Be careful there fellas, it's a rental car," I said as I grimaced, wondering if the extra rental insurance I hadn't bother to purchase in an attempt to save money covered such things as border checkpoint dismemberment.

I was asked about my writing assignment as one of the officers assigned to underwear detail started flipping through the manila envelopes inside my tote bag—each sealed and marked in black marker chicken scratch with labels like: *Possible Entrance Points into the United States* and *Border Security Weaknesses Research*.

"You want to explain this?" the grim buzz cut officer asked through clenched teeth, his gripped fist fanning my folders. I had the strong feeling of being mere moments away from being declared an enemy combatant and transported to Guantánamo.

I T WAS TWO in the morning after clearing another immigration checkpoint where I had been detained for another half-hour. I was thirty minutes outside a small south Texas burg called Crystal City when reality began to bleed. In my rearview mirror, I saw a Chinese lantern off in the distance, papier-mâché bits of orange crepe paper dancing like simulated flame within it. I stretched my eyes, briefly closed them tight, and then reopened them, turning back into my rearview mirror. The Chinese lantern was gone, it was only a distant light, blinking and beckoning in the lonely drawl of the early-morning night. And then, suddenly the lantern was back—always just two hundred yards in the distance no matter how far I drove—no matter how many curves in the road I took. Ahead of me, the various lights and reflections took on spherical three-dimensional illuminated form, shimmering as plastic bulbs or lava lamps.

The high caused by my sleep deprivation had vanished and I was straddling complete collapse, hallucinating now, an acrobat on the high wire in the big circus tent, but flailing my arms and intoxicated and about ready to lose my balance and plummet.

A car drove up beside me, its passengers peering over to examine me, caring little for subtlety or discretion, just staring at the monkey in the zoo. Satisfied I wasn't a real Mexican, or else that I was harmless, a fact most likely gathered from my slightly fearful return gaze, they accelerated and passed me. It was typical behavior thus far. I had seen vehicles with Mexican plates in El Paso, and they had seemingly been offered no additional scrutiny by the other drivers on the road. After all, not all Mexicans weren't allowed into America, some had work visas or legitimate tourist visas. But that had been a border town in a largely Hispanic city where Spanish was spoken just as frequently as English. This was South Texas, heartland country. And out here, the other drivers seemed to involve themselves personally in investigating the strange driver with the Mexican plates.

And couldn't they immediately see that I wasn't Mexican? Was there really a need for the prolonged gawking stares. As I caught my reflection in the rearview mirror, I realized that maybe there *was* a need for a concentrated examination. I was darkly tan now after weeks on the border and I was starting to kind of look, well, not exactly Mexican, but not exactly white, either. A light-skinned Mexican or of European Spanish descent, perhaps.

Well, fuck them. I was Mexican and in their country. So what?

What the hell were they going to do about it, anyway?

I turned on the radio hoping for some coast-to-coast radio, but I could only pick up mariachi music from a station within Mexico.

I WAS DRIVING around Crystal City looking for a safe spot, which I assumed would be in numerous supply in quaintly quiet small rural Texas with its handsome clapboard homes and genteel strip shopping centers interspersed with too many Baptist churches and bars. I just needed somewhere to pull over where I could get a few hours of power napping, shave off the growing bite of exhaustion: a grocery store parking lot, a library, even an empty Dumpster. If I only slept a couple of hours, I still might be able to make it to El Paso by midday, which was quickly becoming a surreal quest of an impossible order.

But why? I asked myself.

Why was it so necessary to get to El Paso?

The answer was, of course, because I wanted to vacate the entire border region of the United States as soon as possible. That and I had to pay for an additional day if my rental wasn't back by noon tomorrow and I was quickly going broke.

And that's when I noticed the red Ford truck pacing me at each intersection, one street down on a parallel avenue. The driver was obscured by interior darkness of the vehicle. Instead of staying on the road, I took a left and immediately looked into my rearview mirror to see the red truck pull up to the intersection, and then also turn left, now behind me and following quickly.

I pulled into the parking lot of a crowded twenty-four-hour gas station. I watched as the red truck slowly circled the gas station, slow and methodical, before it disappeared behind the gas station's left flank.

The gas station parking lot was filled with three brand-new large extended-cab well-muscled pickup trucks, the sort you saw in the television ads that hauled jet planes. They were each filled with white teenagers, laughing with one another, shouting to the occupants of the other trucks.

And what fucking day was this anyway?

I had no idea.

I struggled hard to think, my brain itching as I did so.

It was Friday. I was 70 percent sure it was Friday.

And this was how teenagers spent Friday night in small and rural south Texas. They drove around their small towns in their pickup trucks and hung out at the gas station. Someone had probably smuggled a few six-packs of beer that they would later consume under the bleachers of the local high school.

Sad, I thought to myself.

"Amigo," the voice said.

I didn't think the voice was talking to me as I obviously didn't speak Spanish, but I turned anyway. It belonged to another young man, white and in his early twenties, who was parked a few spots down from me and who suddenly opened up the hood of his truck, pretending to tinker inside, while feigning frustration.

"JUMPER . . . CABLES, NO?" he asked, accentuating each word loudly and clearly so I'd better understand his English.

"Lo siento, no hablo inglés," I replied sheepishly, shrugging my shoulders, not understanding what he was trying to ask me as I moved past him and the eyes of the teenagers in the other trucks peered toward me, their laughter quieting.

I walked inside the gas station where I bought three Red Bulls, drank them in rapid succession on the toilet, promptly urinated, and then moved back out to my Mexican car, temporarily reenergized with an already dying caffeine injection.

The parking lot was empty now, all the trucks gone, including that of the young man who had supposedly needed a jump start. I peered around the gas station in all directions—there was also no sign of the red truck that had been following me. But the silence and the sudden quiet had an uneasy quality to it. It seemed artificial, fake, a facsimile of genuine privacy.

I quickly jumped into my car and started her up, reversing out of my spot with a squealing of my tires as I drove back onto the main road anxious to get out of town. I didn't feel safe catching even a few hours of sleep in Crystal City. I imagined pulling in behind some Dumpster and then while I slept being snuck up on by bored half-drunk testosterone-filled teenagers looking to cause a little mayhem. And wasn't it in rural Texas where they still had the occasional story of black men being lynched even in this first part of the twenty-first century?

Mexicans too, I imagined.

Mexicans, like myself.

T'S BOTH THE wonder and terror of rural Texas that at three in the morning, the highways are all but deserted. If you're looking for solitude, then it's a wondrous break from the claustrophobia of city dwelling. But if you're scared and desperately needing sleep, it's a terrible thing to contemplate, because you realize a side-of-the-road nap leaves you completely vulnerable to the local character. And in gun-toting redneck Texas, it wasn't a character I trusted, what with being Mexican and driving a car with Mexican plates.

I listened to the mariachi music as, somewhere in the distance, behind an early A.M. mist that concealed the bluffs and open fields, a radio tower blinked, reflecting and refracting in a yellow smog that encompassed the road.

The car's headlights bounced off the median and mile markers, appearing to me as twisting sparkling diamonds and spinning miniature light tornadoes. Behind me, in the rearview mirror, the Chinese lantern with the paper flames pursued. The road twisted and bent, and each time I turned the steering wheel, the road jacked itself a few degrees off my intended course, forcing me to make last-minute adjustments to my trajectory as I barreled down the highway.

The shadows bent and dripped and exploded around me in brilliant displays of shaded dark that transformed and crashed upon the interior of my car in a spray of violet amethyst before sliding slowly to the floorboards like syrup.

I wasn't just dealing with severe sleep deprivation, I was also dealing with the legacy of too much lysergic acid diethylamide during college, which kicked back into play whenever I got real tired at typically inconvenient moments like this one.

My eyes bulged, feeling scratchy and itchy and bruised as if blow-dried as I fought against every wink, not trusting even the slightest and briefest of eyelid closures. I was pitched forward over the steering wheel as I laid heavy on the gas in an attempt to more quickly arrive at the next town. I was dropping fast and my third wind was peeling back, and I was unraveling as it went. And when my eyes couldn't stand it anymore, when the dry burning felt like sandpaper, I let them blink shut, a momentary application of moisture.

And then I wondered how long they had been closed.

I reopened them and didn't recognize any of my surroundings.

How long had I been driving like that?

My throat tightened uncomfortably around anxious erratic breaths, squelching and resisting the urge in my stomach to expunge too much acidic buildup. I began to vomit and clenched it off as a pungent red slime of Red Bull residue slid from the corner of my lips down my face.

I put on my blinker and started to pull to the shoulder of the highway. I had wanted to sleep in a town, where there was at least some semblance of protection. The occasional passing car, local police, parking lot lights—but I was past the point of being able to be picky. I would have to take my chances here on the side of the road.

And then, in my rearview mirror, I noticed a distant pair of headlights with their brights on. The headlights crested a hill and its adjacent declining slope in a second and a half. This was one fast-moving vehicle. Behind the first pair of headlights came a second pair. I kept driving with my blinker on. I decided I'd wait for them to pass me before I pulled over.

It took mere seconds for the headlights to traverse the distant horizon where they had first peaked to now closing in quickly one hundred yards behind my car. The vehicle must've been going over a hundred miles per hour and it didn't look like it was slowing as it closed in as if to smash into my rear fender. There wasn't even a slight drop in speed, or a turn signal offering advance notice of a move into the neighboring lane to pass me. The headlights were lifted high, belonging to a truck of some sort, and as the truck accelerated into the position already occupied by my own car, I braced myself for impact, gritting my teeth as my body cringed, my limbs locking out against the wheel and the gas pedal.

The truck was just inches off my rear bumper when it slowed down, maintaining my pace, the light from its headlights flooding the interior of my car in a ghostly white phosphorous. I was trapped!—unable to evade, unable to outrun, and unable to slow down for fear the slightest drop in speed would cause the truck to collide with my own vehicle.

I pumped the accelerator, hoping for some final burst of speed from my rental car, the engine of which was already screaming, as it was revved beyond its capacity. Smoke would start billowing from the engine block any second.

I veered sharply into the lane of oncoming traffic that wasn't and the truck followed, keeping perfect pace, attached like a magnet.

I swerved back, the truck followed.

"JESUS FUCKING CHRIST! LEAVE ME ALONE!" I yelled.

I think I screamed. I'm not sure. Memory loses lucidity without the cushion of sleep.

The road stretched and began to breathe, as if a giant pair of lungs were encased under the asphalt, slowly rising and dropping. The yellow paint hyphenating the highway's center began to smear across the road, exploding like yellow paintball pellets.

I wiped my eyes, blinking them rapidly as I wiped the sweat from my face.

Jesus, I was going fucking bat-shit crazy!

And then, just as quickly as it had arrived, the headlights fell back, as if a bungee jumper had stretched to the furthest edge of its tether and then shot backward. And a second later, the headlights were gone, replaced by red twin dotted taillights turning around and heading back the way they had come.

I gasped silently, heaving for air as I rolled down the window.

In my rearview mirror there were two pairs of headlights in the far distance, circling each other, rotating between red taillights and white headlights as they performed U-turns in the road. And then it was head-lights again, speeding toward me.

"Come on! Come on!" I screamed at my car as I pumped the accelera-tor, hoping for a different result. Hoping that on miracle tap number eighty-six, the car had been secretly programmed like a James Bond vehicle to dump the nitrous and miraculously achieve speeds of two-hundred-plus miles per hour.

This time the truck pulled up next to me. I had the feeling of laughter, of pointing, of yelling, of agitated emotional communication being passed on in my general direction.

I tried my best to ignore it as I struggled to maintain control of the car and stay on the road. It was just another rural Texas welcome to a foreign visitor, nothing unusual.

And then the truck started swerving into my lane, driving me onto the shoulder as I felt myself lose control of the wheel, gravel spraying out from behind the tires. And then, also just as suddenly, the vehicle was gone, just retreating red lights racing into the darkened distance.

I straightened out my vehicle and exhaled a big sigh.

Was this all some type of payback by the universe for quitting?

I laughed at the notion, of course I didn't believe in such things.

I would pull into the next town, get some sleep, return the rental car to Juárez, move on to Denver, return the truck and the gun, head back to Europe, gather my notes, write my book. The only difference being I never actually crossed the border.

There was no such thing as bad luck or cosmic payback.

I noticed the coyote for a single second, my headlights catching it sideways in the face as it curiously looked up, and for the briefest of moments, the coyote and I locked eyes with each other, before I hit it straight on, catching its head with the center of my front bumper.

I skidded to a stop in the middle of the highway, breathless as I stared into my rearview mirror and tried to make out its form from within the shadows, tinged red from my brake lights. I sat there for a moment wondering if I should take a look. And why did I want to look after all? It was surely going to be a horrible thing to behold. But all I could think about was the poor beast panting for breath, slowly dying alone in the desert. It was my fault and I felt the responsibility to bear witness to what I had done. The animal wouldn't appreciate my presence, but I also wouldn't appreciate myself simply driving on, casually shrugging my shoulders and going to sleep on the side of the road.

I opened the door and stepped onto the road. The desert was filled with the distant sounds of crickets and hundreds of other nighttime creatures serenading in synchronistic harmony. I took cautious steps backward wondering if I had imagined the whole thing, if this was simply a part of the hallucination.

And then I saw the smeared blood and I followed the trail of intestines, which had apparently hooked on to the undercarriage of my car and began to unravel like a spool of twine. The intestines ended in a body, cut cleanly in half, the hot organs still glistening and steaming in the cool of the early-morning hour. Its head was eviscerated, its brains smeared pâté and not a cracker in sight.

I stumbled to the side of the road and threw up.

And it was there, pitched over the side of the road, the granules of sand biting into my palm, sinewy strands of vomit hanging from my mouth, that I wondered how much more punishment I was due before my penance for failure was considered paid in full.

Not only was the universe out to get me for quitting, I was being targeted with a vengeance.

Chapter 22

STINKING OF PISS AND PETROL
(NEW MEXICO SECTOR)

I awoke at a Border Patrol checkpoint at three o'clock in the afternoon.

I was hungry, but more than that I wanted a shower. How long had it been since I showered? El Paso when I was with Andre?

But more than a shower, I wanted to get away from the border.

On bare feet I jumped across burning asphalt and thanked the Border Patrol agents for letting me spend the night and then got back into my car and continued on to El Paso.

STILL ON THE ROAD, four days straight now with only a nap at the Border Patrol checkpoint and later at an abandoned business center parking lot on the outskirts of El Paso. But at least I was back in my truck and headed north toward Denver so that I could return the gun and the pickup.

Through the windshield it was an oily sea of darkness—a pitch black nothing that stretched until the end of time and space. I was racing into an empty void. I needed to put as many miles between me and the border as quickly as I could. The truck's weak dim headlights splayed on the highway, the meager shafts of light swallowed and absorbed by the velvet darkness. The truck's interior and dashboard vibrated as the engine chugged, coughing and working overtime on its pistons to maintain my speed, making more troubling noises now than before.

I was veering northeast now, and somewhere off to my left, to the darkened north, was the Trinity Site—the location of the first atomic bomb test. I had decided on the scenic route back because I needed to be alone and the Interstate was too crowded a corridor even at this early-morning midnight hour. I wanted to be alone. It was a fear that on a crowded Interstate, too many others would recognize my embarrassment. They'd look over and instantly know I was the guy who had quit on the border.

I looked at myself in the rearview mirror: I didn't have the courage of even Mexican migrant children. And in this realization, I attempted to glean some meager self-respect. Fine, I hadn't crossed the border. I had failed in my purpose for this trip to America. But understanding one's limitations and one's true character was surely something to be admired—it was an infinitely better proposition than sustained self-delusion.

At least, this is what I told myself.

The speedometer was flat, bouncing at ten miles per hour, but in truth it was seven times that. The gas gauge held at only a quarter full and as I studied it, squinting, I could swear I saw it move, dropping incrementally, moving like an inchworm, slowly but surely. I turned on the truck's cab light and squinted at it again—it *was* moving!

"What the fuck?" I exclaimed to no one. I had just filled up in El Paso. That hadn't been even an hour ago! What was I getting now? Eight miles to the gallon?

I exhaled heavily as I turned off the dome light and peered into the darkness.

I imagined myself stuck on the side of the road in the desert, miles from nowhere.

This was not good. Not good at all.

I performed some quick mental estimates, trying to decide if it was best to turn around and head back to Las Cruces to fill up or whether I should continue on, attempting to coast into Alamogordo on fumes.

And then, as I crested a ridge, I saw the lights of Alamogordo far below, distant but fierce pinpricks, congregated together, collapsing on top of one another into a pale white hue on the horizon, shimmering and taunting. It was what I imagined America looked like to astronauts returning from space, gazing at the clustered city lights.

I felt a small inch of space between the bottom of the accelerator and the top of the floorboard. I slammed the pedal, crunching the difference, and the truck's engine jumped octaves, singing soprano now as I roared through the darkness toward the light.

I was a lost soul, navigating the darkness of purgatory looking for heaven, for redemption.

And also for a fill-up at a gas station.

And maybe too some snacks for the road.

The city lights disappeared behind drops in the road that I couldn't see or predict as I prayed the lights hadn't been an illusion as I gripped the wheel, feeling flushed and feverish. And then, moments later, the lights would reappear at the top of another high point—the lights no closer, still distant, and perhaps maybe even further away, as if the city was playing a game with me—itself racing backward so that I'd never reach it.

The city lights disappeared from view again, and when they reappeared, they were now to the north and my left. I wasn't moving in a straight line; in fact, it appeared the highway was leading me away from the city.

I felt my throat constrict, my breaths blocked and stacking up on top of one another somewhere deep down in my esophagus. How could this be? How the hell could the highway not be going to Alamogordo?

My eyes dropped again to the gas gauge, deeply entrenched in the red now.

COASTING ON FUMES and the phantom memory of gas now, the memories of long-ago vapor.

Ahead of me on the road, construction lights indicated an impending detour that I was to reduce my speed for an approaching stop.

"Shit!" I cried as I let off the gas and dropped the speed as I saw the Border Patrol checkpoint ahead of me.

I came to a screeching halt in front of the Border Patrol agent, squinting through my windshield at the stark fluorescent lighting from the overhead roof of the security checkpoint.

"Where you coming from, sir?" a young Hispanic agent asked me, barely looking old enough to have graduated high school.

"Look, Officer, I have no gas left! I need to get to Alamogordo!" I argued, slightly panicked as my eyes darted back and forth between the officer and my dead gas gauge. The officer peered into the interior of my truck, unexcited by my revelatory statement of condition.

"Where are you coming from?" he asked again.

"What does it matter where I'm coming from?" I barked angrily, upset that there were now militarized checkpoints deeply entrenched behind U.S. soil where citizens were required to state their purpose and reason for being.

"Where are you coming from?" he asked again, each of his questions reminding me of what I was trying to forget. He motioned his buddy a few feet away to join him.

I didn't know how to respond to his question. Where was I coming from?

Europe? San Diego? Phoenix? El Paso? Mexico? Take your pick.

"El Paso," I replied angrily.

"Where were you in El Paso?" he asked, the second officer now by his side, shining his flashlight into the interior of my truck.

"Where was I in El Paso?" I broke into maniacal crazed laughter. "I was lots of places in El Paso, what, do you want me to list the streets I was on?"

The flashlight broke from my truck's floorboards to my pupils. I winced and cowered, squinting at the contact.

"This your truck?" the officer asked calmly.

"Yes, it's . . ." I started to reply before realizing that was a lie. "No, it's not my truck."

"You have any weapons in the vehicle with you?"

"No, I don't . . ." I started to reply before realizing this too was a lie. "Yeah, I've got a gun here somewhere," I said, looking around the interior of the truck and wondering where it was.

"Is it yours?"

I sighed. "No . . . no, that's, that's not mine either."

Both officers studied me for a moment, the flashlight on my face, highlighting and amplifying my numerous facial imperfections.

"Pull into bay number three," the officer said.

I SAT IN the holding cell, my hands against the wall, my legs spread, while two new officers searched me. The first one, the young one, overseeing their search.

Of course, I was being detained in a cell. I had quit the border. This was just the latest in what would be a long line of payback. Not from the universe, I had decided. But rather from the Border God, an angry and vengeful deity that hated being teased.

"Look," I replied sighing. "I'm a reporter, okay? I was covering illegal immigration? I've written a book and everything, I'm legit, okay?" I sighed. "Dude, I'm a fucking writer. I'm an author. Books and shit?"

The Border Patrol agents all snickered.

And as I turned, I caught a reflection of myself in the one-way mirror. Me with the wild askew crazy hair and the rumpled clothes and the stench of cigarettes and body odor.

They didn't believe me.

I wouldn't believe me either.

"Why didn't you just tell me that before?" the young officer asked.

"Because I shouldn't have to, I'm in goddamn America and we still have rights don't we?"

The officer shrugged. He wasn't sure.

A fourth officer entered and explained that my vehicle was clear. The dog hadn't found anything but the gun.

They opened the door for me to leave as they handed the pistol back.

I walked across the asphalt, buried in the reflective glare of the overhead fluorescent lights, when I saw the cluster of six officers stand behind me, talking and laughing with one another in the low-decibel giggles reserved for little girls on the playground. Laughing at the pretend writer who wasn't, at the strange and peculiar skinny stinky mess of a man who claimed to be a journalist. I felt the thick burn of shame licking at the back of my neck as I opened the driver's side door, flung the pistol to the floorboard, and dug into my rucksack, throwing its contents all over the interior of the cab until I found a copy of my first book, tucked away at the bottom.

I grabbed a pen and autographed it and, with a wide smirk, started back toward the Border Patrol agents in a confident cocky little strut. They had to know that I was somebody, a goddamn author, a real fucking person. Not a nobody failure who didn't have enough courage to cross a single Mexican border.

As I approached, the giggling cluster of officers quieted, their hands dropping to their sidearms in unison.

"SIR! GET BACK IN YOUR VEHICLE!" an older officer shouted.

I paused halfway across the tarmac, distressed and dejected and confused.

"BUT I WANTED TO SHOW HIM MY BOOK!" I cried. And then, as if to offer proof that this was indeed my intention, I raised the book and shook it. See? A book!

"GET BACK IN YOUR VEHICLE!" the officer shouted again.

"BUT I'M—" I started to say before one of the officers made several threatening steps toward me and I raised my arm in defeat and moved back to the truck.

I collapsed behind the steering wheel, quietly fuming as I turned the key in the ignition. Nothing. Not even a good-faith guttural grunt on behalf of the engine. I sighed and searched through the mess in my passenger seat for my cell phone to call a tow truck.

No service, not even a single bar. Dead phone.

I cringed and got back out of the vehicle and inched my way toward the halfway point across the tarmac where I had been turned back last time, feeling for the imaginary line that I had been banished to.

"SIR, GET BACK IN YOUR VEHICLE! THIS IS THE LAST TIME I'M GOING TO TELL YOU OR I'LL PLACE YOU UNDER ARREST!"

"CAN YOU CALL ME A TOW TRUCK?" I cried a little too weakly. "I'M OUT OF GAS!"

"WE'LL CALL YOU A TOW TRUCK. NOW GET BACK IN YOUR VEHICLE!"

I nodded and moved back to the truck, where I slumped in the driver's seat staring out at the darkened desert for several long moments. And then in a furious and sudden fit, I grabbed the steering wheel, gripping it tightly as I yelled and tried the ignition one more time. The trick was to surprise the truck, catch it off guard and unsuspecting during a moment of lulled weakness.

The truck roared to life!

I threw it into reverse and squealed backward out of my spot. I leaned out my window to see an approaching Border Patrol agent say, "A tow truck is on its—"

"SO LONG SUCKERS!" I yelled, laughing crazily as I gunned the gas and lurched forward, stalling out, and coming to a halt only a few feet away.

The Border Patrol agent moved up to my window, his mouth smacking gum, his eyes suspicious as he eyed me warily. "You want the tow truck again?"

"I don't know," I replied meekly, feeling as if I wanted to cry. "Give me a second." I turned the ignition several more times, and the engine caught on the last try. "No, I'm fine," I responded quietly, politely this time.

The Border Patrol agent said nothing, only watching me as I pulled forward and back onto the highway. In my rearview mirror I saw him walk back toward the office as he shook his head in disgust.

I FOCUSED ON the city lights, still on the horizon, but looming closer second by second.

The gas gauge needle had entirely disappeared now, buried somewhere inside the interior of the truck's dashboard.

And then, a few miles past the Border Patrol checkpoint, the truck started to heave, convulsing as if choking. The wheel shuddered in my hand as the steering became rigid. I pulled over to the side of the road where the truck came to a dead halt.

And then silence. Nothing but open desert in all directions. I sighed and stepped out onto the highway. Not even the headlights of distant vehicles on the horizon. And then, remembering that I needed to urinate, I moved in front of the truck and started to relieve myself, sighing in satisfaction at the proportional relief in pressure against my bladder, the warm piss steaming in the cool early-morning hours.

The truck started to roll backward into a drainage ditch on the side of the road.

"SHIT!" I screamed, running toward the cab of the truck as I felt the warm flood of urine splash my crotch. I scrambled into the driver's seat and slammed on the brake at the same moment I felt the truck's tailgate make contact with the edge of the ditch.

I stepped backward into the middle of the highway to see what the damage was. My truck was at an angle, fully in the ditch, only its front engine sticking out. I fell onto the middle of highway and laughed as I pretended to make snow angels, my head flat against the cool asphalt, bits of gravel embedding themselves as my cheek turned one way and then the other. I stared back toward the Border Patrol and then forward toward Alamogordo. I estimated Alamogordo was still miles off, but I would endure it, what I wasn't going to do was shame myself with another appearance at the Border Patrol station. I stood up, did a few jumping jacks in the middle of the highway to get my circulation going, reached inside the cab for my jacket, closed and locked the door, and then set off down the highway.

The desert was quiet, just the crunch of my footsteps on gravel, a tickle of a breeze on my face, and somewhere in the distance the careening scream of a circling hawk. I looked up into the darkened sky to see the bird hovering straight overhead, floating with ease on strong currents, suspended within a vacuum. Jesus, it was a beautiful creature.

The hawk screamed, this time louder, as if reading my thoughts and annoyed. I looked up to see that it had dropped in altitude, not thirty feet above now, swooping toward me as it examined me for moral deficiency of character.

"Hey get the fuck out of here!" I yelled as I waved it off. That's how you got rid of birds of prey; you waved them off and used profanity.

The hawk screamed again. I looked up to realize it was matching my speed and pace directly overhead.

I felt the distant tinge of anxiety as I broke into a panting trot, and overhead the bird matched my pace. I turned and ran backward, and overhead the bird changed direction and matched me. I turned and ran back the other way, and again, the bird matched me. I turned back, toward the truck, and this time the hawk swooped in closer; its scream sounding right in my ear.

I made one final dash, correcting my route, and quickly unlocked the door of the truck and jumped inside, winded and out of breath as I peered out the front windshield into the night sky trying to ascertain the location of my attacker.

I locked the doors as I pulled out my sleeping bag from the mess on the floorboard of the truck and laid it out over the seats. I was pretty sure the bird wouldn't be able to open the doors, but you never knew about these sorts of things.

I leaned forward off the seat and sorted through the mess on the truck's floorboard as I searched for my iPod. At the very least, I could listen to some music before I fell asleep. Eventually finding it wedged under the passenger seat, I put on the earphones and listened for exactly two minutes before the battery died.

And when I slept, I dreamt again of the desert, but no euphoria was to follow.

ONLY RAN out of gas four more times.

With the truck only getting six to seven miles to the gallon, I made piecemeal progress across New Mexico, filling up at each and every opportunity for gas, where I'd also fill up cardboard gas cans, setting them in the bed of the pickup. And then, after I ran out of gas, I'd walk forward or backward to the nearest town. There I'd fill up my two cardboard boxes with gasoline to the brim, necessarily needing every last drop I could manage, and then walk back to the truck, spilling the extra gasoline I had been so intent on acquiring over the front of my clothes as I clasped the two boxes to my chest with tired arms. I'd fill the truck with fuel, drive some more, run out of gas, and then rewalk back toward the same town I'd already walked to.

It was only four walks across the desert, thirty miles in total, no big deal. I wasn't even tired after twenty miles. It was a morose realization to discover that I was trained after all; physically hiking the Amnesty Trail wouldn't have been a problem.

And as I arrived at each gas station filling up my cardboard boxes, those on either side of me, filling up their Pathfinders and Explorers, surmised my condition and frowned, stinking as I was of sweat and piss and petrol.

"SIR, I'M AFRAID your card's been declined," the clerk told me, sliding the card back toward me across the chipped counter with the chicken-scratch pen marking. As he said this, his face took on a gaze of practiced and sincere empathy.

I felt my face redden and flush. "Are you sure? Could you try it one more time?" I asked desperately as I leaned over the gas station counter.

He nodded and swiped the card again. He shook his head. Sorry, no good.

"It could be just something wrong with the card," he offered, trying very hard to reassure me, to relieve me of my embarrassment.

"Well, I would think so!" I yelled too loudly, causing some of the gas station's other patrons to look in my direction. "I know I have lots of money on there!"

"Sometimes it's just the strip, you know?"

"Yeah," I smarmily replied. "Goddamn strips."

"I could try punching in the numbers for you?" he offered as he reached for the card, wondering, for a single moment, if perhaps it was just the strip.

"Oh, that's okay," I replied, quickly grabbing the card before his hand could reach it. "I'll just pay in cash. I'm going to go out to the truck and get your money. I'll be right back." I walked slowly out of the gas station backward, surveying the patrons and the clerk, to see how many witnesses would be present when I drove off without paying. But because of my outburst, everyone was looking at me, their faces filled with pity at the smelly disheveled man, stinking of body odor, gasoline, and urine.

Back in the parking lot, I counted out the few remaining bills in my wallet, laying them neatly on the dashboard. I was three dollars short. I swallowed hard as I scoured the glove box and under the seat for change.

I walked back inside, cupping the pile of wrinkled bills and coins as if a small treasure that I didn't want to spill. I laid the amount on the counter, my eyes trying very hard to appear nonchalant and indifferent, all too aware that I was fifty-seven cents short.

The clerk started to count the change and then, seeing desperation in my eyes, smiled warmly and said, "This is exact, yeah?"

"Yep, that there is exact change, my friend," I replied hastily.

The clerk winked at me and slid the money into his cash register uncounted.

I nodded him a thank-you, and he nodded back. He and I had an understanding.

AS I DROVE north toward Denver, still south of Pueblo and several hours from Colorado Springs, I ignored the rumbling in my stomach. My mouth was parched, swallowing what little remaining spit I had left, a low-rent soft drink. As I passed billboard advertisements for various restaurants, I wondered if they would give me some water for free. Or perhaps I could pretend to be contemplating a purchase from the menu, get access to the free water, and then quickly leave. And, maybe, if I was lucky, it'd be one of those restaurants that offered complimentary tortilla chips and salsa, and maybe they'd bring it out before they asked for my order.

The gas gauge was already back to half-empty and I wondered what I would do at the next gas station. How was I going to make it back to Denver? I did have a gun with me, I reminded myself. I could always commit an armed robbery. Get myself some gas and clean out the cash register, that'd put me back in the black for at least a little while.

My eyes scanned the billboards for a hotel with wireless Internet so that I could sit in the parking lot, access my online banking, and rearrange some dollars and debt to put some liquidity back into my straining credit cards.

And then the smoke started billowing from the engine—thick and pungent and noxious.

I pulled over to the side of the road and opened the hood.

The engine was on fire.

I studied the fire for a moment before deciding it was the sort of thing I should probably move away from. Trucks on fire blew up in the movies. I didn't know about real life, but I didn't want to take any chances.

I grabbed up my belongings and threw them into the field behind me as I retreated to the safety of the dirt and sat down watching my step-father's truck burn.

I peered up curiously at the sky with a devilish smile.

I sighed. The Border God had won.

I was going back to the border.

And this time I would cross.

I was 90 percent sure.

Chapter 23
A TIMID ENTRY INTO MEXICO
(TUCSON SECTOR)

My rented Jeep Cherokee pitched at a toppled velocity as we sped through the dirt roads of the Coronado National Forest. The rain slammed across the windshield, the wipers keeping pace in an anxious dragging jarring. A sign on the side of the road warned of flash floods ahead, but there was no time to heed such warnings, I only had seventy-two hours until I was due in Los Angeles. I had arrived in Denver, returned the gun, freed up some emergency funds, which now meant I was effectively broke, and had driven back to Arizona.

The Cherokee slammed headfirst into a surging overflowing stream that pummeled a gutted ravine as I felt the undercurrent grip hard, threatening to pull me off the road and deep into the woods. The engine screamed and, propelled by my previous momentum, the tires reached the opposite bank where they dug at the mud. I let off the accelerator and felt the Cherokee start to slide into the stream as I let myself fall back a few inches to give the tires a different grip before flooring the gas pedal, propelling myself out of the cascading stream and back onto the road.

The forest streaked by my windows in hyphenated blurring green flashes of foliage as I gripped the steering wheel with both hands and watched the accelerator climb. I had made some phone calls—because I was connected now, plugged in as a player on the border—and word was that a big offensive was occurring right at this moment in the Coronado National Forest. That Border Patrol had sealed off Highway 82 and all roads out of Patagonia, and another citizen's volunteer movement was flanking on the east outside and just south of Sierra Vista. And together they were trapping hundreds of Mexicans inside.

And I was speeding because I had the feeling of being late for a very important date—of being left behind. The Mexicans had left without me! I needed to be trapped in the forest too! It was dreadfully important that I also be trapped in the forest.

On my right-hand side was a fortified ranch, a sign outside the road leading to its interior asked, "Is your space defensible?"

I looked around the interior of the Jeep. I wasn't defensible. I reached over as I drove and locked all the doors, briefly taking my eye off the dirt road.

I rounded a corner where a large pickup truck was speeding toward me. The other driver sounded his horn in a long pitched recurring wail and I jerked hard on the wheel to avoid him. I felt the Cherokee jump into the air, a declining drop of fall-away forest on my right-hand side. I gripped and tightened my body, prepared for what I expected was an imminent tumble, as the vehicle crashed down the side of the hill, bouncing side over end. The Jeep's tires touched down and I pulled hard, sending me back onto the road with a bouncing jerk as in my rearview mirror the truck swerved to a stop in the middle of the road, the screaming driver getting out of his vehicle.

I controlled my breathing as I maintained the pace. The Coronado National Forest was perfect for a border crossing, all thick forest and heavy foliage. This was exactly the place where I wanted to be doing a border crossing and I wondered why and how I had previously overlooked it. I was headed for Lochiel, an abandoned ghost town on the border that was only sometimes open to the public.

I pulled out my GPS and stuck it out the window to get a reading.

It said I was inside Mexico.

I slammed on the brakes as I approached a T intersection in the road, which, I was guessing, was the border. An abandoned farmhouse stood just south of my position. My breath came in heavy hungry gasps as I observed the border. This was perfect. I could jump out of my car, run across, and run back. I was willing to settle at this point, nothing fancy, just something simple, a technical crossing.

And then, seized with the sickly paranoid feeling of being watched, I turned to my left out the driver's side window to see an RV and collection of pickup trucks, a smattering of lawn chairs outside filled with border watchers, Minutemen, all of whom were quiet in paused conversation as they studied me.

I screamed at them as I drove by, hollering obscenities and berating them for their strict devotion to border security.

I PRETENDED TO CAMP a few miles further back near Duquesne, my plan being to sneak across the border at night, until I was forced to leave under the threat of arrest by a Border Patrol agent who correctly viewed my singular habitation of the otherwise deserted camp site as a suspicious and threatening gesture.

It was nighttime when I circled back around on Highway 82 through Sierra Vista and past Fort Huachuca. I hit the forest, turned south on Highway 92, and was boxed in by a squad of Border Patrol vehicles, one pulling forward onto the highway blocking my escape, with two more vehicles in the rear. As they approached with guns drawn, I attempted to explain that it was a goddamn national forest and I was a goddamn American citizen and I had only wanted to utilize our nation's parks as they were intended, for dubious night drives at one in the morning while alone and appearing frantic and fearful. They had responded that the Coronado Forest was closed to the public after dark and that I had better get the fuck out of the area and never come back. I assured them that I would as I crossed my fingers behind my back.

I spent the night in a desperate frantic binge, traveling on border roads, looking for my perfect moment—a junkie looking for a fix.

I was pulled over by Border Patrol five times.

By morning, I found myself back in Sierra Vista as I reneged on my previous night's promise to never come back and took a right-hand turn off Highway 92, headed for the border again. I passed a few local residents out jogging, another couple on a morning bicycle ride. I moved slowly until I reached the entrance to the Coronado National Forest at the center of a T junction, the left-hand turn advertised as leading to a picnic area, the right-hand turn leading to a nature center and park ranger station. But straight ahead, where I wanted to go, the Coronado Forest was closed now, vehicle barrier in place. My intelligence report had been correct: they were closing down the forest—too many Mexicans trapped inside.

I had missed my opportunity.

I sighed with a heavy heart as I took the left-hand turn, traveled for a quarter of a mile, and then pulled over into an empty small gravel parking lot next to a series of picnic tables. I got outside and stretched, still aching from my nocturnal slumber curled in the fetal position in the Cherokee's back seat as I laid my map of Arizona on the picnic table. I was a desperado—a fleeing anxious archetype of the Old West looking for an escape into Old Mexico, the only difference being that instead of running to Mexico with my stolen bank loot, I wanted to turn around and come right back into the United States.

I felt anxious and sick to my stomach. I felt hungry and tired and lean. Surely, there was somewhere on the border where I could cross while hedging my bets, perform a pseudo-crossing without necessarily committing to the entirety of the experience?

I looked at my watch.

Nine A.M.

My flight was in exactly sixty hours. And it would take me at least twelve hours to get back to Los Angeles.

I pulled out my GPS.

And a curious grudging cautious smile appeared on my face.

I was less than a mile from the border.

I peered into the forest and then back around at the small gravel road I had taken to drive to the picnic tables. I squirmed under the opportunity as I moved to the back of the truck and gathered up some items to take with me—not a border crossing, merely a small nature hike—a simple commune with nature in federally designated open space under the control of the Forest Service.

Nothing more.

No reason to get one's hopes up.

I locked up the Jeep and started hiking through the brush. A few meters beyond the picnic site, in a dried ravine, was a series of cement vehicular barriers and a line of tattered clothing and abandoned trash. I pushed through a briar patch that tore and ripped at my clothes as I moved into position just above the ravine, walking parallel to the dehydrated creek high and above on the hillside.

The distant traffic from the highway was funneled as a reverberating echo to my position between the hills, an exaggerated hum of tires over asphalt. Grasshoppers jumped out from under each of my impending steps as I moved through the wild waist-high grass that covered the hillside. Insects buzzed and screamed in synchronized electronic chorus as the heat of the day started to take hold.

Overhead a plane was flying back and forth, expunging a frothy trail of contrails in its wake as it paced. Surveillance, probably. I stopped and took a seat as I realized my new distance. A quarter of a mile from the border. I gritted my teeth, stood, and then moved forward, climbing over and under and through several gnarled thin wire fences, and then a few minutes later I was at an open field, the large hills on either side of me dropping suddenly away, and the forest ending . . . Mexico.

And no fence whatsoever.

I stood there for an irresolute amount of time listening to the insects, making sure I was alone.

There was no Border Patrol, no Minutemen, and as far as I could see, the plains of Mexico were empty, free of characters of devious intention.

I looked both ways as if crossing a street.

And then I gripped my guts as I crossed the invisible line on my GPS that separated Mexico from the United States. As I walked, on Mexican soil now, I wondered how long I would have to stay in Mexico before a return to the U.S. counted as a separate crossing. As originally envisioned, the crossing was going to originate from the Mexican side of the border, not the U.S. side where I crossed and then quickly jumped back the two feet over to American soil. Two feet didn't count, that was for sure.

But what did?

One hundred feet? A thousand?

In the distance, about two hundred meters out, there was a cluster of bushes and trees. Those bushes and trees, I decided. If I made it there, that would pinpoint a geographic insertion into Mexico. I broke into a running trot and upon reaching the trees I fell into the grass on my back laughing. I chewed on grass and crumbled clots of dirt with my hands.

And the new question now was, How much time had to go by before a return crossing was made distinct and separate from my crossing into Mexico?

Two minutes? Two hundred?

As I pondered this question, I stared up at the surveillance plane in the sky, moving back and forth in slow rotating circles.

It hadn't been that bad after all.

All of my worried constipation when all I ever really needed was to have gone ahead and done the damn thing!

I closed my eyes and smiled.

I WOKE UP HOT and uncomfortable, my face glistening in beaded precipitated surrender to the overhead sun, which was churning in its nuclear fury. My mouth gagged on expired mildew saliva as I sat up and looked at my watch. It was noon; I had been asleep for two hours. Well, a nap constituted a break in the sequencing of a day, which meant enough time had passed for me to cross back.

I stood and turned around facing America. Behind me, just on the U.S. side of the border, was a large thin looming tower, electronic monitoring of some sort. And I hadn't seen it before because it had been hidden on my left-hand side by the hill as I had emerged out into the fields of Mexico. And atop the tower was an eye of some sort, a head, which I knew was looking at me, monitoring me—not unlike that magical tower in the *Lord of the Rings* movies.

I dropped down into the tall grass as I considered my next move. Should I low-crawl through the grass all the way back to my Jeep? That would take the rest of the day!

"Fuck!" I exclaimed to myself as I chewed on a piece of grass and contemplated my situation.

It was thirty miles in any direction to a town within Mexico, and while I didn't mind being in Mexican towns, I certainly didn't want to be noticed out here in the hills alone where anyone who came by me would correctly assume I had been up to no good. And this is what they called a pickle of a situation, nothing to do but face the consequences.

And so, I stood up and walked slowly toward America.

I WAS ALMOST to the Jeep when I heard the scream of the sirens, exaggerated by the shape of the valley and the surrounding hills. I dropped under the cover of a canopied bush and scanned the hillsides and then I saw them: three distant Border Patrol trucks with lights and sirens on, only their top halves visible from my position as they circled the hillside roads, moving toward my position!

I felt my bowels loosen as I contemplated an imminent arrest for illegal entry into the United States. It was the certainty that sometimes occurred during stressful moments where the mind didn't have time to second-guess itself, to doubt its intuition and the source of its surety. And in that moment, the only thing I could think of was to race back to my Jeep, to make it there before the Border Patrol did, where I would be able to offer the pretense of . . . what?

What purpose would I have being out here?

Picnic. I was on a goddamn picnic.

I broke through the brush, exercising an awkward lurching sprinting gait, my lungs heavy and wounded as I gasped, pumping my legs. My arms were in front of me acting as a shield, brushing away branches and overreaching thistle that exploded at contact with my body. I tripped twice, tumbling headfirst into the dirt where I slid, propelled by my own momentum. I rapidly informed myself of the necessary actions needed to create the false pretense of the appearance of a picnic.

A picnic by myself?

Well, sure, Officer. I always go on picnics by myself!

I'd lower the tailgate, throw some food and Gatorade on a picnic table, and most importantly, I'd act completely fucking casual.

I reached the ravine and barreled in headfirst, branches ripping and clawing at my head.

In the distance, screaming sirens. But closer now.

At the ravine's edge, I leapt over the vehicle barriers and charged up the slope to the parking lot. I threw open the tailgate. I emptied my rucksack of food on the picnic table. I sat and assumed a deliberately bored pose of one picnicking by himself and hating it. I froze in a position of contemplating the food before me as I pretended to consider its consumption. From my peripheral vision, my darting eyes strained at the gravel road leading to the picnic area, ready on a moment's notice to begin my practiced pantomime should the Border Patrol trucks suddenly appear.

Ten seconds passed.

I pretended to eat a little.

Another ten seconds passed.

I took another imaginary bite.

"Fuck this!" I exclaimed to no one as I broke from my plan, jumped in my Cherokee, and turned the ignition.

A ND AS I APPROACHED the T intersection and the barricaded entrance to the Coronado National Forest, I saw the Border Patrol vehicles with their silent red strobe lights flickering, parked one after the other on the side of the road, the agents who drove them off in the woods trying to intercept me.

They had erroneously assumed the normative modus operandi of border crossers, of moving through the woods. They hadn't suspected that I would have had my own vehicle already parked at the picnic area.

I sped past the trucks, and back onto the asphalt road, laughing as I went.

I had successfully crossed into the United States.

Kinda. I had kinda successfully crossed into the United States.

By about two hundred meters and two hours.

Which, if you were being technical, counted.

I drove through Tucson high on the euphoric psychology of imminent redemption, one hand on the wheel, the other managing the cell phone tucked into my chin as I called Gus, somewhere out in the desert tracking Mexicans as he planned his retirement in Mexico.

The thing of it was, I couldn't leave well enough alone.

Now, after the Coronado National Forest, I was encouraged.

And being encouraged meant an honest attempt at the Amnesty Trail, what with it being the closest route to the Coronado National Forest and all.

"Gus, how's it going?" I asked. "How's business?"

"Caught twenty-three last night," Gus replied.

"Great! That's really great, Gus. I'm real happy for you. Listen, the reason I'm calling is I had a crazy idea. I was thinking of running the Amnesty Trail myself . . . as a social experiment, you know? An empathetic experience to re-create what the Mexicans have to go through, and I just wanted to know your thoughts, if it was possible."

Gus was silent for a moment as I fumbled with the scrap of paper my directions were written on, looking for the name of the street I was to turn onto.

"Yep, I can see why you'd want to do that," Gus responded. "But that would take days of planning, of course."

"Oh, yeah, of course!" I responded, a bit offended that Gus felt the need to remind me of such considerations as I turned onto the wrong street. I looked at my watch. I had another three hours of planning before I needed to be on my way toward Mexico.

"I mean, this wouldn't be something you could do today," Gus added. "The Amnesty Trail is a three-day road trip."

"No, of course not! Of course not! This is like far in the future. You know, when I'm properly prepared," I responded.

"And you'd want to make sure you took that sidearm of yours with you. We spotted some more drug mules day before yesterday."

"Of course, I'd be armed. Always, man. Always."

My cell phone buzzed. A call on the other line.

"Gus, I'm going to have to place you on hold for just one moment," I said as I quickly switched between calls and put the phone back up to my ear. "Hello?"

"Johnneee!" Anna cried. My wife.

"Hey, baby, how are you?"

"Fine. I miss you! How many more days until you're home?"

"Uh, three," I replied, swallowing hard. "I'll be home in three days, baby."

"Johnny, if you miss your flight, I'll divorce you, do you understand?" she said as she laughed. Anna was always threatening to divorce me for slight infractions.

"Where are you?"

"Uh, I'm on my way to Los Angeles."

"Oh good," she replied, her relief palpable that my mission was over.

"Anna, this isn't a good time for me, okay? Let me call you right back." I clicked back over to Gus.

"Gus, tell me everything I would have to do."

"ANYTHING ELSE?" THE CLERK at the gun store asked from behind the glass counter as he eyed me suspiciously, sensing my nervous nature and bewildered character. The clerk was a sporting man, a hunter, which meant, of course, that he was potbellied with a grizzled beard—the type of sportsman weaned on a special diet of light beer and bratwurst.

"Uh, yeah, how about that night vision scope?" I asked, pointing behind the case. "Is that a good scope?"

"Depends. What do you need it for?"

"Um, hunting. In the dark. In the desert."

A scowl curled onto the clerk's face. "Hunting in the dark is never a good idea."

"I understand. Let me take a look at that there scope."

The clerk frowned and handed over the scope. "What are you hunting?"

"Uh, elk."

"It's not elk season."

"I understand." I added the night vision to the water bladder and the boots already on the table and cleared my throat as I asked, "Let me take a look at that .45 pistol."

The clerk hesitated, his face assuming wary and wise hesitation.

"You can't hunt elk with a .45."

"I understand. Let me take a look at that sucker," I said, pointing beneath the glass counter to the shiny one.

"You live in Arizona?"

"No."

"Can't sell it to you then. In-state license only on handguns."

"I understand."

I silently cursed the nation's stringent gun laws.

"Well, what could you sell me then?" I asked, sighing.

The clerk put both hands on the countertop as he quietly assessed me before replying quietly and after a long delay, "I could sell you a rifle or a shotgun." He pointed to a series of long-barrel rifles mounted on the wall behind him.

"Do you have any smaller rifles, perhaps? Something more compact?" I collapsed the distance between my hands so that they held the space for only a small pistol, which is what I desired.

The clerk shook his head and moved away and came back a moment later with a small .22 rifle. It was pink. He handed it over to me.

Further down the counter, I saw another customer moving a rifle around in his hands before he moved it up to his shoulder and aimed at the wall, testing it, which is what I should've been doing if I wanted to pretend that I was serious.

I fixed the butt of the petite pink rifle into my shoulder and pretended to aim at some imaginary deer or whatever it was that people used rifles to hunt as I aimed it at the wall, appraising the weapon as I licked my lips.

"You right-handed?" the clerk asked.

"Yes."

"It's the other shoulder then."

"What's that?"

"Put the rifle up to your other shoulder."

"Right. Right."

I switched shoulders.

Sometimes even I forgot I had been an infantry soldier in Afghanistan.

"Yeah, that feels good," I replied, handing the rifle back.

"That's a rifle for children," the clerk said, his words contemptuous and mean.

I tapped my fingers rhythmically on the counter as I looked for different weapons. Small nonpink rifles that weren't for children, perhaps. And what the fuck did they even make rifles for small girls for anyway? What type of goddamn country was this?

"I need something small," I said. "Something not a pistol, but also not for children."

"How small?"

I swallowed hard. "Um, something that could be easily concealed in a backpack."

The clerk turned to a fellow employee who was stocking bullets in the case, listening to our conversation. The two shared a concerned look and the one stocking the bullets shrugged his shoulders.

"How about this?" the clerk said as he handed me a short-stocked rifle that looked like a machine gun of some sort.

"Perfect!" I replied, a leering smile spreading over my face. "What is it?"

"It's a .22 rifle."

"It looks cool, though."

"You don't buy guns because they look cool."

"I understand."

A moment later and he's asking me strange curious questions, "Have you ever been adjudicated mentally defective?" As he asked this, he stared at me with unflinching eyes, thinking I was.

I averted my gaze and stared at a display of plastic decoy ducks. "Not that I know of."

The clerk lingered over the paperwork, wondering if he should refuse the sale, before he sighed and asked, "Anything else?"

I tossed a pack of gum on the counter.

"Yeah, I'll take some gum too. No law against that is there?"

IN A HOLIDAY INN along Interstate 19, which ran south from Tucson to the border at Nogales, I sat on the bed as I searched through the archives of Google Images, looking for training aids for illegal aliens as I attempted various sequencing of words like "Altar" and "Smuggler" and "Training Aid."

After an hour of searching, I found what I was looking for. I saved the picture to my hard drive and opened it under Windows Media Player so that I could zoom in to get a proper look. It was a map on the wall of a church in Altar—a map that cordoned off the southern Arizona desert south of Tucson into concentric circles, each level representing a day of travel. Reaching Arivaca, a small mountain hamlet, that was one day.

Reaching the Titan Missile Museum just south of Tucson, that was another. And on the third day, immigrants were expected to make it to Tucson or Three Points, where Gus lived.

I had only fifty hours to work with.

I decided that, given present time constraints, I'd try for Arivaca.

Mostly, because I didn't want to miss my flight and end up divorced.

I PAID THE ATTENDANT for parking and, rucksack on my back, joined the throngs of pedestrians filing across the street, slowly making their way a few streets over to where Nogales, Arizona, ended and on the other side of the fortressed customs center, Nogales, Mexico, began. I gazed at the spot where Agent Thomas, Andre, and I had parked next to the border wall a few streets up on the side of a hill.

And then, as I arrived at the crosswalk, Mexico just fifty feet on the other side, I saw the sign that warned against bringing firearms into Mexico lest the owner of the firearm in question wanted to spend some time in a Mexican prison.

I didn't want to spend time in a Mexican prison.

I moved back to my Jeep, opened the rear, made sure no one was looking, and unloaded the .22 rifle and covered it with clothes. I cursed myself for so much wasted money.

I WALKED THE carnival-themed streets of Mexico slowly, taking it all in, moving past the street vendors and the hustlers and clever salesmen trying to practice their respective trades, not even offering them the benefit of a polite no and simply glaring as I brushed past them.

I didn't know where it was that I'd find what I was looking for, or even what it was exactly that I was looking for besides a tenuous connection that could possibly, theoretically lead to eventual contact with a coyote.

To lend myself some courage, I reiterated to myself my new self-appointed title of Border Crosser. No different than Jedi Knight. It was an austere position of ancient reverence. Holy, even. Blessed by God. I pretended that Border Crossers had been admired for thousands of years across all cultures.

I decided that I quite enjoyed pretending holy sanctimonious qualities and endowments that I didn't actually possess, as if a warrior priest moving through the barter town on some fringe planet in the outer rim of a science fiction novel.

I took a turn and moved to a street filled with scuttlebutt bars and lowlife cantinas, the type of place where a fellow could get into real trouble if he wasn't blessed with the mark of the Lord on him as I was, if he wasn't protected by magical spirits.

I felt a hand grab hold of my collar and pull me backward. And although externally I appeared to be passively submitting to the force, in my mind I was prepared on a moment's notice to do some sort of karate chop deal.

"Girls!" the man with the backward baseball cap and oversized NFL starter jacket spit into my face. "You like girls! Naked girls! Big titties!" Next to him, a bouncer with cornrows and a purple dress shirt winked at me as he guarded the entrance to the strip club.

"Why, yes," I replied. As luck would have it, the gentleman who had propositioned me had assumed correctly that I did indeed like naked girls with big titties. I marveled at his intuitive foresight and ability for precognitive assumption.

"Five dollars, man!" the hustler replied.

"How much is that in pesos?" I asked as I attempted to do the math in my head.

"Just five dollars, man!" I handed him a ten, the hustler pulled five from his sidewalk cash register and held it out for himself. "A little somethin' for the help, bro! A little somethin' for the help!"

I glared at him as I grabbed my five dollars change from his hand and went inside.

The inside was desolate, only two other men, both Mexican, sitting by themselves at opposite corners staring to the far stage where a big-breasted woman also endowed with fat rolls slid around on stage, completely bored and contemplating her evening after she got off work. The mirrors that lined the walls, which were leveraged in a bid of exotic respectability, were smeared and dull, cracked. The flashing lights blinked randomly in irreverent patterns.

I ordered a drink and took the third corner so that you could draw a straight-edge triangle between the three of us gawkers and took brief silent polite sips before folding my hands and staring at a point on the opposite wall of cracked stained plaster. The music blared, the volume so loud that the lyrics and the band were indistinguishable.

An honest attempt at Altar was where I had my best bet of finding a coyote, but Altar was too far away, too isolated. In Nogales, I felt a bit more secure, protected by the penumbra of frequent American tourists, however tenuous that protection may have actually been. The police here were used to dealing with American tourists who crossed over for cheap shopping and to buy drugs at the farmacia. And only a few blocks from the border and the customs station, I felt safer making inquiries than I would in a place like Altar. Hell, here I could sprint home if I had to.

All I needed was some organic conversation with the right Mexican, someone who was savvy to the criminal underworld. Or at least knew people who were. It was the type of person that it seemed reasonable to find in a place like this.

And as the hustler working the door opened it for another customer, this one an elderly American, an idea came to me.

I walked back across the room and leaned out the door. The smile on the hustler's face disappeared and turned into one of nervousness as he saw me point at him and this was because I was purposefully sampling the facial expressions that I imagined a cold heartless indifferent serial killer might model. I motioned for him to come forward with my little finger and he slowly approached.

So far, everything was going well and, psychologically speaking, I had the upper hand, which was good. I would need it for what I was about to attempt.

Between two fingers I held out a twenty-dollar bill.

"You're right. I should've given something to the doorman. My apologies."

He offered a hesitant smile and reached for the money.

I pulled the twenty away.

"But I need some information."

His hustler's swagger reemerged as he snapped the money from my hand. "Shit, what ya need, bro?"

"I need to find something," I replied.

"I know what you need. Coke." He sniffled his nose. "Want some coke, I can do dat. Want some meth, weed, what you want, bro?"

"Coyote," I replied evenly and with about as much confidence as I could muster.

His smile vanished again for a moment, reappearing more slowly as he cocked his head curiously. I understood what he was thinking—I didn't need drugs, I was *already* on them!

"Yeah, hol' up, yo, I git back to ya, bro," he replied, offering me some type of street sign that meant much love or brotherhood or some such shit.

I moved back to my table to await the coming consequences.

I reiterated my new mantra in my head. *I am the Border Crosser.*

From a side curtain, another stripper, this one with stretch marks, wide-berthing hips, and low-hanging swinging breasts slid in next to me as she started licking my ear, "I'll suck your dick for twenty bucks."

"Oh, thanks anyway, but I'm married," I cheerfully replied, holding up my ring finger where I had no ring. "Thanks for the offer though."

Thirty minutes later, the hustler reentered the room, this time with two shifty-looking young men, both sturdy and strong in T-shirts and jeans. They crossed the room to my position and slid into the booth next to me. They introduced themselves as Sam and Bob. Some type of alias type of deal, I figured.

Hi, Sam. Hi, Bob. I'm John.

Bob said something to Sam about me in rapid-fire Spanish and Sam laughed. I collapsed into my chair offended when I heard it, waving them off.

Bob and Sam shared a surprised look—did I understand Spanish?

Bob turned to me and asked me something in Spanish.

Sam and Bob and the hustler waited for my response, to see if I really understood.

I swallowed hard and then, with a stern confidence, I replied, "Sí."

But I said it in a way that conveyed, not an almost nonexistent grasp of the language, but rather the certainty of one who has little appreciation for mindless chitchat, of one who appreciated minimalism and getting straight to the fucking point.

"Now can you help me or not?" I asked, setting the tone for the rest of the conversation to be conducted in English and hoping like hell that what I just said made sense in light of whatever it was they had just asked me.

Sam said little, hiding behind a cocky confident smirk as he kept looking me over, disapproving of my condition, like a woman wincing at the identity of her undesirable secret admirer. I responded to this with unflinching resolve, staring back coolly, refusing to respond uncomfortably for even a moment.

Bob was grim.

What did I want a coyote for? Well, hell yeah, he can get me a coyote, who the fuck do I think he is anyhow? Of course, he can get me a coyote. That's not what he's asking though, he wants to know why the fuck I want one?

To Bob, I also responded with unflinching resolve, stating that I wanted one for the same reason everyone else wanted one, to cross the border and why I was doing that was really none of his business.

The hustler stayed behind them, hovering, intrigued by the strange gringo as he made trips to the entrance to conduct the necessary business of working the door.

I asked how much it would cost.

Bob said four thousand.

I said it was a deal.

Bob said he needed to see the money.

I had the money, the last of what I owned.

I showed it to him.

Bob said he had to make some phone calls and for me to sit tight as he went outside where he could hear.

I ordered another beer.

Sam asked me some questions in Spanish.

I nodded. Yeah, sure.

Sam asked some more questions in Spanish.

"Sí," I replied again.

Bob reentered and Sam and Bob both talked in rapid-fire Spanish.

Now Bob asked me some questions in Spanish.

"Sí," I replied again, confident and casual. I sipped my beer.

Bob and Sam both laughed.

They elbowed each other in the side, pointing at me.

They knew I didn't speak Spanish.

Approximately seven minutes. That's how long I had been able to hold my own, to maintain any semblance of respect. They both laughed at me easily now, talking freely to each other in Spanish, knowing I didn't understand a word of what they were saying. My stress tic started to pound in my temple and I could feel events slowly sliding out of my control, careening toward disaster.

"What's going on?" I asked Bob, a bit too needy now, too eager.

"We got some people coming, we're not coyotes, but these people . . . they can hook you up."

"Is it safe?" I asked.

I immediately regretted my question.

It had been accidental, a slip of the tongue giving birth to private thoughts. It marked me as even more of a rank amateur than they had already assumed me to be.

Before I had asked that question, they knew I didn't speak Spanish, they knew I was foolish, but they also thought, just perhaps, just maybe, that I was also a bit loco, a bit crazy, reckless. The type of person who you couldn't anticipate and whom you therefore couldn't dismiss.

"Sí! Sí! Is very safe!" Sam replied as he and Bob both broke out laughing, enunciating the *sí*, the only word they realized I understood. Sam put his hand on the back of my neck and rubbed it playfully in the way an uncle might a nephew; it was affectionate, but tinged with condescension and an assumed position of authority. When you freely rubbed the neck of a male you didn't know, it demonstrated you had absolutely no fear of him.

I felt my face flush with embarrassment.

Bob patted me on the back and winked at me. You know, to reassure me.

Yeah kid, don't worry. It'll be all right. Everything will be just fine.

And is this your first time flying by yourself? Are your parents going to meet you at the airport?

"It's four thousand, for the coyote, yeah? And one thousand for us, five hundred for the doorman," Bob added as an afterthought before he moved to the door to make another phone call.

"Whoa! Whoa!" I called out after him, obviously flustered and standing, ready to follow him outside and argue. Sam forcefully pushed me back down to my seat.

And at the feeling of Sam's forceful push, at the realization that they were past the point of affectionate neck nuzzling but had moved on to forcibly and physically directing my actions, the stress tic in my temple surged and I felt as if the floor had dropped out from under me. My guts were filled with lead and my head was filled with helium; I was as firmly planted in my chair as Bush was when he heard about the planes slamming into the World Trade Center.

I looked across the room and two strippers were staring at me, talking quietly to each other.

The look on their faces was one of worry.

I sat sipping my beer as an Usher song started playing. The volume was so loud that it sent the mirrors that lined the walls trembling. I needed to think of how I would escape this mess, but the music drowned out all my thoughts. I couldn't even hear myself talking to myself.

As I stood to get another beer, Sam's arm went across my chest like a seat belt, forcing me back down. I nodded at my beer. All I need is another beer, bro.

Sam shook his head. Nah, bro, you're all right. You don't need anything, bro.

I nodded silently, understanding that this was what they called a bad situation.

I wondered if they even knew coyotes or if this was just a shakedown.

I wondered what they would say if I told them I was a journalist on assignment.

I wondered what would happen if I just started screaming for help, crying out like a little girl. Would they just become embarrassed and quickly leave, or would they accelerate their plans, punching me in the face perhaps before forcibly rushing me outside and throwing me in the back of a car that would subsequently speed off?

I had to come to terms with the fact, rather shortly, I assumed, that it could quickly come down to necessarily screaming for help. As much as I was loath to admit it, it might either be that or slowly finding myself further along this chain of events, amazed at each moment that I still hadn't yet attempted anything that would save my life.

And what would Anna, my wife, think when she got the call that I was dead or in the hospital? I wasn't even supposed to be in Mexico, I was supposed to be on my way to L.A.

I thought forward to my funeral after these Mexicans killed me. At my funeral, one of my friends would surely get up and explain that "we should not weep, for Johnny died doing what he loved, engaging in yet one more adventure. And it was while traveling, which was always his greatest love." I closed my eyes, wishing for sudden time-traveling ability so that I could emerge suddenly and surprisingly at my own funeral and scream at all my friends and family that they were fucking idiots, that they should very much weep for me, that I had died scared and lonely and desperate and regretting every stupid choice I had ever made.

From the corner of my eye, I saw Bob reenter the strip club, this time with two more men, both serious contenders, a third hanging back outside the door. And behind them, a plethora of curious onlookers from the street stuck in their heads for a look. Word had apparently gotten out that a crazy white boy in the strip club wanted to hire a coyote.

I didn't know whether to shit or take a breath.

The world was spinning, casting off the shackles of gravity, and I was losing my balance.

Bob and two men at the doorway started walking toward me as I stood abruptly, pushing past Sam's arm, which reached out too lightly to stop me.

"Be right back," I said as I grabbed my rucksack from the floor, momentarily recapturing my psycho-cool demeanor. "Gotta take a leak." I pointed to my penis, which is the organ I used to conduct such transactions in case he hadn't known.

He nodded and let me go.

I took long forceful strides across the bar as I made my way to the bathroom, hyper-aware that all eyes were upon me.

Inside the bathroom, I closed the door and stared into the streaky mirror. There was a toilet with no lid and a wastebasket filled with shit paper. The bathroom mirror vibrated to the beat of Usher.

I supposed that the trick they would perform in the movies was either to squeeze out the window in the bathroom, or else to trigger the fire alarm with a cigarette lighter, thus clearing the building where the protagonist could escape amid the crowd. The strip club bathroom, having neither a window nor a smoke detector, quickly made both of those options unviable.

Another option was to just run. Run like there was no tomorrow. Run out of the strip club, run onto the street, and run all the way back to the international border crossing where there would be Mexican federales and U.S. customs agents within shouting range.

But there was a problem with running—it was provocative. There were certain breeds of people in which running triggered an escalation in conflict. Not unlike a dog, sleepy one moment, but then the second they saw someone running, they were up and sprinting, barking and excited. I didn't know these men outside waiting for me, but I suspected that might be their sort of character.

But speed-walking, however, speed-walking was a different story entirely.

Not walking, not running. But still fast.

I took in several deep breaths, left the bathroom to see them all laughing, raucously laughing, tear-inducing knee-jerk laughing.

I smiled casually and waved as I speed-walked straight from the bathroom to the front of the strip club where I exited as I heard my name being shouted from behind me. Outside the strip club, on the street, the hustler called after me, "Where ya going, bro? Bro, where ya going?"

A hand grabbed my arm. I shook it off.

I paused in the middle of the calle, looking back toward the United States, which is where I should've gone if I was being smart. But instead I got into the back of a taxi pulled to a stop in front of the strip club.

The driver turned around with a smile, "Where you going?"

"Sasabe."

I was going to Sasabe. Directly south of the Buenos Aires National Wildlife Refuge. Dead center in Mexico for the Amnesty Trail.

His smile fractured into a frown. "Three hundred dollars."

"Fine, fine."

And then, at the idea of earning three hundred dollars, he smiled again. Never knowing I would've happily paid him four thousand.

Outside the taxi, my strip club business associates were knocking on the window, their hands attempting to open the door, which I was bracing shut as they yelled at me.

"Go! Go!" I screamed.

The taxi driver shot me a concerned look, he didn't know what I was involved with, but he didn't like it, not one bit. The light turned green and the taxi driver pulled forward.

Chapter 25

THE BORDER CROSSER
(MEXICO SECTOR)

We stopped at the edge of town where I filled up my rucksack with fluids and snacks.

Back on the road, the taxi driver kept watching me in the rearview mirror.

"Why you going to Sasabe?"

"Business."

"Sasabe ain't safe."

"I know."

"It ain't safe at all."

"I know."

The taxi driver was quiet, realizing he wasn't going to get much else out of me.

A slight and terrible silence overtook the car as we drove and I watched rural Mexico pass by outside the window. I breathed in deep, I was ready for this. I had performed two crossings, after all, one with Little Dog, and one in the Coronado Forest. I had performed formal training deep in Mexico, I had spent time working the trails with the Minutemen in Arizona, and I knew the government's border security apparatus. I was fitted with the proper gear, GPS with too many labeled grid points, night vision, food and water.

And there it was. That old familiar urge to retreat, just hanging there. All I had to do was tell the taxi driver I had changed my mind and instead wanted to go to the international border. And so well practiced and rehearsed was this urge that it almost happened, it almost became spoken word without my realization or intent.

"Can you get there any faster?" I asked.

THE TAXI IDLED as the driver turned around in his seat, frustrated at my indecision. We were in Sasabe, a dirt-road ghost town of cinder-block buildings and dubious dwellings, no one on the streets except for a man in military camouflage with an M16 slung across his back using a pay phone as he watched us.

"I gotta go," the taxi driver whined, apparently not liking being in Sasabe any longer than necessary.

"Just hold on, okay? Just hold on! I'm going to get a soda."

The taxi driver mumbled under his breath as I got out and crossed the street to a small barren storefront. Inside, a total of six items on empty shelves. The floors were concrete and the glass windows smeared. Four people inside stopped working as I entered and quietly huddled at a doorway that led to the interior of the store's rear—darkly lit without electricity.

"Una Coca-Cola, por favor," I said, pointing to a Coke in a barrel.

I paid a few pesos and drank heavily as I surveyed the town and sighed.

I was stalling and I knew it.

I looked back the way we had come, toward the three pickups with the tinted windows that had been congregating along a crumbling graffiti-covered cement wall. They hadn't followed, which was something.

I walked back to the taxi and told the driver to take the rural country road back toward Nogales. The taxi driver protested, this wasn't an off-road truck and I had asked for Sasabe and he had taken me here, goddammit.

The back roads required additional compensation. We negotiated a price and were on our way.

The taxi driver moved slowly in an attempt to adjust for the uneven terrain. I held my GPS out the window to get a fix on my position, an understanding of my place within the world.

And then, when we had traveled just a couple of miles, I told the taxi driver to pull over to the side of the road. He whined again and berated me from the front seat as I got out and climbed to the top of a small ridge, evaluating the land for possibility.

I climbed back down and moved to the taxi, lighting up a cigarette as I considered the matter.

"I got to go!" the taxi driver squealed.

I was quiet as I didn't reply.

"We got to go back to Nogales," the taxi driver whined once more.

I was quiet as I didn't reply.

I looked at my watch, two in the afternoon.

The sun burned furiously in the sky.

I grabbed my rucksack and shut the door to the taxi . . .

EPILOGUE

I climbed in my Jeep with less than a day to make it to Los Angeles.

As I drove north toward Tucson, I decided that, academically speaking, from a position only motivated by journalistic curiosity, which, of course, was what I had been intending all along, U.S. border security sucked.

Nothing I had learned boded well for America.

I was reminded of the scene in *Jaws* when Roy Scheider was shoveling chum into the water and finally saw the size of the beast.

In other words, *we were gonna need a bigger fence* . . .

I had one conclusion from my trip, which was that it might be time to start learning Spanish as a second language.

Which, being that I didn't even live in America, really wasn't something that even concerned me. But other Americans, Americans who still lived here, they needed to start worrying.

And right now, at this very moment, Little Dog, both excited and ferocious, was calling in a group of seven who had just hopped the fence by the 240 marker. I hoped he was snaring his daily quota. I smiled and felt just a bit better knowing that at least one portion of the country was being protected by him and Freckles. Unless, of course, Freckles had already been killed by the cartels, which was definitely a possibility.

The girls of Humane Borders were probably in the desert, filling up the water for the migrants (not the illegals, because no human being is illegal). Mark was in Phoenix hoping desperately that someone would buy one of his damned cars as he silently cursed the line of Mexicans visiting their government's consulate while obtaining ID cards. Gus was in the desert, tracking Mexicans while planning his retirement in Mexico. And Salvador was inside the safe house, fearfully looking out onto the world, trying to build the courage to leave since nothing less than all of his family was depending on him.

I clicked on my audio recorder to offer final comments.

Which, mostly, consisted of how bad I felt for all involved.

I felt bad for the Minutemen, demonized as they were, old retired military vets who only wanted to do the right thing by protecting their country and having the laws that were already on the books enforced—an ostensibly simple request—the sort of thing they had grown up believing was what governments were supposed to do: enforce the law. And them not understanding how the country had changed, that enforcing existing law had become a thing of complication now.

And I felt bad for the Border Patrol, decent and hardworking men and women tasked by the American people with nothing less than the impossible. Criticized, in regular and frequent rotation, for being both too lenient and too lax.

But, mostly, I felt bad for the Mexicans. They had done nothing wrong but to have owned the bad luck of being born in an economically depressed country where they were forced into the role of villain for only wanting a better life, caught between the laborious momentums of corporation and government, and with no one in charge at the helm as we pitched slowly toward disaster.

But these weren't my problems.

I was done with the Mexican border.

There were other borders to cross. And up next was a race across Europe, the Middle East, and the former Soviet bloc countries to Mongolia for a magazine. The concept of the race was simple: get into as much trouble as possible. It was a concept that greatly appealed to me.

Ahead of me, the traffic pulled to a stop at the Border Patrol checkpoint between Nogales and Tucson. On the left-hand side of the road, a Wackenhut bus took another load of Mexicans back south toward the detention center outside Nogales where they'd get their chicken burrito and maybe some crackers. On the right-hand side of the road, a slim Hispanic kid in his early twenties was pulled over to the side of the road, casting fearful looks back at the Border Patrol while he opened the hood of his car and pretended to worry about an imaginary problem, a meager attempt to delay his necessary processing at the checkpoint where he'd be discovered.

Just business as usual on the border.

As I approached the checkpoint, I felt overcome by fictitious and imaginary feelings of guilt. I saw the German shepherd moving between the cars and worried that the dog would sniff out the kilo of cocaine in my trunk. Which, of course, I didn't really have.

I pulled to a stop and the Border Patrol agent leaned into my window as he looked around the interior of the car.

"You want a driver's license or passport?" I asked.

"Passport," he quickly replied.

I handed it over, snickering at the thought that showing one's passport, a document typically reserved for crossing borders, for international travel, was now the preferred document of choice for movement within my native country.

Like some type of goddamn police state, or something.

Not that I minded, of course.

I realized there were Mexicans to catch.

ABOUT THE AUTHOR

Johnny Rico is the author of *Blood Makes the Grass Grow Green* and works as a freelance writer for magazines as diverse as *GQ*, *Penthouse*, and *Men's Journal*—where, among other assignments, he's gone undercover in the U.S. Army's CONUS Replacement Center, interviewed mercenaries in Nepal, and raced across the earth as part of the Mongol Rally. He lives in the United Kingdom.

www.johnnyrico.net

writejohnrico@aol.com

ABOUT THE TYPE

This book was set in Scala, a typeface designed by Martin Majoor in 1991. It was originally designed for a music company in the Netherlands and then was published by the international type house FSI FontShop. Its distinctive extended serifs add to the articulation of the letterforms to make it a very readable typeface.